TAKING THE STAND

TAKING THE STAND

Rape Survivors and the Prosecution of Rapists

Amanda Konradi

Westport, Connecticut
London

Library of Congress Cataloging-in-Publication Data

Konradi, Amanda.
    Taking the stand : rape survivors and the prosecution of rapists / Amanda
Konradi.
        p.   cm.
    Includes bibliographical references and index.
    ISBN 978–0–275–99718–2 (alk. paper)
    1. Rape—United States—Trial practice. 2. Rape victims—Legal status,
laws, etc.—United States. 3. Trials (Rape)—United States. I. Title.
    KF9329.K66 2007
    345.73'02532—dc22   2007027859

British Library Cataloguing in Publication Data is available.

Library of Congress Catalog Card Number: 2007027859
ISBN: 978–0–275–99718–2

First published in 2007

Praeger Publishers, 88 Post Road West, Westport, CT 06881
An imprint of Greenwood Publishing Group, Inc.
www.praeger.com

Printed in the United States of America

∞

The paper used in this book complies with the
Permanent Paper Standard issued by the National
Information Standards Organization (Z39.48–1984).

10   9   8   7   6   5   4   3   2   1

Copyright Acknowledgments

The author and the publisher gratefully acknowledge permission for use of the following material:

Chapter 5 was adapted from two articles: Konradi, Amanda. "Preparing to Testify: Rape Survivors' Negotiating the Criminal Justice Process," *Gender & Society*, Vol. 10, No. 4 (1996): 404–432; and Konradi, Amanda. "Understanding Rape Survivors' Preparations for Court: Accounting for the Influence of Legal Knowledge, Cultural Stereotypes, Personal Efficacy and Prosecutor Contact." *Violence Against Women*, Vol. 2, No. 1 (1996): 25–62.

Chapter 6 was adapted from the article Konradi, Amanda. "'I Don't Have to Be Afraid of You': Rape Survivors' Emotion Management in Court," *Symbolic Interaction*, Vol. 22, No. 3 (1999): 45–77. © by The Society for the Study of Symbolic Interaction.

Chapter 9 was adapted from the article Konradi, Amanda, and Burger, Tina. "Having the Last Word: An Examination of Rape Survivors' Participation in Sentencing," *Violoence Against Women* Vol. 6, No. 4 (2000): 353–397.

Portions of Chapter 10 were adapted from the article Konradi, Amanda. "Pulling Strings Doesn't Work in Court: Moving Beyond Puppetry in the Relationship Between Prosecutors and Rape Survivors," *Journal of Social Distress and the Homeless*, Vol. 10, No. 1 (2001): 5–28.

For sexual assault survivors, their supporters,
and their advocates.

CONTENTS

Contents

ACKNOWLEDGMENTS

I am indebted to the rape survivors interviewed for this project for their trust and honesty. I am extremely grateful to Joanne Salinger, as well as to the assistant district attorneys, rape crisis advocates, and sexual assault nurse examiners in urban and rural counties in California for telling women about my study and for providing information about the workings of the process. Laura Mizel's careful transcription made my analysis possible.

Amazing friends and colleagues at the University of California–Santa Cruz encouraged me through the initial stages of this research and pushed my thinking. These include Norma Wikler, Pam Roby, Nancy Stoller, Josie Mendez Negrete, Lynet Uttal, Patrice Meriwether, Robert Thompson, Megan Boler, Virginia Draper, Sara Williams, Travis Silcox, Miriam Wallace, Margaret Villanueva, Candace West, and Elizabeth Carter. Colleagues at the Ohio University who helped me expand my analysis and provided laughter and essential diversions while working on this material include Mary Beth Krouse, Diane Ciekawy, Christine Mattley, Debra Henderson, Nancy Tetarek, and student Tina Burger. I am grateful to department chairs Eric Wagner and Martin D. Schwartz for helping me secure release time and to the staff at Ohio University Child Development Center and the Towson YMCA for taking great care of my children and making my work time worry free. Academic colleagues whose commentary shaped my earlier academic publications include Patricia Martin, Lisa Frohmann, Jennifer Dunn, Edna Erez, Claire Renzetti, Elizabeth Schneider, Elizabeth Scheel and others who remain anonymous. This book is much more user-friendly thanks to guidance from agent Stan Wakefield and editor Suzanne Staszak-Silva and to the amazing feedback I received from my mother, Isabel Konradi, and the great friends who waded through my lengthy first draft: R. L. Silver, Cathy Winkler, Mary Beth Krouse, and Becky Dolinsky. Maureen O'Driscoll's thoughtful copyediting smoothed my prose.

A number of organizations provided me with financial support at critical junctures: the Woodrow Wilson Foundation, the Society for the Psychological

Study of Social Issues, TDK Electronics, the University of California-Santa Cruz, Ohio University, the Women's Leadership Program at George Washington University, and Loyola College of Maryland.

Many thanks to the friends in Philadelphia who helped me cope with rape and the justice process, in particular Mimi Grimes, Karen Walker, Sarah at Philadelphia WOAR, and two very decent prosecutors. Finally, Barry Ochrach, your love and support through the entire justice process and subsequent data collection and analysis, as well as your constructive criticism, dinners, and shared parenting, kept me going.

CHAPTER 1

WHY TAKE A STAND?

Rape is a devastating kind of victimization that destroys a person's sense of safety and self and frequently produces emotional trauma that outlasts physical injuries.[1] In the United States, women who survive rape have one formal avenue for holding attackers accountable: the criminal justice process. But national data on crime reporting collected by the Federal Bureau of Investigation (FBI) and Bureau of Justice Statistics reveal that a little more than half of attempted and completed rapes are brought to the attention of law enforcement agencies.[2] And academic studies of crime incidence that use less-restrictive definitions find as few as one in six rapes are reported.[3]

Over the last five decades, many social scientists, policymakers, legal personnel, victim advocates, and feminist activists have debated whether women should report rape, arguing both for and against encouraging it. Two key arguments for reporting are that (1) it is a victim's social obligation to activate the justice process to protect others from harm and (2) punishments available through the criminal justice process offer the only real means to deter rapists. Arguments opposing reporting include the following: (1) the process as it currently operates in the United States is not effective in deterring rape or in rehabilitating rapists, (2) blatant racial and class biases in the application of law restrict justice to a narrow band of the citizenry, and (3) participation in rape prosecution damages many women because it fails to produce justice and subjects them to blaming. Rape survivors have not established a group identity and have not substantially shaped the development of the debate about reporting. But, maybe they can and should.

Between 1991 and 1993, I interviewed approximately 50 rape survivors about their experiences prosecuting their assailants. They had pursued their own agendas and, in the process, experienced themselves as more than "resources" employed at the discretion of prosecutors—the formal role they occupied as crime victims. Although their participation was personally difficult and the prosecution failed some, they were not left with nothing.

Rape survivors' narratives of prosecution have great relevance to the debate about whether or not women should report their victimization to police. They provide critical data for women who have been raped and are pondering tough questions: Is it worth it? What choices can I make? What is it like to talk to and work with detectives and attorneys? What is it like to testify in court? Am I going to be vilified by the defense attorney? Is there anything that I can do to prepare myself for interaction with police, prosecutors, and defense attorneys or to make testifying easier?

Rape survivors' accounts provide tremendously useful data for prosecutors and police considering equally tough questions: Does the criminal justice process have an unjustifiably poor reputation? Why don't rape survivors seem to trust me? Are there ways I can better use my resources to secure good outcomes for the state? What can I do to make the prosecution experience better for rape survivors?

Similarly, these narratives help rape crisis and victim-witness advocates and counselors see more clearly when and how their interventions are of value to rape survivors and how supporting rape survivors' needs can serve both prosecutorial goals and long-term societal interests. Finally, rape survivors' narratives provide a resource for the friends and family of raped women who want to support their loved one's decision making, but know that she cannot yet tell them how best to do that. They will learn what they can do of value and when and why their heartfelt efforts to help might be rejected. By bringing together the experiences of varied rape survivors in this book, I seek to provide information from which these questions can be answered and action can follow.

A User's Guide: Where Is It?

In August 1985 I was raped by strangers and began a journey through the criminal justice system in Philadelphia, Pennsylvania, that would last several years. This research project came into focus as my knowledge about the rape law, court procedures, and gaps in the social science literature on rape grew.

When the police entered the house at 1:30 A.M. one Saturday, my journey through the criminal justice process began. I was one year out of college, but I knew almost nothing about how courts and trials worked. It was not something I had learned about from my parents, in public high school, or in my college major. While I knew that other women had gone through rape trials before me, no book existed that could tell me what it was like to testify in court, what it was like to talk to and work with detectives and attorneys, what choices I could make, what I could refuse to do, and what feelings I might have about my whole experience. Sometimes not knowing was in itself frightening.

By the time I entered the University of California in the fall of 1986, to begin a Ph.D. program in sociology, I had testified in two preliminary hearings and a trial and two defendants had been sent to prison. I concluded that my experience was frustrating, but less difficult and harmful than I had expected. My involvement with the Philadelphia criminal justice process was not over, however, because a third defendant was in detention awaiting trial and a fourth suspect remained at large. After I flew back to the East Coast to testify during the winter term, I decided that I wanted to do independent research to find out if the reform of rape laws had contributed to my "better than I expected" impressions. Associate Professor Norma Wikler agreed to oversee such an independent project, and I began the initial stages.

After exploring the law of rape and the process by which it was prosecuted, I wanted to know more about the part that rape survivors played in bringing their assailants to justice. I immediately found *The Victim of Rape: Institutional Reactions* written by Lynda Holmstrom and Ann Burgess,[4] which followed 146 girls and women from hospital emergency wards, to meetings with prosecutors, and into court. The authors described their observations of rape victims' interactions with legal personnel and the women's and girls' comments. It documented the stress of participating in the prosecution effort caused by repeated trips to court, lengthy waits, harassment by defense counsel, courtroom contact with the assailant, and general lack of control. Reading this text allowed me to see that many raped women endured great emotional discomfort to see the prosecution through to its conclusion. This willingness to endure suggested a high level of commitment to the legal process on their part.

The Victim of Rape also raised many questions in my mind. If participating in the legal process was traumatic, in whole or in part, what kept women involved in it? What or whom did survivors hold responsible for their discomfort? What did rape survivors do about their discomfort? I thought it was unlikely that women who were emotionally traumatized would not respond to the conditions that created the trauma in some way. Were rape survivors not doing anything to reduce or alter their discomfort or did the research method miss what they were doing? It seemed to me that there must be women other than myself who did not only feel traumatized by their involvement in the process.

Studies that picked up where Holmstrom and Burgess left off, documenting rape survivors' involvement with the criminal justice system after the main push for rape law reform, did not exist. Studies that explored the meaning the legal process had for rape survivors, documenting the activities in which they engaged when not in the presence of legal actors, and that questioned how differences among women came to matter as they progressed through the legal system, also did not exist. How rape survivors took on the victim-witness role in the criminal justice process needed to be examined. The reasons that they carried out their obligations to the legal process, from giving statements to investigators to testifying in court, needed to be explored and not assumed. I decided to embark on that exploration.

Survivors Pursuing Justice in the Wake of Rape

Methodological Overview

This book is about women taking part in the criminal prosecution of rapists who attacked them. It is based on interviews with 47 women and explores their experiences from sexual assault through reporting, investigation, probable cause hearings, plea bargains, trials, and sentencing. The sample of women is varied. It includes survivors raped by strangers, acquaintances, and past and present intimates; white women and women of color; upper- and middle-class women as well as those supporting themselves on marginal work or state aid; women with college degrees and high school educations; teenagers and women over 50; and women from a range of states in the United States. The only common experience among the survivors is sexual violation—an intrusion on their physical being and sense of personal safety—that presented them with a common problem. Each woman had to define what had happened and decide whether a criminal justice response was warranted. And, ultimately, each did.

I chronologically took rape survivors through their legal experiences.[5] Their accounts were transcribed verbatim, and I developed my analysis by systematically coding these accounts.[6]

I approached rape survivors as goal-directed problem solvers.[7] I sought to understand how women involved in a particular kind of forced sexual interaction come to interpret it as a criminal event and claim a role in the criminal justice process. I assumed that rape survivors behaved on the basis of what they knew and believed as a result of their membership in particular social worlds. I assumed that police, prosecutors, defense attorneys, and judges shared a common understanding of the criminal justice process as a result of their training and working together daily. I sought to learn how the extent that a survivor did or did not share the meanings common to criminal justice personnel shaped her strategies for interacting with them and the success of her interactions. Likewise, I sought to learn how the extent of a rape survivor's knowledge of the specialized rules of interaction that govern courtroom conduct shaped her strategies for engaging with the attorneys that questioned her there.

Rape survivors' pursuit of legal recourse involves asserting a social identity that may or may not be supported by others: victim. In taking on this identity, the rape survivor must contend with how she is viewed by legal personnel engaged in the ongoing prosecution and defense of alleged rapists. If the prosecutor or defense attorney challenges her victim identity, she must respond to maintain her claim on the victim-witness role. I sought to learn what rape survivors perceived as identity challenges and how they responded to them.

Because I did not assume the boundaries of the criminal justice process as it is known by the personnel who work within it, I could learn how rape survivors' memberships in multiple social worlds and multiple role obligations were both resources and obstacles for their participation in the criminal justice process. I could also learn what aspects of rape survivors' biographies and motivations led some to greater success in working with criminal justice personnel and testifying in court.

In chapters 2–9, I will discuss rape survivors' participation in and experiences of distinct phases of the criminal justice process. As I move through these phases, I will highlight continuous and changing features of rape survivors' behavior in the criminal justice process. In the next several pages, I will provide an overview of what my research revealed.

Overview of Themes

Cultural stereotypes about rape victimization and rape victims shape how rape survivors enact the victim-witness role, all the way through the process. At the outset, stereotypes influence the ease with which women apply the labels "rape" and "rapist" to an event they experience as a sexual violation and to the men who perpetrate these violations. During the investigative phase, they are attentive to whether investigators and prosecutors judge their actions or their character negatively. Later, concern with judges' and jurors' acceptance of stereotypes motivates survivors to prepare before court events. As trials loom, legal personnel orient survivors to specific matters, such as behavioral expectations for victims, community racial dynamics, or the potential meanings others may attribute to their speaking patterns and vocabulary.

Cultural ideals of competent witnesses and "rape victims" establish parameters for survivors' courtroom behavior and require women to do more than construct convincing answers to questions. As a result, most women seek to moderate what they are feeling, what feelings they express, and how intensely they express them when in court. Prosecutors and judges generally facilitate this emotion management, while defense attorneys seek to hinder it.

Even rape survivors' decisions about whether to participate in sentencing are based on their understanding of what kind of investment is appropriate for victims of crime to express in penalties.

Rape survivors' existing social relations and associated role responsibilities shape their actions: they evaluate their options as mothers, daughters, wives, daughters-in-law, girlfriends, ex-partners, and so forth. Women who feel morally and legally responsible for others seek to continue to protect them in the aftermath of rape, and this affects what they do. Some seek counsel or emotional support before initiating legal action, some extend their protection to the men who raped them, and some make reports primarily to appease others. Following reporting, some women reconsider role obligations that are at odds with full participation, but others cannot.

Family members, friends, and even strangers influence when and how women initiate contact with police and provide moral and physical support for making formal reports. Friends and family members later influence women's ongoing strategies of engagement: fostering contact with law enforcement during the investigations, assisting with precourt preparation, helping them maintain composure while on the witness stand, helping them understand how their testimony fits into the overall case being built by the prosecutor, and granting legitimacy to their motivations to participate in sentencing or other court events.

Women have concerns about involving family and friends in court events, however. These occasions expose supporters to detailed testimony about the rape that may offend or emotionally injure them and also can result in changing their attitudes and behavior toward the survivors. Thus, some survivors limit would-be supporters' access to court events, but others resolve the conflict posed by their need for support by constructing their testimony in ways that shield listeners from painful truths.

Victim-witness and rape crisis advocates are widely recognized as experts by rape survivors and strongly influence women's reporting decisions. Victim-witness advocates also present an alternative form of court support. When advocates are aligned with prosecutors' agendas, however, completely relying on them for support causes problems for survivors.

Fear of rapists returning to harm them or their loved ones delays some rape survivors' reporting. This fear can be managed through redefinition of the rapist, and it need not depress survivors' desires to be visible participants in the process.

Strong trauma reactions make it difficult for women to process information and contribute to reporting delays. Yet, debilitating trauma reactions are not predictive of rape survivors' later involvement in the process. Some severely traumatized women are quite active in pursuing prosecution and are assertive in their relationships with legal personnel.

Survivors apply what they learn about the legal process in their encounters with legal personnel and in courtrooms. Sometimes their learning unfolds over a period of weeks; other times, it unfolds by the minute, as they use trial-and-error methods to develop an effective way to counter defense questioning tactics. They can and do get better at being witnesses, and their perceptions of self-improvement are coupled with greater confidence in fulfilling the witness role.

Frequently, rape survivors' motivations to engage with the criminal justice process exceed prosecutors' focus on establishing guilt and securing a sentence. Women act to resolve the power imbalance the rape establishes with the rapist so that they can achieve an accurate formal label for their injury, move beyond their feelings of fear, and achieve a sanction that is comparable to the wrong they experienced. In some cases, their goals lead them to support the prosecutor; in others, it may lead them to resist his or her efforts on behalf of the state.

The problems that rape survivors face in the criminal justice process are not simply the result of the adversarial nature of court, defense tactics, or their own emotional reactions to violent sexual domination. Problems emerge from several factors including the following: (1) the social networks in which they are situated, (2) their variable access to emotional and financial resources, (3) their lack of knowledge about the formal and informal practices of court-rooms, (4) their lack of structural power in the criminal justice process, and (5) standard procedures employed by prosecutors and police.

Rape survivors' satisfaction with the criminal justice process ebbs and flows as they confront and negotiate solutions to obstacles. If participation in the process can be used to achieve some desired end in regard to the rapist, then dissatisfaction with the resolution of the case is somewhat offset. However, rape survivors' dissatisfaction persists when it emerges from interactions in which legal personnel use their structural power to force them to respond in certain ways—interactions the women experience as a second assault. These kinds of distressing interactions occur with prosecutors as well as defense attorneys. Whatever the cause, such dissatisfaction leads to defensive behavior, and this had the potential to undermine the prosecutorial mission.

Understanding the basis of rape survivors' problems, their impact, and rape survivors' own efforts to solve them opens the door to resolve or reduce them and, thus, to increase rape survivors' satisfaction with the criminal justice process.

The Social Context of Rape Prosecution

A woman's ability to use the criminal justice process to pursue her rapist is limited by laws that define specific sexual violations as a crime and by rules that specify what counts as evidence, what attorneys may ask victims/survi-vors, and what jurors may or must consider. Historically, laws hampered the prosecution of rape by delineating a narrow band of behaviors as criminal and holding victims/survivors of rape to different and higher standards of conduct than victims of other crimes. Few women who experienced forced sexual vio-lation were able to access the criminal justice process and, of those who did, fewer saw jurors hold their assailants accountable. Throughout the latter half of the twentieth century, altering problematic rape statutes was high on the feminist agenda.

Gender Expectations and Bias Against Women Encoded in Law

When early U.S. legislators created a criminal justice process for the new North American country, they adopted the adversarial fact-finding practices employed in Britain. They also adopted their criminal codes from British Com-mon Law.[8] The criminal laws went unexamined and unchanged over centuries. Thus, well into the twentieth century, the legal definition of rape reflected the thinking of the men of a much earlier period of time.[9]

Eighteenth-century thinkers who established the U.S. criminal codes and procedures understood rape as an act of "carnal knowledge." It was a sexual

transgression of a woman by a man who was not her husband. Rape involved forcibly taking sexual intercourse, but it was not explicitly understood as an assault
or a violent attack against a person. Laws distinguished the crime of rape from
other crimes of assault through the exclusion of spouses and a number of ele-
ments of proof that were required to corroborate a complaining woman's story.

Into the 1970s, many states required raped women (1) to pass a polygraph,
(2) to show proof of their resistance of the utmost (bruising, torn clothing,
other evidence of a struggle), (3) to provide verification they had cried for help
(witnesses who could testify to that effect), (4) to make their complaint
promptly to legal authorities, and (5) to provide physical evidence the assailant's penis had penetrated their vagina.[10] In addition to these corroboration
requirements, many statutes also specified that in cases of rape—but not other
crimes—the judge read to the jury an instruction that traced back to a
seventeenth-century jurist, Sir Matthew Hale: "rape is an accusation easily to
be made and hard to be proven and harder to be defended by the party
accused, tho never so innocent."[11]

Specific assumptions about women and their proper social role are the
source of this narrow definition of rape and requirements of proof.[12] Excluding a woman's spouse followed from the belief that it is her proper marital
role to submit to sexual relations on demand. Three general stereotypes about
women's nature are the source of corroboration requirements and the Hale
Caution. (1) Women are deceitful and vindictive: they will fabricate stories
about rape to achieve power over specific men. (2) Women ask for it: they
seduce attackers by the way they behave or dress, which is a subliminal or
unconscious expression of their true desire. (3) Women want it: women fanta-
size about being overcome and, in general, desire aggressive sexual relations.
Given these perceptions of women, their word could never be sufficient to
convict a man who maintained his innocence. Hard corroborating evidence
was necessary to prove sexual intercourse occurred and was unwanted.

Socially, in the past, woman's moral character was assumed to be linked to
her history of chastity and the likelihood she would consent to extramarital
intercourse. Women who were not chaste were suspect for being more likely
to consent to sexual relations and, in turn, to be less moral and likely to lie
about it—to "cry rape."[13] This link provided additional support for the Hale
Caution and was the impetus for the final piece of evidence that made its way
into rape trials: past sexual history. While prosecutors could not use the past
sexual history of a male to impeach his credibility, it was generally accepted
that "evidence of the 'unchastity' of the female [was] admissible for the purpose of showing the *probability of her consent* to the act of intercourse."[14] Thus,
the virginity of a woman was considered relevant when determining whether
she was a credible witness—if she was likely to lie—*and* if she was a willing
sexual partner generally.

The special corroboration requirements, cautionary instructions, and the
use of past sexual history made prosecuting rape difficult. Women who had

submitted to attackers out of fear, who remained silent during the rape because of threats, whose screams of terror or pain were not heard by others, whose assailants violated them with an object or did not ejaculate, and who delayed reporting for several hours, days, or longer were without "proper" evidence to gain convictions. Women who were married had no prospect of securing legal action against husbands who raped them, no matter how brutally.

Social researchers documented that the legal requirements had a significant cost in that the majority of rapes brought to the attention of authorities never came to trial.[15] Even if police made an arrest, prosecutors frequently would not file a criminal complaint and grand juries would not indict. Conviction rates for rape in the early 1970s were lower than those for all other violent crimes, as low as 10 percent in New York and 11 percent in California.[16]

Progressive Reforms and Their Limits

In the late 1960s, feminists organized to bring public attention to the private issue of rape and to increase the success rate of rape prosecution. They pursued several approaches at once.[17] Community activists publicized violence against women by organizing Take Back the Night marches and speak-outs, created rape hotlines and counseling services, and established ties with law enforcement groups to change procedures for dealing with raped women. Lobbying groups such as the National Organization for Women funded Rape Task Forces to collect information about rape, publicly criticized problematic aspects of the laws on the books, proposed model legislation, and joined forces with legislators concerned about a rising tide of crime to push changes through the legal system.[18] For example, women in Michigan wrote and pushed a Model Sexual Statute through the legislature in 1974 and the Philadelphia Center for Rape Concern (PCRC) proposed another in Pennsylvania in 1977. Academic feminists also brought the deficient nature of rape law into the consciousness of attorneys and judges by publishing critiques of existing legislation and legal procedures in influential law journals.[19]

Feminists were most successful in getting state legislatures to eliminate the requirements that a woman must make an immediate report of rape to police and that her testimony be corroborated by physical damage or witnesses.[20] It took a lot longer to get the spousal exemption removed.[21] Some states made rape law gender neutral and unwanted sexual contact, including intercourse, was combined with other assault crimes. Some states lowered penalties to encourage juries to convict and others raised them to emphasize the seriousness of the crime. New laws to limit the kinds of information that could be brought into court to discredit a witness, known as rape shields, became effective in many states.[22] Through litigation, rape trauma syndrome became evidence of victimization in some states,[23] and survivors' reports of rape to any person became evidence of prompt disclosure (required by law) in others.[24]

Education about symptoms of rape trauma and about the lack of evidence supporting myths about rape and rape victims significantly changed police procedures for handling rape cases. By the mid-1970s, researchers found that fewer women reported that they were treated with insensitivity by police.[25] Feminist pressure helped police departments secure state and county funds to pay for medical exams that provided forensic evidence of rape.[26] The information feminist reformers collected about case attrition also led some district attorneys (DAs) to rethink the way they handled rape cases. Some formed special teams of experienced prosecutors to handle child molestation and sexual assault cases and some shifted to a standard of "vertical prosecution," which meant that rape survivors dealt with a single prosecuting attorney rather than being shifted between attorneys as their assailant's case made its way through the system.

Supportive agencies for rape victims were created in many places as well. County and state treasuries built special private emergency room facilities, funded rape crisis hotlines,[27] and subsidized the training of sexual assault advocates who met rape survivors at the hospital and helped them handle the immediate demands of the medical exam and the police report. Other products of women's vision and organization included Sexual Assault Response Teams (SARTs), groups of advocates and specially trained medical practitioners, and Sexual Assault Nurse Examiners (SANEs), who were specially trained evidence collectors.[28]

The reform of rape laws removed many statutory obstacles to prosecution and sent a symbolic message that rape was a crime of violence. However, changes in the law did not produce dramatic effects in the short term: the percentage of rapes that were charged and the conviction rate did not increase dramatically.[29] This is because the felony trial process exists through the decisions and behavior of legal personnel: police officers, detectives, DAs, judges, and jurors.

Feminist reform of laws did not result in dramatic shifts in the prosecution rate of reported rapes because many legal personnel continued to make decisions *as if* the unreformed laws were still in existence. They chose to fully prosecute alleged rapists only when corroborating evidence was abundant and the survivor's character was unassailable. Some decision makers still believed the assumptions that underlay the old laws. Others felt pressured to rely on stereotypes because the jurors and judges who would be making decisions about probable cause and guilt believed them. If they hoped to advance professionally they needed to rack up "wins."[30]

Even the new courtroom protections for rape survivors had little impact. Unless prosecutors kept "rape shields" in mind and raised objections in cross-examination, witnesses had no protection from questions about their past sexual history. If the new laws were not applied by prosecutors, it was *as if* they did not exist. Most rape shields allowed sexual history to be introduced under certain circumstances, and some judges broadly interpreted the exceptions allowing defense attorneys wide latitude.[31] If judges did not uphold prosecutors' objections, it was also *as if* they did not exist. In addition, rape shields did not counter the flexibility of the English language, which allowed defense attorneys to imply rape survivors were untrustworthy and promiscuous without actually asking prohibited questions.[32]

Situating Survivors in Their Contexts

The experiences of the survivors I interviewed reflect the history of gender bias in rape law and feminist reform efforts. Rosanne, who was raped in 1969, dealt with unreformed laws and procedures. Five women prosecuted in the mid- to late 1970s, after their state eliminated corroboration requirements, but before it added a rape shield. The rest of the women had both forms of protection.

The survivors prosecuted rapists in 11 states.[33] Several comparisons show the scattered nature of state law reform in 1987.[34] First, spousal exemptions remained for the crime of rape in Arizona, Louisiana, and Virginia. Thus, two women who participated in the prosecution of their spouses in California could not have done so in any of these three states.[35] Second, Arizona still allowed a defendant to bring up a rape survivor's past sexual history with others without restriction. In California, such information was admissible for the purposes of establishing consent but not for establishing a survivor's credibility; while in Illinois and Louisiana, a defendant could not introduce any evidence of a survivor's past sexual history with others. A third point of comparison is age of consent. Before such an age, sexual intercourse is automatically a criminal offense. The rape of 17-year-old Megan, which California prosecutors charged as a statutory rape, could not have been similarly handled in Louisiana, where the age of consent was younger. Fourth, sentences for similar forms of sexual violence differed by state. While Natalie and the other Louisiana survivors had the prospect of seeing their assailants sentenced to life, convicted rapists in Arizona, Illinois, and Kansas faced minimum periods of incarceration of five to six years, and those in California were ensured of only three years.

Most of the women had support services available to them. However, some smaller cities and rural areas did not have a Rape Crisis Center (RCC) or a hospital prepared to conduct rape exams. For example, Urban County in California had only two hospitals located in the urban core that were set up to perform evidence collection, and women living in outlying rural areas had to travel to be examined there. Francine, who lived in a rural area of the county, was more than an hour's drive from the hospital that conducted her rape exam and over a half hour's drive from a crisis center.

Rape Stereotypes

Stereotypes are characteristics that are attributed to individuals on the basis of their membership in particular social groups. Humans use stereotypes to develop a behavioral line toward others in the absence of direct knowledge (academic or experiential). Stereotypes provide a logic to initiate or refuse to initiate interactions with others, to grant or deny others status in interactions, and to assume shared meanings once interactions are under way. The more that humans lack knowledge of certain groups or group experiences the more they tend to rely on stereotypes to guide their behavior.

In spite of being common social knowledge about members of a particular group, stereotypes are inaccurate. First, stereotypes are false. They associate an attribute with a group of people that is not unique to them and not universally shared among them. Second, stereotypes imply that all people in a particular group place the same importance on their group membership.

Gender stereotypes explain women's generally lesser social status relative to men as a matter of natural differences between the sexes. Women follow their preferences and make choices that lead to their fewer educational and employment opportunities, to their lesser influence over religion and politics, and to their greater family responsibilities. Gender stereotypes ignore men's individual and group control of institutions—economic, legal, and religious— and their physical violence. Rape stereotypes are a special class of gender stereotypes. Collectively, they support the ideas that (1) rape occurs because women fail to heed men's natural tendencies and to adequately protect themselves and (2) unwanted sexual contact is not itself violence. Some of these distorted stereotypes are as follows: It is in men's normal nature to be overcome by a woman's appearance. It is normal that men can't make sense of women's frequently mixed signals. It is not harmful when a man forces himself sexually on a woman, because heterosexual intercourse is a naturally desirable interaction. When written into law or applied by legal personnel, these stereotypes absolve rapists of responsibility for much of the sexual violence they perpetrate.

Because women have always reported violent sexual encounters, our society has had to acknowledge that rape exists. Thus, coexisting with stereotypes that absolve all but the most violent and sadistic rapists are stereotypes about the impact of rape on women victims. These stereotypes of rape victims demand a postrape reaction that is responsive to the mythic qualities of a real sexual attack. It is a response that decisively names the event as "rape." It involves the display of intense emotions—assumed to arise from the irrationality and unprovoked nature of the attack—and an immediate desire to unleash the power of the law upon the offender. When these social expectations of rape victims extend into the courts, they also absolve rapists of responsibility.[36]

Women and men living in the United States are aware of stereotypes that explain the causes of rape and the responses of rape victims. Some may accept them. But others may reject them as myths, because of their direct experiences with rape and rape victims or their exposure to feminist education that provides accurate information about the causes and consequences of rape.[37] This book explores the ways in which rape survivors and others—supporters and legal personnel—respond to rape victimization in the context of rape and victim stereotypes. My discussion expands on the scope of beliefs that frame rape.

Defining "Rape"

All women in this book experienced some kind of forced sexual penetration by a body part or object: vaginal, oral, or anal. These women did not distinguish significantly between forms of invasive sexual domination and all agreed with characterizing their experience as "rape." The men who attacked these women were, however, charged under a variety of statutes, because criminal laws pertaining to sexual crimes vary by state.[38] The differences between how the women experienced the sexual attacks and how prosecutors charged them in formal complaints and, in many cases, reconfigured them through plea negotiations are a topic of inquiry.

Survivor or Victim?

It is conventional in the social science literature on rape to describe women who have been raped as "victims" and those who become involved in the legal process as "victim-witnesses." Counselors are more likely to refer to women who have been raped as survivors, which emphasizes a woman's strength in the face of adversity and her potential to adjust to the physical and emotional damage she experienced. I use "survivors" and "women" in this text when I refer to the participants in my study, as these terms separate the experience of being sexually violated—victimization—from what women do about it. While "victim" is often heard and read as passive, survivor is more open, and because agency is the focus of my investigation, I prefer this term. Identifying a woman as a survivor of rape also facilitates (1) analytic separations between the event that is her impetus to make a claim on the criminal justice process and her naming of that event; (2) the prosecutorial characterization of the event and her legal role; (3) the legal contest the prosecution and defense conduct over the nature of the alleged criminal conduct and the woman's legal status; and (4) whether the woman experiences the way medical and legal personnel respond to her claims as domination.[39]

In no way do I intend my use of "survivor" to undercut the very real physical and emotional damage caused by rape or the real structural inequalities associated with women's positions as witnesses in the organizations the justice process comprises. In many instances, raped women *are* re-victimized in their interactions with members of the broader society in which they live and in their interactions with legal personnel. However, how and why this re-victimization occurs deserves study. It does not directly follow from the rape event and cannot be assumed in all cases.

Pseudonyms

Someday, there will be no shame in publicly identifying as a survivor of sexual violence. Right now, however, this is not the case for many.[40] Thus, to protect the privacy of interviewees, I use pseudonyms throughout this book. I have replaced the names of real individuals or real places with pseudonyms or relationship descriptors (such as, [her husband]). I've left intact rape survivors' use of my name. By writing this book, I hope to shed more light on the experiences of rape survivors and reduce the stigma they experience.

CHAPTER 2

"I Knew I Had To . . .": Reporting Rape to Law Enforcement

When I asked women to tell me about how they decided to contact the police, I learned that they reached the point of telling officers that they were raped in very different ways. Consider the unique qualities of Natalie's, Maria's, Sandra's, and Marlene's stories.

A stranger forced his way into Natalie's house, beat her with a flashlight, and raped her on the floor in front of her toddler. This 26-year-old, white, married legal secretary decided that she would report to police while her attacker was still present. Despite being so brutally beaten that police later transported her to the hospital in an ambulance, she sought to look for and remember information that would ensure he was caught and brought to justice.

> At work they had offered us, um, crime prevention seminar and said like if this would happen to you, that you have to remember his race and any tattoos or any of, you know, what he looked like, and I can remember thinking that while he is in the house that I really have to look at him [. . .] I never had a doubt you know, am I gonna do it [report] or aren't I.

The man who raped Maria was her husband. This 26-year-old, Mexican-American clerical worker and mother of two small children went to police primarily to get herself and her children to safety. She told them about her husband forcing sex acts only because it seemed necessary to secure their help to get to a shelter.

> I knew that I'd have to, that you know that I'd have to do something, somehow, to . . . to get free of him. 'Cause he was probably gonna perform anal sex on me next time [he threatened this] or whatever. It's gonna be worse and worse, it was just getting worse and worse. I decided to sneak back in my room, get my clothes, turn the alarm off, 'cause [. . .], it was still on [. . .] and then got my purse, quietly shut his door, went into the kids' room, quietly shut their door, got dressed, snuck out their window, and I walked and like ran to the police station. And I just told them that I want to get my kids and, well, they wanted a valid

reason. I told them that my husband ... you know, he hit me and I want to leave him. I wanna go to a shelter or something, you know. I just want to get away from him, I just want to get my kids. [...] They're like well, we need ... they wanted to know the story, so that's when I reported to them the story of what he did. [...] I told them the whole story, I told them the sexual acts that he made me do, yeah, it was pretty blunt, you know. I knew that I was in [a] way doing that [to get them to help].

An acquaintance overpowered and raped Sandra after she had fallen asleep on a couch. This 22-year-old, white, childless, single college student and rape crisis counselor recalled an extended period during which she was disoriented and paralyzed. Telling a rape crisis hotline volunteer that she was raped finally helped her break through physical and mental trauma responses that rendered her incapable of rational thought or action.

My mom was like, "Call Thelma [who directs the rape crisis line]." I called the line. I was [very] embarrassed to call the line (like I know these people). I'm [thinking], "I can't call them, you know, this is for rape victims!" You know, I mean, my thoughts I had going in my head are to this day, I don't even comprehend it. But I did [call the crisis line], and it was this girl Nancy, and um, you know, I told her it was me. I'm just all, "I think I was raped," and I started to tell her what happened. *Then* right there, *I knew*, right there. She's all, "I'm calling Thelma right now." So, right there, I knew, I said, "Take me back! Take me back, I'm calling the police." I wanted to be at Inga's [where it happened]. And I called them [the police], and I said, "I've been raped, please come." [...] That's when I knew, that's when everything started hitting me. Like, this really happened, Sandy, I mean, this really happened. Then the pain started to really, I didn't realize that I was like, bleeding [vaginally], you know, and I couldn't walk.

Marlene's ex-boyfriend broke into her apartment and raped her. This white, 20-year-old, childless, single college student quickly concluded that she ought to report the sexual attack, but knew also that she needed to get emotional support to ensure she would carry through her decision.

I mean, when I was walkin' around my apartment, delirious wondering what to do, I thought to myself if I stay here I won't report this, but if I go upstairs and get help from her [the lady Marlene baby-sits for], I know she'll make me, and I know she will help me with it. I just knew I had to, you know, it was just something [I had to do]. I mean, I had been raped before and not reported it, with this it was just different. [...] She right away insisted that I call the police, and that I needed to report it, so I did. I called um, 911, and I said that I, I just said that someone had broken into my apartment and had raped me and they just left. And she went downstairs with me and waited for the police with me.

In combination, these quotations illustrate that rape survivors follow different paths into the criminal justice process. Natalie, Maria, Sandra, and

Marlene were all in their 20s, but their lives were distinct. They had dissimilar concerns and capabilities to act during and after sexual assaults, different social supports available, and varied knowledge of the U.S. legal system.

The primary purpose of this chapter is to explore how the full spectrum of survivors in this study came to the attention of police. It focuses on the kinds of dilemmas they faced and the decisions that they made in light of the kinds of victimization that they experienced. It traces the centrality of cultural stereotypes, from what rape is and who rapists are, to decisions about reporting rape and the ways that knowledge of the U.S. justice process shapes these decisions. It shows how the emotional trauma of rape affects decision-making capacity and the important ways that family, friends, and sometimes strangers facilitate reporting rape and shape the survivors' decisions to contact police.

Violent Sexual Violation Experienced as Reportable Rape

Forty-three percent of the survivors who decided on their own to report the rape said that they did not actively deliberate or weigh pros and cons.[1] They experienced the interactions they had with their assailants as reportable rapes. That is they recognized them as sexual violation and as criminal in nature while they were taking place. In general, the sexual assaults they reported conformed closely to cultural stereotypes of "real" rape. Their assailants brandished or threatened to use a weapon they claimed to have or physically subdued them by beating or strangling them. The 20 women perceived the force used or threatened by their attackers as the *sole* cause of the sex acts that took place and accepted *no* blame for the rapist's actions. Many said that they feared for their lives and considered it a distinct possibility that they would be killed during the assaults. Eighty-five percent of these women labeled their assailants strangers. Two other women in the group, raped by their ex-boyfriends, said that they "acted like strangers" during the sudden attacks: completely without regard to their prior positive relationships. The parallel between what these 20 women experienced and knew to be worth bringing to the attention of police is demonstrated in the speed of reporting. All reached police through some means within 30 minutes of their escape or the rapist's departure.

Two quotations help to illustrate the nature of the assaults that led to these solo reporting decisions. Despite their different social relations with their assailants—stranger and roommate's houseguest—Cindy and Sara's descriptions highlight the assailant's violence and their own immediate fears of death or serious bodily harm.

Cindy, a 37-year-old, white single parent and clerical worker, was raped in an empty apartment by a gun-wielding assailant who pulled her off the street. The attacker forced her to perform oral sex and raped her vaginally, but she talked him out of raping her anally. After the assailant left her, Cindy hopped over a low fence and ran to a neighboring house. She describes the circumstances leading up to and aspects of the sexual assault:

So as we approach on the street: I step towards the street to like, step around him, right, and he stepped the same way, so then I stepped back and then he stepped back. [...] And just then, you know, as I started laughing, he put his hand on my shoulder and a gun up to my head, and then he said, um, he ... said look down, look down, don't look at me, and then he pushed me over towards the houses. [...] As he's leading me down this um, alleyway, he kind of paused for a minute, and was telling me that this was a test, "You can get an A or a B or a C, or you can flunk this fuckin' test and I'll blow your fuckin' brains out." [The assailant took Cindy to an empty apartment where he continued to threaten her, verbally abuse her, forced her to disrobe and raped her vaginally and orally.] [...] At this point I'm figuring this guy's just gonna kill me you know. [...] 'Cause I didn't see how he could do this and then let me live, you know. I mean I really thought he was gonna kill me, and I kept thinking about my son, um, back at the apartment, wondering where I am, why I'm not home yet, and I had this image of you know, him you know, at 3 or 4 in the morning, still wondering where I am, and maybe the cops coming to say that you know, they just found his mother murdered in the apartment down the street. [...] I'm thinking I'm gonna do anything I can to try and get out of this alive, you know?

After she had gone to bed, the rapist made a surprise attack on Sara, a middle-class, childless, white teacher in her 30s. He beat and attempted to suffocate her when she resisted his efforts to rape her.

I walked into my bedroom, shut the door, and took off my clothes and got in bed and just as I was ready to turn out the light, he walked through the door. [...] He says, "I didn't get um, any pussy at that club so now I'm going to fuck you." I said, "Hey, just leave me alone, just ... just leave." [I'm] thinking that would have been enough [to stop him], and instead he immediately um, jumped on top of me, and squeezed my nose shut, covered my nose. I was struggling with him, and it was very difficult because I couldn't breathe. So I was trying to get his hands off of my face, and every time I would get his hand off my face, he would start cursing at me and saying things to me, and um, then he would squeeze my nose shut or my mouth again and then he would start striking me if I'd get his hands off of me. [...] What kept running through my mind was the fact that this man really wanted to kill me, and I could tell he really wanted to hurt me, that this was what this was all about. It wasn't about—in a way it was about sex—but it wasn't as much sex as it was the violence, I could tell he was really getting off [on] the violence. [...] Every time I could talk, I kept trying to make myself not just an object. I kept saying you know, "Don't do this, your wife will find out," you know, "F—— [Sara's roommate] will find out.... This is rape, you're raping me, you're hurting me."

None of the 20 women who experienced "reportable" rapes recalled ever considering not contacting police. Their clarity about the logical course of action underscores the congruence between what they experienced and knew to be a matter for the criminal justice system. Nine of the 20 women described reflexively calling the police when they got away from the rapist or he left. It was inconceivable that they do anything else. For example, Crystal, a white, single, middle-class professional, attacked in her home by a man who gained entrance through a window in her apartment, explained,

> No. No, there was never an option, [...] I didn't think about that [not calling police], I didn't think it over. I mean it was like, just instantly, this is what you do. [...] I was up off the floor the second I thought it was safe and on the phone to police. There was never a second of "Should I report this?" I mean it wasn't even an option.

The 11 other women thought through activating and participating in the criminal justice process before contacting police. Seven of them said that they decided to report the rape while they were still under their assailant's control and their decision influenced how they behaved during the rest of the attack.[2] For example, Natalie, Wanda, and Lauren worked to identify and remember unique characteristics of the rapist, while he was in their presence. Susan and Wanda also tried to protect the evidence of the rape that was left on their bodies.

In the first opening quotation to this chapter, Natalie explained that an education program for victims of crime influenced her behavior during the rape. A legal secretary, she was generally familiar and comfortable with the legal process. Wanda, a 46-year-old, white masseuse, said that she made the decision to dial 911 right after she awakened to find her rapist on top of her. Wanda imagined a future interaction with police during the assault, and noted the rapist's unique characteristics so that she could provide accurate information to them.

> I knew immediately [that I would report]. I mean, even while it was going on, I was aware I was gonna call 911 [...] because I was trying to think okay, he's obviously not muscular because I'm a massage therapist. He didn't smell like alcohol. I was processing information because I knew I would report it. That [not to report] never, ever was a consideration. I knew I would testify if it became necessary. I knew I would go through the system. There was never a doubt. [...] Um, my determination was so great, [...] that I go through the process, and that I do everything: I mean I didn't go to the bathroom or I didn't shower or anything before going to the hospital, because [of] my determination that all of this evidence be, uh, retained.

Like Natalie, Wanda understood that she could contribute to the apprehension of her assailant by providing good information about him. Her comments about avoiding the shower and the toilet indicated that she also understood that the specific kind of victimization she was experiencing—rape—called for her to protect evidence of her assailant that was left on her body. Wanda could not pinpoint the sources of information that led to her particular understanding of her part in the criminal justice process; however, Susan could.

This white restaurant manager in her mid-20s and mother of two small children made her decision to report to police while she was under the control of the knife-wielding assailant who hijacked her car at an bank machine. After escaping, she drove straight to the hospital following the directions that she received from a rape crisis volunteer, who came to her door seeking donations and offering information. Susan's full acceptance of the volunteer's expert knowledge and her conviction to carry out her rape victim role in a manner that helped police led her to reject the hospital receptionist's efforts to make her feel comfortable.

> She [the volunteer] had kinda briefly went over, if you are ever raped you should go to the hospital and call the police. Don't have anything to eat or drink. And don't wash up, and [don't urinate.] And that is what I did. [...] The receptionist [at the hospital], she says, "Can I get you some water or some coffee or something?" And I go, "No. No."

Several other women were less explicit about their motivation, but nevertheless, described behaviors during the assaults aimed at apprehending the suspect. For example, Candace, a 43-year-old, white immigrant enrolled in college, repeatedly was punched in the face by the rapist because she refused to comply with his commands to look away from him. Then when he fled the scene, she followed him out under a street light to get a good look at him and picked up the beeper that dropped from his belt.

Survivors' efforts to attend to the needs of the legal system while they were in danger show both their own mental fortitude and the strength of their commitment to their anticipated role in the criminal justice process. Their descriptions also demonstrate (1) that despite the terror and trauma of rape, some victims are alert and calculating and (2) that survivors readily label rapes that conform to stereotypes as crimes and as legal matters.

The Discovery of Sexual Violation as a Crime

Recognizing that acts of sexual violation are crimes can also be a complicated process involving multiple interactions. Theresa, a white, 48-year-old clerical worker; Megan, a 17-year-old, African American, first-year college student; and Joanna, a 20-year-old, white college junior, knew they had not consented to sexual activity and felt personally violated, but they had trouble making sense of their experiences. Inconsistencies with cultural stereotypes made it difficult for these women to label the disturbing interactions as rape: The women had initially chosen to be with their attackers—a date, another dorm resident, and a mentor. Their assailants' greater physical strength ensured the completion of the assault, but the men did not hurt them with weapons or threaten them with death or bodily harm. Each woman had verbally resisted her assailant, but none had put up sustained physical resistance. Consequently, all three women had some reservations about reporting to police and each disclosed her feelings of violation to many others to determine an appropriate course of action. Unfortunately, Theresa's and Joanna's confusion about what to do was increased when the "experts" they sought out failed to endorse quasi-legal labels they tentatively gave to the assaults. In the end, others' arguments to make police reports strongly influenced the women. To convey the ambiguity that survivors may experience and how they commit themselves to a legal solution, let's examine Theresa's and Megan's accounts of the assaults and the interactions that followed.

A date became a rapist for Theresa. After he took her out for the evening, he invited himself into her house and assaulted her. She described his behavior and her own thoughts and efforts to physically and verbally resist:

[He] started to kiss me. I pushed him away, said "No, I can't do this." I did that three times. And he ... the third time he stood up and I thought he was leaving and that's when he pushed me down on the couch. And got on top of me and my one arm was pinned on the side of the couch and the other arm was out and hitting, [but] I couldn't bring it up [and make contact]. And he um, was just pushing his body on me and it was very painful ... It hurt a lot, and um, probably not too long after that, I uh, I shut down. And I just was gone. Um, he um, first he kept doing that [kissing] and he took my clothes off ... everything off except for my panties and his, and he used his hands on me. [He] put his hands in my vagina and hurt me a lot. At one point he asked me if I wanted him to um, have oral sex with me and I said "no." And he kept trying to put my hand on him and I wouldn't, I'd pull away and I wouldn't let him do that. And um, it just went on for a long time and then um, he um, hurt my breast really bad. It was so painful I think I screamed. (voice drops) Um, and then eventually he um, stood up and pulled me up and took me this way [by the arm] and said, "Lets go into the bedroom where we can lay and hold each other." And so he walked behind me and he walked into my bedroom, laid on the bed. [...] He was masturbating himself, plus, doing me, and I tried to pull away a couple of times and he had his arm on the side of me and would pull me back. And then um, he asked me to have oral sex with him and I said "no." And he said, "It's no big deal we're just finding out what we each like, what turns us each on." And um, then he started pushing my head down on him and I decided just do it, whatever it takes [to] get him out of here. [...] After oral copulation he ... he laid there and um, masturbated until he ejaculated himself and then he got up and left.

After her date left, Theresa felt violated, believing that something was done "to" her, but she was also ambivalent about her own behavior.

And it's like, I wasn't sure what had happened to me, I really wasn't sure. [...] I know I kept saying no. (Theresa sighs.) I wasn't really sure what had happened. But I know I was very upset and I called my best friend. (Theresa's voice drops.) I called her and she says all I did was cry.

The morning after, Theresa described the interaction to a coworker who labeled it rape. To verify the label, she called the local RCC. She asked the

hotline volunteer who answered the telephone what constituted rape and the
volunteer read her a description. The description centered on the penetration
of the vagina with a penis and did not encompass the specific sex acts that
Theresa experienced: digital and oral penetration. Theresa recalled,

> She said that unless ... he had had intercourse with me, that it was not rape. So
> what it did was it ... it told me I was not raped. This is the rape crisis center,
> these are people who are supposed to know this stuff, and she told me no, I
> wasn't raped, so she must be right.

Theresa hung up believing that she had not been "legally" raped, and she
decided that she did not have a reason to make a report to police.

Several days later, Theresa disclosed to her doctor who gave support for a
legal interpretation of her experience, in spite of its differences from the definition supplied by the rape crisis worker. He also referred Theresa to a therapist who was specifically trained to handle rape cases. Still, Theresa explained
that personally it didn't seem worthwhile to pursue a legal remedy, because
her past direct experience with county prosecutors was negative.

> I have had [prior experience] ... (sighs) My sons were sexually molested. And
> the district attorney in this ... in Urban County decided not to prosecute, I do
> not have a lot of faith in the justice system. And I have seen it victimize victims
> over and over again. And I wasn't sure I was strong enough to go through that.
> It wasn't worth it to me.

Nevertheless, learning that she had contracted herpes from her assailant shifted
Theresa's assessment of the damage he had caused. The vaginal lesions gave
her great physical pain and required her to spend money on medications, but
the nature of the disease also made her think beyond her own situation to other
women. The arguments the doctor and her therapist made became persuasive:

> Someone who's not sexually active, like myself, 48 years old, been with two men
> in her whole life, could end up with something like this. So, on the thought of this
> happening to someone else. They were telling me that ... they were encouraging
> me to do it for myself too, they were saying I *needed* to do it.

Twenty days after she was sexually assaulted, Theresa called the police. She
was still not sure what crime had occurred, but believed her experience of sexual violation was within the domain of the criminal justice system.

Megan also took some time to reach a decision to report. One evening in
her first week at college, Megan spent an evening walking about her dormi-
tory visiting students. A senior man invited her into his room, offered her
alcohol, and engaged her in a series of drinking games. After she had con-
sumed a lot of peppermint schnapps and had lost most of her ability to com-
mand her body, he attempted to rape her vaginally and forced her to orally

copulate him. She gave the following account of her physical incapacity and her efforts to verbally resist his coercive behavior:

> I would tell him like, "Oh, my hands feel numb, and the floor, the room is spin-ning." It was like a new experience I think because I never drank. [. . .] I was really, really, really drunk. So then I was laying down on the bed for a little bit, like a few minutes, um, I never lost consciousness or anything. And he came and sat down next to me. And he started kissing me, and I said, "Wait, we can't do this, um, I have a boyfriend, and this is just totally against my morals." I said, "I told you earlier that I had a boyfriend and we were going to stay faithful." I told him "No." But still, I was laughing and just completely out of it. [. . .] Eventually he started kissing me again, and I kind of pushed him away and said, "No." Then he just . . . he just kissed me again and um, I kind of gave in. I mean I was really out of it, I felt really gross. He asked me to lift my arms and take off my sweater, and I said "NO, I have a boyfriend and this is wrong you know, just totally against my morals." He said "Okay" and he started kissing me again. And then, eventually he just . . . he just took my sweater off and the rest of my clothes and, um, he got up and he turned off the light, he locked the door, and he took off his clothes and he got on top of me. And I said, "I really can't do this, I have a boy-friend, it's against my morals, and I'm a virgin, NO, you can't do this to me." And he said, (pause) "Don't worry about it, no one has to find out about it, I'm not gonna tell your boyfriend or your parents, and it can just be between you and me, if it feels good then that's okay." So, (sigh) I kept saying, "No, this is wrong," and he got on top of me anyway. He was about 6'7", he weighed about 230 lbs., was a *big guy*. And so he got on top of me and he tried to have sex with me and it really, really hurt, so I said, "Ow!" I was screaming and I said, "Ow this hurts!" He got up and he would say, you know, "Baby don't worry about it." (laughs) He would like stroke me and everything. I was just kinda laying there not (pause) not really with it. [. . .] I was outside of the situation looking at myself. It wasn't even like I was making any decisions. It was like totally a weird experience. I haven't gotten drunk since and so I don't know if this is how I'd always act, but it just seemed like I wasn't thinking of like, consequences, or I didn't even give a thought to like, I could scream really loud and get up and *leave*. I just felt like, so trapped in the situation that I couldn't think of any way out of it. Eventually he got back on top of me, and um, it hurt again, and so I was screaming and he said, "Ok, don't worry about it" and he lay down next to me and said, verbatim: "Well, if you won't let me put it in you, will you at least kiss it?" So then he like, was guiding my head towards his penis and he made me put it in my mouth, and [he] ejaculated in my mouth. I got up and I spit it out, it was really gross, it was all over my face and my neck and everything.

Megan put her clothes back on (inside out) and stumbled from her assail-ant's room to a bathroom on her own floor, where she brushed her teeth and washed her face. She was still very inebriated and incapable of doing much. She was also crying uncontrollably and several women who found her in the bathroom tried to console her. Megan did not tell them what had hap-pened; however, when a resident assistant (RA) whom they sent came to the bathroom, Megan described what had taken place. The RA did not label Megan's experience, but suggested that medical care was important and offered to take her to the health center in the morning where she could be "checked out." Megan recalled her conflicting feelings of violation and self-blame and the reason she told the RA:

> I felt a lot, you know, to blame for what had happened because I knew that I didn't drink. [. . .] Afterwards I felt like I should have known that I would be getting into a situation that I couldn't handle, so I really blamed myself. But during the whole thing when he was getting me drunk, I said to him, "Oh, I bet you do this to all the freshman women and you're trying to get me drunk." In the beginning he would deny it and then as the evening, I guess went on, he said, "Well yeah, I've done this to a couple of freshman women before." So, what I was just upset about was that the same thing might happen to my friend, so I said [to myself], I was just really angry, I said, um, "You know, I have to tell someone because I don't want him doing this to my friends."

In the morning, Megan went with the RA to the Student Health Center and talked to an advocate from the Campus Sexual Assault Response Recovery Team. Learning that Megan was not yet 18 and a minor, the advocate had a legal duty to report to the police and did. This was a surprise to Megan and was quite upsetting because she did not want her parents to find out about the rape. She agreed to describe what happened to police and go with them to the County Hospital for a rape exam to keep open the possibility of prosecution. However, believing that *she* had the authority to control charging and seeking to retain some control over future events, Megan made it clear that she was not sure she wanted to participate in prosecution.

Megan spent the bulk of the day with the health center staff and the police. When she returned to campus in the afternoon, she was ready to make a commitment to the legal process. The police and the health center workers had consistently defined her experience as a legal issue and treated her like a legitimate rape victim. Moreover, they described benefits to offset the costs of the reaction she perceived her parents would have to her disclosure and they placed importance on *her* participation in the criminal justice process. The contribution Megan could make by participating in the criminal justice process, in the context of a good reception from legal personnel, came to outweigh her feelings of guilt and her fears about her parents.

Megan's and Theresa's stories show that when rapists' and survivors' actions are inconsistent with cultural stereotypes of rape, sexual assault events are not readily labeled "rape." Sustained support for legal action by others helps survivors recognize that their nonconsent and feelings of violation are legitimate indicators that a crime occurred. However, survivors' recognition of others as experts can delay or even halt reporting, when the experts fail to recognize survivors' questions and behaviors as representing (constituting) tentative assertions that a crime occurred.

Taking Assailants' Threats Seriously

Fear and the perception of danger shape the way we make choices daily. Generally, we try to avoid acting in ways that will expose ourselves and our loved ones to injury. A sense of sustained danger guided the decision making of seven survivors. The level of threat and harm they experienced during rape differed, yet each came away from the assault with a strong feeling that her assailant's threats were credible.[3] They were unwilling to take on responsibility for exposing themselves or others to increased danger and did not make reports until they were convinced that the danger of contacting the police was less than the danger of not doing so.

The six adult women in this group were clear that the sexual activity that took place was entirely the result of the assailant's force or threat of force and perceived their experiences to be legal issues. The length of time it took them to resolve their concerns ranged from three minutes to one day. Fourteen-year-old Nellie was concerned that she might have contributed to her victimization, despite the rapist's use of a gun, and delayed two months in making a report. I present the reasoning and behavior of the survivors raped by strangers and acquaintances, and then consider the reasoning and behavior of women attacked by men with whom they were intimate.

Weighing the Threat of Retaliation by Strangers and Acquaintances

Barbara, a 33-year-old, white, upper-middle-class single parent, was attacked by a rapist who broke into her bedroom. Immediately, she defined the attack as rape. However, she took some time to consider whether to call police because her assailant threatened to return to hurt her son if she did. Ultimately, Barbara decided that not reporting presented a false sense of security: the rapist might return anyway. The only active way to protect herself and her child from danger was to work to get her rapist off the street.

Rosanne, a 30-year-old, white single parent, was also raped by a nighttime intruder. This man threatened to return and rape her daughter if she called police. Acting with concern for her daughter's safety foremost in her mind, Rosanne telephoned her priest. The priest endorsed reporting and Rosanne did so immediately after she hung up. Yet she continued to give the rapist's threats credibility, and she asked that the police obscure their identity as law enforcement officers when they arrived. Rosanne described her actions as follows:

> He told me when he left and he was holding a knife to my throat, he said, "If you call the police, I will come back and I will ... I will get your daughter and I'll get you too and I won't be gentle next time." Well, I, he left and I laid on the bed, I got back up on the bed and I wrapped myself in blankets and I sat there and shook, and I can remember feeling just panicked, you know, not knowing

what to do. He told me not to call the police. The first person I called was a priest who was a friend of mine, whose name was Father G——, and I asked him if he would come out to the house. I told him what had happened and he said, "Call the police anyway." He said, "Go ahead and call the police, you need to report this." He said, "I'll be out." So he came out, um, and by the time he got there the police were already there. I asked the police if they would come in plainclothes and in an unmarked car and I told them what the man said.

Unfortunately, the rapist did return to attack again. This time, however, Rosanne had laid claim to a victim-witness role, and she set up the rapist to be caught by police.[4]

Rosanne: All of a sudden I wasn't afraid of him anymore, and I felt like, for the first time, I felt like I was in control, even though—I'm 4′11″ and at that time I didn't even weigh a hundred pounds—there was no way that I could defend myself against someone that weighs almost 200 pounds. I wasn't fearing for myself physically, you know. I started thinking, I could be dead, he could be really hurting me, this could be worse, I'm going to get through this, and I'm gonna catch him and I don't care how I do it. I told him, I said, "I am moving, so if you want to see me, you're gonna have to call me, and I'll give you my phone number, you call me, and I'll tell you when I can see you again." [. . .] About the last hour he was there, I said I need a cup of tea, and I went into the kitchen and I turned on the light, he followed me in, and he did not have my face covered at that time and I saw him.

Amanda: Did you do that intentionally?

Rosanne: Yes, I'm an artist—that will fit in later—he left and I called the police and I said I am not going to city hospital, I'm going to my own doctor. I told them he came back. I had the officer's name, so I asked specifically for him. I told him I was gonna go see my own doctor and uh, after I saw my doctor I would come to the police station and that I wanted to make a report and I wanted to tell them exactly what happened.

Rosanne called the police without hesitation after the second attack. Having become knowledgeable about the evidence collection that took place after rape, as a result of the first assault, she asserted her right to select the medical provider that would make her most comfortable. Her different behavior during and after the second rape stemmed from her lack of fear and mental commitment to report the rape on the second occasion. This contrast in Rosanne's response to the second assault underscores that it was a perception of future danger, not concern about the seriousness or legal status of the first rape, which initially made her resistant to initiating police contact.

An acquaintance held 31-year-old Jennifer hostage in his truck and forced her to perform oral sex. When he released her, she returned home and immediately told her husband that she had been raped. Jennifer also told him that she did not want to call the police because the rapist had threatened his life and those of their children, if she did. Jennifer's husband accepted her description of the rape at face value, but argued that the police should be contacted anyway. However, Jennifer's concerns about her family's safety were greater than her husband's influence and she refused to take the initiative. Jennifer explained her reasoning:

> Now, he had threatened my family, threatened everyone if I told anything, that "the hit was still on me," but he could get it off. [...] I had to ... be, one of his as he calls it, "girls." So I went home, I was terrified. I didn't want to call the police, my husband insisted. And I kept telling him that I would rather just leave town, and go to his parents' house 'cause he [the assailant] didn't know where it was. 'Cause I was still under the assumption that he was, as he called it, a Mafia leader. And so [my husband] called the [assailant's] niece. She came over, she said she wasn't sure [about the assailant's affiliation]. Then we called the niece's mom [the assailant's sister], and she said that she didn't think so, to go ahead and call the police. At that point we called the police.

With the issue of danger resolved, Jennifer and her husband reported the rape. As with Rosanne, Jennifer's dramatic shift in focus underscores that it was danger, not concern about the seriousness or legal status of the assault, that made her resistant to initiating police contact.

Jennifer successfully resisted a powerful pressure to make a report, her husband's insistence. That he made telephone calls to address her concerns, rather than calling police directly, suggests that he accepted them as valid and that he possibly viewed reporting as something that ultimately was her decision. Not all people who were in a position to act for a survivor showed such restraint.

Weighing the Threat of Retaliation by Intimates

Maria, Louisa, and Katherine had intimate relationships with their rapists: Maria, a 26-year-old Mexican-American mother of two and clerical worker, was legally married to him; Louisa, a 23-year-old Mexican-American mother of two, had a long-term common-law marriage; and Katherine, a 31-year-old, white, childless dental hygienist, had lived with her boyfriend for several months. These women had been experiencing escalating violence from their partners, and their reporting deliberations revolved around that danger. Maria, Louisa, and Katherine weighed the threat of remaining with their assailants and doing nothing against the threat of reporting to police and making a move to leave their relationships. On the one hand, the rape demonstrated to each woman that her partner did not value her as a human being and also suggested to her that there was no limit to his violence if she stayed with him. On the other hand, each rapist had threatened his victim about talking to the police, making reporting a risk as well.

Maria, Louisa, and Katherine's partners had all previously battered them. Each woman acknowledged that before the rape the occasional physical abuse had become more frequent and more dangerous. In addition, Louisa's and Maria's partners had, over time, extended the means of their domination in the relationship from physical to sexual. For example, Maria's husband had started pressuring her for intercourse at times he knew were inconvenient to undermine her growing independence of him. However, none of these three women said they had experienced anything they identified as rape before. Their intimate partners crossed a threshold of decency when they used violence to gain sexual compliance and this was a catalyst to action.

As the abuse in their relationships increased, Maria, Louisa, and Katherine said that their positive feelings for their partners dissipated proportionally. As they grew to see their continued participation in the relationships as very dangerous, each woman had considered going to the police for help. However, none had followed through. Maria explained that she never could bring herself to act during a battering episode and test the threats her husband made.

> He had threatened me for a ... a period of time, years. I ... I've been like trying to go to the police, and it's just [that] I was afraid because, you know, he ... he would ... he would say well, before they get here, I'll make sure it's worth it. You know?

Katherine recalled that she had once attempted to call the police to stop a battering episode, but her boyfriend escalated his violence and left her tied up for hours. She believed his threats to kill her if she tried to call again.

Maria and Louisa also lacked trust in the criminal justice system's ability to assist them. Maria explained that her husband had been in and out of jail, and was living openly in their community despite having several outstanding warrants for his arrest. She had observed the revolving door of the justice system firsthand:

> I have like just a little bit of knowledge, like I guess from my husband getting in trouble and him explaining to me what happens to him in the court. I was afraid, I was fearful because I knew how the legal system worked. I know that a lot of times that my brother-in-laws, you know they violated probation and like nothing [happened.] Like a slap on the hand. They go to Disneyland, ... or something, for like maybe two months. Their number comes up and they're out again on the streets again, doing the same old thing.

Additionally, a past occasion in which the police did not protect her anonymity when she reported a disturbance led her to believe that they were not willing or not able to protect her. Although she was almost certain that her husband's drinking would lead to violence on the night he raped her, she could not bring herself to call police before anything happened.

To accomplish rape, the women explained that their intimate partners subdued them through physical force and the threat of additional injury. Maria's husband punched her twice in the face, "hard like he would hit a man," and threatened to beat her further to force her to orally copulate him. Katherine's partner, who had beaten her and tied her up the night before, pinned her down and jerked off her clothes. She resisted verbally but limited her struggle to protect herself from additional injury. Louisa who had just been battered by her husband, complied with his orders to remove her clothes when the tone of his voice warned of further physical violence. These women experienced the sexual assault as an act of violence that qualitatively surpassed anything their partners had previously done to harm them. By forcing the women to engage in sexual activity under threat of injury, their partners betrayed their intimate relationships and exhibited their complete disregard for them as human beings. Maria cried when she described the feelings of degradation that led her to name her husband's assault "rape."

> He made me, you know, you know, perform oral sex, and all the whole time while I was, he was saying things to me like, "I don't feel sorry for you, don't expect me to feel sorry for you." [...] That just stuck in my head. And I thought: this guy is sick. [...] He says, "You're not going to go to work tomorrow. That's right. You're not going to go to work tomorrow." It ... it was all about the job. It was the act of controlling and he was you know, trying to have this power over me, to control me through ... through forcing sex on me, and other physical violence. He was saying all kinds of other stuff like, "Don't ever try to leave me" don't even try to bite him or anything like that because he'll *make sure* I'll never even leave the room. [...] He was saying stuff, really sick stuff like, you know, "lick it right," [...] just, so sick, I couldn't believe. He didn't ... he had no respect ... regard ... and every way he lost total respect from me, that's why it was so degrading, that's why I say it's rape. [Maria's description of vaginal rape followed.]

Experiencing such disregard caused the women to reassess the balance between the dangers posed by reporting to police and staying with their abusers. To do nothing was to accept an absolute lack of control and to be in perpetual danger of continued sexual invasion, severe injury or even death. Alternatively, contacting police might result in increased safety. Fairly rapidly, each woman concluded that she needed to contact police quickly to escape her assailant's violence.

Although the women experienced their partners' attacks as forcible rape, they also recognized that their relationship with their assailants was inconsistent with cultural stereotypes of rape. This made each woman cautious about making claims as to the legal status of the sexual assault. Katherine explained that she did not consider using "rape" to describe the attack to police because she understood it to refer to interactions between strangers.

> To me, um, just throughout the years, you usually hear of rape and the person doesn't know the person who'd been raped and um, that's what I've always thought of as being raped. Then you hear about the ones, you know, husband

rapes wife or that situation, so when I went to the police, they um, I used the word "forced sex." And I think I used the word "forced sex" is because I knew the person.

Louisa wondered if anyone would believe her story of "boyfriend-girlfriend" rape. All three women understood, however, that domestic violence was legally actionable. Thus, each began her report by describing the general physical abuse she experienced and asked police for help getting protection from her partner. The women focused on their own safety and, for Maria and Louisa, the safety of their children. They revealed the details of the sexual assaults to expand on their initial claims of harm. This contrasts sharply with the way survivors whose assaults were more consistent with stereotypes directly asserted their definition of sexual victimization to police.

In the second quote that opens this chapter, Maria described her decision to go to the police and her interaction with them at some length. Having fled her home on foot to get to the police, her first concern upon reaching them was getting her children out of the house and to a shelter. This is what she asked them to help her do when she arrived at the station. Only when the officers seemed reluctant to give her assistance did she recount her husband's sexual violence. Maria's recitation of the sexual acts her husband physically forced on her led the police to agree to help her get her children. They also told her that her husband deserved to be charged for rape, thereby reinforcing her definition of her experience and her understanding of the event as more serious than battery. However, this created a new distress for Maria because, in her understanding of the legal system, the victim had the responsibility to press charges. She told the officers that she could not take that responsibility and potentially set herself up for future harm when he was released. They responded to her concerns by redefining the legal process and her victim role within it: she was a witness for the state, and they and the DA were responsible for any charging that took place.

Katherine also asked the police for protection and, as she answered their questions, she revealed the details of what she called "forced sex."[5] Louisa initially told police she was battered. After she found the police were attentive to her, she posed her definition of her experience to them as a question, asking, "Isn't that like rape?" The police verified her label.

Survivors' deliberations about danger were not abstract or philosophical, but concrete. All these women were thinking in terms of harm to themselves or ones for whom they felt responsible. Their deliberations involved weighing the costs of not telling versus telling: Could or would the rapist direct future violence toward them? For women assaulted by strangers and acquaintances, recognition that the rapist was unlikely to reattack led to reporting. For women raped by their intimate partners, certainty of reassault led to police contact, even in spite of a lack of full faith in the justice process. These interviews show how other people are crucial contributors to helping rape survivors interpret their experiences and weigh information, and even when women aren't sure what to call their experience of sexual victimization, these interviews show that the circumstances of the assault may lead survivors to feel that the support and protection of law enforcement is necessary.

Weighing Obligations to Others Against a Public Remedy

Women deliberated about "prosecuting" their assailants before they made contact with police.[6] This occurred when a survivor knew the rapist intimately, the sexual violation was accomplished solely through his greater strength and will to ignore her cries and pleas, and she did not place the rape in the context of increasing violence.

Julianne, a 23-year-old, white college student, recounted how her boyfriend, S—— overpowered her and framed the interaction as consensual intercourse—indicative of his love for her.

[He was] kind of tugging at my pants and stuff and I'm pulling the opposite way and struggling. So finally I said, "You know, I've gone to counseling because of you, I want you to realize this, I can't have you in my life, I want you out of my life forever." Well, right then and there he freaked. I mean that was like *it*. [...] He just [...], grabbed me and turned me around. So I was laying out on the floor, and um, [he] undid my pants and I don't remember my pants ever coming off completely. [...] We were constantly back and forth. Me going, "No, don't do this to me! Please." [I was] begging him not to do this to me. And he said, "I love you, you know I love you." [...] So it just was back and forth you know, him ... him justifying basically what he's doing, you know. [...] So um, he did what he wanted to do, got up [and] pulled up his pants. I'm just like, crying, just laying on the floor, I'm putting on my pants. He says, "I know we don't spend enough time together but tonight we'll spend ... we have all night together and we'll talk then." So um, he got up and walked out of my room and [...] I was bawling. [...] So I got up, I went out to my roommate [Grace] and her boyfriend [Tim] in just shock and the words came out: "He raped me." There was no question in my mind what had happened to me.

Despite feeling violated and labeling the attack as rape and a crime, these survivors felt unsure whether entering the criminal justice process was the most appropriate response. Their view of the criminal justice process as both public and impersonal conflicted with their intimate history and emotional attachment to the rapist. Unlike the battered women discussed previously, they initially viewed the rapes as isolated episodes of violence in nonabusive relationships. They described the assailants as behaving out of character during the rape. Julianne said that her boyfriend "freaked." Carmela explained that her ex-boyfriend's attack was irrational: "I thought that um, he must have snapped or something." Lacking premeditation, the attacks were initially excusable.

When survivors' perceptions of their past relationships were not altered by the attack, they considered their response options in light of their preexisting social ties with their assailant. They sought resolutions that would not harm him and initially rejected contacting police, because they viewed his incarceration as the probable result of prosecution. Julianne recalled her resistance to framing the rape as a legal matter:

> I didn't, I just didn't want to do it. [. . .] I . . . I guess in a sense it was . . . this was a person that I had loved for so long that I couldn't . . . I could not see you know, the *legal system*, the police, you know. It just seemed like it would have just been easier for me just to say, "Okay, it happened, I'll never talk to him again."

In addition, these women experienced a conflict between finding a meaningful response—a formal recognition that harm was done to them—and the very public forum of the courts. In part, this reflected their awareness that the rapists and their mode of attack did not conform to stereotypes of rape. From the standpoint of protecting themselves from scrutiny, doing nothing was a logical choice.

The women were not ashamed of themselves, however, and quickly told others about the rape. These confidants moved the women to reconsider a legal solution and report to police. First, they led survivors to redefine the relationship they had with the assailant and helped them see the rape as a step in a pattern of controlling behaviors exhibited by the assailant. Viewed in this way, the defendant's aggressive behavior was no longer excusable as a "mental break" and the women's desire to protect him decreased. Second, others offered to stand with the survivors through the criminal justice process. In doing so, they provided the survivors with an alternate intimacy that counterbalanced the public venue of the courts and made up for the likely loss of their relationships with their assailants. I will discuss how this redefinition process worked for Julianne and Rachel.

When Julianne revealed the rape, Tim immediately suggested that she report it to police. When Grace then supported Julianne's private orientation to the matter, he underscored the appropriateness of a legal remedy, trying to shift Julianne's perspective. He emphasized the seriousness of the attack and implied that it was an escalation in S——'s behavior toward Julianne.

> He [Tim] didn't want to make the decision for me, but he really wanted me to call the police. He just kept saying, "You can't let him get away with this. Hey, this guy's gone to the ultimate limit with you, why aren't you calling the police?"

This still did not motivate her to act. Two of the rapist's close friends finally led Julianne to reevaluate her effort to protect him. When she disclosed to them, they told her: "If he did it, you have got to call the cops." Unlike Tim, however, they offered Julianne a way out of abandoning the rapist. They

expressed their investment in and continued commitment to the rapist, enabling her to withdraw emotional support from him. Additionally, their commitment to stand by *her*, in spite of their support for the rapist, made Julianne
feel that she had the necessary emotional resources to follow through with
prosecution.

> I said, "Will you come with [me to report]?" They said, "We'll be with you, we'll
> stand by you, we're gonna get through this 100 percent, we'll be . . . we're on
> your side." But they also said, on the other part that still loved S——, "We're his
> friend too, so we're gonna be fair, we want you to know that." And I needed to
> hear that, I needed to know that there was gonna be some equalness there, a
> balance.

Three hours after S—— walked out of her apartment and left her crying on
the floor, Julianne made a decision to call police and was accompanied by his
two best friends.

Rachel had many conflicting feelings after her ex-husband's attack. She
knew that he had raped her and had told him so, but her first response was
not to make a report to police. She explained how the social ties that she felt
toward him bound her, in spite of the fact that she would soon be marrying
someone else:

> [I was] shocked, um, bewildered, I felt pity for him. And I felt scared. Um, God,
> you feel so much . . . like instantaneously, it . . . it's hard to explain but I felt like I
> wanted him to pay but yet . . . what kept going through my mind was: "He's the
> father of your children. How can he have done this? How can you do this to him?
> What's my next step? What about Peter [her fiancé]? How is he gonna feel?
> How, how is it going to change my relationship with him?" I had to be honest
> with him, I couldn't hide something like this, yet I knew how he'd feel about it.
> He'd be angry, I was angry. Um, but I also thought about my other relationships.
> Um, his . . . his [the assailant's] family, that I've kept, not close relationships, but
> . . . but they are grandparents of my children and they have close relationships
> with them. How is that going to be affected? How will my children be affected?
> [. . .] Um, my first response was *not* to report it.

Coincidentally, Peter called Rachel shortly after the rape, and she described
the attack to him. He immediately drove to her home and called 911 when he
arrived there, demonstrating his support for a legal remedy. Yet, his action did
not help Rachel work out her conflicted loyalties, and she did not cooperate
fully with the police when they arrived. Probably aware of her initial reluctance and concerned about her willingness to participate in the necessary
investigation, the officers eventually forced the issue. They asked her whether
she would press rape charges against her ex-husband. Rachel explained that
she decided to pursue legal action after weighing the past relationship with
her assailant against her present relationship with her fiancé and considering

the likely personal toll of letting the event pass without taking action: loss of her future marriage. She explained, "[If I didn't press charges] I would have lost my dignity, which I'd lost anyway, [and] my pride. I would have been injured and I would have lost Peter."

Interviews with Julianne, Rachel, and Carmela show that even though rape survivors experience sexual activity as forcible and label it rape, they may excuse their intimate assailants if they do not perceive that they behaved stereotypically as rapists—that is, with a predatory intent. When the survivors could excuse rapists' behavior within the context of a generally positive intimate relationship, they did not sense future danger and limited their search for solutions. A personal solution to the injury was preferable to a public solution. Other people played a crucial role in breaching the personal-public divide and providing these women with alternate sources of emotional support.

Trauma-Induced Incapacitation

The physical invasion of rape proves a victim vulnerable, fundamentally challenging her sense of bodily integrity and safety. Furthermore, because rape necessarily involves domination of a victim's will, it undermines the stability of her self and sense of place in the world.[7] It is not surprising that a sense of chaos reigns for many women after the rapist's immediate physical threat to them has ended.

Since the 1970s, a set of physical and cognitive symptoms has become recognized as the impact stage of rape trauma syndrome.[8] A woman whose sense of self is fundamentally shaken is often unable to speak in complete sentences or to convey whole thoughts. She may appear incoherent, disorganized, and dazed. If her sense of time is also warped by rape, planning future action can be difficult or even impossible. In a physical state of shock, she may shake uncontrollably, experience nausea and vomiting, feel numb, be breathless, and have heart palpitations and elevated blood pressure. Depending on how she typically manages her emotions, a survivor may be hysterical or dispassionate, appearing to be running on "automatic pilot."

The traumatic impact of rape comes through in many of the stories already presented in this chapter. However, the survivors introduced thus far fairly quickly were able to regroup mentally and physically and take action after their assailants left.

This section is concerned with eight women whose ongoing emotional, physical, and cognitive trauma responses left them disoriented and unable to deliberate about a course of action for some time following the attack: "hysterical," "stupid," "in shock."[9] To understand how the incoherence created by rape can affect reporting, let's closely examine Arlene's and Sandra's experiences.

Immediate trauma responses disconnected Arlene, a 34-year-old, single, white, working-class woman, from the physical experience of violation and left her unable to act in relation to it. When the stranger who hijacked her car and raped her stopped driving and told her to get out, she did not bolt away. In a daze, Arlene collected her purse, her pepper spray (which she had not used), and a library book that she had offered to return for a friend. Then, she calmly got out of the car and sat down on the curb with her pants around her ankles. She recalled:

> I remember watching the car drive off, thinking this is so unreal, this cannot possibly be happening. I mean I had that sense through the whole thing. There was definitely five minutes or so of denial when the thing first started happening, that this wasn't happening, this *can't* be true.

Arlene remained seated until a man and woman walked down the sidewalk in her direction. When the couple approached, she got up, pulled up her pants, and told them that she had been raped. They, in turn, asked if she wished to call police and offered their telephone. She accepted:

> I said, "I guess I have to [call police]," because I knew that I had to report my car was stolen. [...] Um, it was like a big deal, the only new car I'd ever had, the only new car I'd ever bought, all of that.

She placed a call to police, but as she talked to the officer about the stolen car, she began to comprehend the physical domination she experienced and her calm dissolved into hysterical tears. Arlene could not complete the conversation and one of the passersby took the telephone and told police what she had told him.

One might think that a rape crisis counselor, of all people, ought to recognize and immediately report sexual victimization. However, that assumption rests on the expectation that the counselor can maintain her cognitive and emotional self-control after being raped. The story of Sandra, a rape crisis counselor, demonstrates that an attack on self can overwhelm a person's capacity to process information, making what she knows not of paramount importance.

Sandra spent an evening visiting Inga and other friends. She stayed late into the evening, as did F——. Because neither had transportation home, Inga gave them each a blanket and told them to sleep on the couches in her den. After Inga left them alone, Sandra responded to F——'s attempts to kiss her, but stopped this activity quickly because she felt he was pushy. Sandra told F—— that she had some things to do early in the morning and went to sleep on one couch fully clothed. She awoke with a start to find F—— on her back. He overpowered her and raped her with his penis and his hand despite her verbal and physical resistance. Sandra's screams went unheard by Inga, who had gone to sleep with her television on. Sandra experienced anger first, then disbelief that the attack was happening, and finally terror and fear of death. As soon as F—— let her up, she ran from the room and beat on Inga's bedroom door. Sandra remembered climbing onto Inga's bed, unable to speak and sitting there with her mind whirling.

> She's looking at me, she's like "Oh my God what is going on?" I couldn't even talk. [...] I'm [thinking]: Was I raped? Was I not? What happened? Am I dreaming? I mean, I didn't even believe that it just happened to me, I did *not* believe it. I sat on the bed, probably for 10 minutes. [...] [I was] just frightened beyond belief. But mostly shocked.

Sandra demanded that Inga place a call to Renee, another friend, and Sandra told Renee "I was raped by F——." Saying these words, she started to cry. Renee came over to Inga's house and together they told Sandra that she should call the police, but Sandra refused. She also refused to take their suggestion to call the rape crisis line where she volunteered. She recalled that her mind was overwhelmed with all the contradictions between her experience and the classic stereotype of rape. The rest remains fuzzy to her.

> I was too scared to call the police. I didn't want to, [I thought] no one's gonna believe me. I started doing that immediately. They're like "Sandy, call the [rape crisis] line!" Renee was saying, "Call the line," 'cause they both know what I do. And I'm like, "No. No." You know. They're like, "What are you going to do?" [...] I was freaking and I wouldn't let them call the police yet, and I was like, this didn't happen to me. I mean, they told me that I was like, like a multiple personality was the way Renee described me. She's all, "You were like insane or something, you were babbling and ... and you weren't even talking to anybody, you were just flipping out." I mean, I flipped, I don't even remember. [...] I didn't think I was raped yet.

Eventually, Inga drove Sandra home to her mother's house. Her mother also suggested that she call the rape crisis line and she did so. As described in the quotation that opens this chapter, when she named her experience to the volunteer on duty, the reality of domination sank in. Physical sensations returned to her body and she became aware of her injuries. In accepting her status as a rapist's victim, Sandra also recognized the immediate need to call police.

I found that resolution of survivors' immediate trauma responses—a return to present reality and, in some cases, reconnection with the body—all followed contact with others. The conversations that helped particular individuals break through trauma reactions were each unique. When survivors recognized the reality of their victimization, reporting was an obvious choice for some; other survivors needed to deliberate about whether the attack was criminal.

Reacting to Others' Reports

Megan, Joanna, Rachel, and Elisa disclosed being sexually victimized to individuals who contacted police without consulting them. Each of these survivors then had to negotiate the criminal and legal definition someone else gave her experience. Elisa, who was cowering in her house, was grateful that her friend took over. Megan, Joanna, and Rachel, who were not debilitated by trauma reactions, saw others' calls to police as an intrusion and a continued loss of control. These women sought to assert themselves by refusing initially to commit to prosecution. However, with consistent strong support for pressing charges from the people to whom they disclosed their experiences and from the police officers, these women reinterpreted the relative costs and benefits of participating in the legal process. Sincere, accommodating, slow, and gentle police demeanors, which indicated belief in their stories, helped them accept that the sexual violation they experienced was a crime.

The victimization of five additional interviewees was reported to police by other people. Aware of the inconsistency between features of the assaults and cultural myths of rape, Josephine, a 25-year-old, white student nurse, raped by a date while vacationing outside her home state, and Karen, a 16-year-old white girl, raped by her boyfriend, were not sure how to interpret their experience of violation. However, believing that the criminal justice process generally worked on behalf of crime victims, they accepted the "help" presented by others whom they trusted.

Yolanda, Twyla, and Pamela all confronted police because someone else saw their physical condition as serious enough to warrant a call to 911. A stranger who observed 16-year-old Yolanda walking down a street between two men carrying chains and a bat called the police. A coworker who saw Twyla come into her workplace in torn clothing, openly crying, and bleeding from a neck wound, dialed 911. Pamela's assailant used a pay phone to call for medical help when he realized that she physically could not get up from the ground where he left her.

Police broke in and stopped the gang rape of Yolanda. She was grateful to be saved from further abuse and cooperated fully. Twyla was on her way to call police and she interpreted her co-worker's act positively, because it matched her thinking. Pamela, who had previous bad experiences with the legal personnel, stonewalled the police who arrived with an ambulance. When officers asked what happened, she lied: "I told them I fell down; they didn't believe that (she laughs)." Only after doctors and nurses at the hospital sympathetically treated Pamela's other injuries did she reveal the truth to them and agreed to allow them to perform a forensic medical examination. She subsequently agreed to talk to police.

What if these others had not stepped in? Twyla was certain she would have placed the call to police herself. Pamela, Josephine, and Karen were equally sure they would *not* have made reports. There is really no way of knowing whether Yolanda, a dependent ward of the court, would have trusted police to believe her story of multiple assailants or even if she would have survived the gang attack.

How Others Help Survivors Carry Through

Even when survivors decided to report rape themselves, others played important roles. Marlene, a 20-year-old, white college student, and Mary, a white bookkeeper in her mid-30s, both were raped by their ex-boyfriends and had no difficulty naming these sexual assaults as rape. The rapists physically overwhelmed them and both men acknowledged, after the fact, that they had used force to accomplish intercourse. Both women experienced the attacks as credible threats of future harm, and this made reporting necessary. They had difficulty standing up to their ex-boyfriends, however, and saw the potential reversibility of their decisions to treat the rape as a crime. Thus, each sought the company of a friend to help her follow through with the police.

Eleven survivors, who were raped by strangers and decided to make reports to police, were left in or escaped to physical spaces without usable telephones—empty buildings, vacant lots, automobiles. Sara ran and Isabel drove herself to the police station; the remaining nine sought out others to access telephones.[10]

Some women found that, after they identified themselves as rape victims, others instructed them how to treat themselves as evidence. Such input certainly protected forensic material later used by prosecutors, but it also reaffirmed the initial legal definitions they gave their victimization and their decision to report. Jennifer received guidance from her husband, confirming what she had read and seen on television. Candace received advice from her roommate: "I got up and I went to the bathroom. I said I'm going to wash myself; he says 'Do not'." A rape crisis hotline volunteer reminded Frida not to wash. The stranger who made his phone available to Arlene stopped her before she almost destroyed evidence: "The woman offered me a drink and I said, 'Yes.' And the man said, 'You probably shouldn't have anything to drink now'."

Conclusions and Questions for Further Consideration

Rape survivors make different kinds of decisions about initiating contact with criminal justice personnel depending on features of the assault, their immediate emotional response to it, their relationship with their assailants, their awareness of cultural stereotypes, and their legal knowledge and experience.

Statistical researchers have consistently found that sexual assaults that resemble cultural stereotypes of rape—vaginally penetrative attacks by strangers with weapons that produce injuries—are more likely to be reported than sexual assaults that do not match these stereotypes. On this basis, many people have argued that survivors must think in terms of cultural stereotypes when they evaluate what happened to them and what to do about it. My research on reported rapes provides evidence that cultural stereotypes do influence the ease with which women apply labels to an event they experience *as* a sexual violation and how they label the men who perpetrate these violations.

Twenty interviewees explained that their experience of sexual violation so clearly fell into the category they recognized as rape that they reported to police without consciously deliberating whether to take action. These automatic reporters experienced attacks that were consistent with rape stereotypes—that is, attacks that were perpetrated by strangers with significant physical violence.

The remainder of the women in my study, subject to a nonconsensual sexual attack with bodily penetration that was physically or emotionally painful, hesitated to call it rape, or to call their assailant a rapist, or to report to police. Their awareness of inconsistencies between what they experienced as sexual violation and what they understood to be rape required them to deliberate before initiating contact with police. Several kinds of inconsistencies were evident, including the following: (1) When the physical assault involved oral but not vaginal penetration or involved penetration with a hand or an object, rather than the attacker's penis, some women were unsure whether it was a prosecutable crime. (2) Women who were not obviously injured by the force used by men they knew also weighed whether the sexual assault event met a criminal definition of rape. (3) Some survivors, forced into sexual activity by men they considered current or ex-boyfriends or spouses, were also hesitant to label the attacks as rape and their attackers as rapists, even when the assaults were accomplished through the application of significant force. Some were unsure whether the law allowed for prosecution of spouses. (4) Other women were unwilling to assign the label rapist to their assailant, because he was different than the stereotypical images they held of sexual predators. Their history of generally positive feelings for their attacker, resulting from their prior relationship, led them to excuse the attacks as anomalies.

Conversation was critical. (1) It defined the attacks as rape. (2) With police, it clarified that survivors' relations with their assailants did not exclude them from prosecution. (3) It helped women step back from their relationships with their assailants and see the attacks as part of a pattern of controlling and/or violent behavior. Conversations that strongly influenced the women to use the legal process focused on their capacity to protect others from similar victimization.

Despite statistical evidence that the vast majority of rapes are intraracial—perpetrated by a man upon a woman of the same racial ethnic group—the widely held U.S. stereotype is that the perpetrator of rape is a black man and his victim is a white woman. Yet, in terms of deliberating about reporting, none of the women in the sample indicated that race was a salient issue for them.[11] No survivor indicated that she explicitly considered her own or her assailant's race or class while determining whether she had experienced a crime or while determining whether she should enter the criminal justice process. Furthermore, nonwhite women expressed the same range of reasons for delaying reports as white women.

While cultural constructions of rape form a key context within which sexually violated women make decisions, the women's existing social relations and associated role responsibilities form another context of equal importance. That is, women made their decisions while considering their relationships. Women who felt morally and legally responsible for others sought to continue to protect them in the aftermath of rape. Obligations to a spouse or children made women particularly sensitive to rapists' threats to return or to retaliate for reporting. They delayed activating the criminal justice process while they evaluated the rapist's capacity to carry through threats. Alternatively, a serious ongoing concern about their safety and a feeling of obligation toward their children led two raped wives to seek assistance from police. Their intimate partner's commission of rape fundamentally underscored their degraded status in the relationship and their inability to protect the children for whom they were responsible. Fear of *certain* future harm overcame both their hesitancy to name their sexual violation rape and their reservations about the justice system's capacity to meet their long-term needs.[12] The existing obligations survivors felt toward the rapist or his social network—if the rapist was a current or ex-intimate—led these women to be cautious about activating the criminal justice process. They did not report until they could justify a punitive public response that rejected their prior social relationship with the rapist.

Despite labeling the sexual violation they experienced as rape, all young women in their teens and several in their early 20s did not independently make a formal claim on the legal system. Their behavior was consistent with their economic and social dependence on others. They lacked the experience to make important decisions on their own and they lacked the experience to make claims on people in positions of authority.

The comprehensive knowledge of the law and legal process available to survivors—their own experience, reading, television watching, and that of others with whom they consulted—shaped both their reporting decisions and how they handled their bodies. I found several consistencies among survivors' views of the legal process and personnel. Aside from possible retaliation by assailants, few women viewed contacting law enforcement officers negatively. Almost all assumed that the individuals responding to their telephone calls for help would treat them with compassion and consideration. Only the few who had had negative past experiences with police said that the indifference or rudeness they expected from officers delayed their reports. This pattern supports previous research that found women who report to police expected to be believed.[13]

Including those women who had expected some rudeness, none in the sample viewed police as a potential obstacle in the progression of their case through the system. Some, however, delayed contacting police while they considered how prosecutors might respond to their claims and how they would stand up to testifying obligations. Specifically, they worried about their ability to talk about the details of the rape or to handle cross-examination, and they worried about their need for emotional support over a lengthy period of time. Before they made contact with police, women who had prior bad experiences with prosecutors or the courts said that they had to convince themselves that these difficulties were unlikely to be repeated.

Survivors' general lack of concern about police is consistent with research that suggests law enforcement officers' reputations have improved.[14] The interviewees' greater concern about testifying reflects shared cultural knowledge about the criminal justice process. Relatively greater media attention—factual and fictional—focuses more heavily on the visible aspects of crime victims' involvement in the criminal justice process than on aspects occurring behind closed doors. In short, these women thought about those aspects of the criminal justice process of which they were most aware: court events. And those without experience relied on factual and fictional resources.

Finally, physical and psychological responses associated with trauma delayed reporting. Survivors who described dissociation could not fathom the rape as a personal experience and had difficulty applying meaning to it. Until they were able to recognize and label their experience *as* their own, they could not act.

The majority of women followed Greenberg and Ruback's three-step chain of decision making to sort out whether to bring their injuries to police attention. They (1) labeled the assault event criminal; (2) labeled their injuries as serious; and (3) then decided that initiating the criminal justice process was a way to stop their attacker. However, I found two interesting deviations from this pattern.

First, some women took on what they perceived to be the legal role of crime victim during the attack. Their focus on resisting rape shifted to a focus on surviving rape and apprehending the rapist. Assuming they would report and making a mental claim on a legal role guided their subsequent interactions with their assailant. The varied natures of the rapists' attacks resulted in different kinds of strategic behavior on the part of these determined reporters. Some acts escalated the rapists' violence and others decreased it. Increased violence made the attacks more consistent with rape stereotypes, presumably increasing their ability to be prosecuted and possibly elevating the seriousness of charges filed.[15] On the other hand, strategic acts of acquiescence, initiated to ensure survival and future ability to report or to obtain a better view of the assailant, were inconsistent with victim stereotypes. Such inconsistencies viewed out of the context in which rape survivors gave them meaning were fodder for defense attorneys.[16]

Second, several women raped by their spouses initiated contact with police before they labeled the *sexual attack* as a crime. They knew that their spouses had forced sex on them and knew it was intolerable. Such an act of violence demonstrated their partner's complete disregard for them and punctuated their perpetual danger. But they did not know if the violence constituted the legal matter they knew as rape. It was police, from whom the women sought safety, who defined the sexual attack as rape and as the most serious of their injuries. In these cases, Greenberg and Ruback's second step followed the third.

Statistics from Greenberg and Ruback, Dukes and Mattley, and the Bureau of Justice Statistics[17] suggest that people other than the rape survivor bring a sizable proportion of rapes to the attention of police. My interviews reveal that two groups of others made reports to police on behalf of rape survivors.

The first group was strangers who confronted survivors with obvious physical injuries. These strangers likely sought medical help for a person in obvious distress more than they sought to initiate a process of criminal prosecution. Yet, their acts of compassion set the legal process in motion. The second group included people socially close to a survivor or in a position of responsibility for or authority over her: parent, adult friend, host, boss, fiancé, and rape crisis advocate. They labeled the survivor a victim of a crime and sought to bring the criminal justice process to bear on her assailant. In some cases, the survivor was coherent and capable of defining her reality, and in others, trauma impeded her response. Either way, from their positions of authority and responsibility, these socially connected others felt that they could determine the best course of action for the survivors.

Although these others made police aware of rapes and brought them into contact with survivors, victimized women did not simply adopt their application of labels to the assault event and to the assailant. Thus, the periods of interaction immediately following others' reports often were awkward as officers and the survivors sorted out "what's going on here." Sustained interaction with caring and considerate law enforcement personnel and their continued support for a legal resolution resulted in women eventually calling the sexual attacks crimes.

Although survivors made the majority of reports themselves, others played key roles in the process by serving as physical intermediaries, helping survivors carry out their reporting decisions, and helping them apply the labels rape, rapist, and crime victim to the attacks, their attackers, and themselves. Even when others did not press their own definitions on survivors, they affected reporting behavior by referring survivors to RCCs or rape counselors. Eight women chose the legal process after consulting with rape crisis personnel who validated the seriousness of their experience and supported a legal definition of the assault. Six women were referred to the crisis centers by others. The number of referrals to RCCs and the credibility survivors gave the advice that they received indicate the growing social recognition of non-legal rape authorities in U.S. culture. Others also increased the likelihood of reports without imposing their definitions when they helped the traumatized survivor reconnect with herself and comprehend the reality of the rape. This connection enabled women to make decisions about how to label the event and whether to contact police.

In the next chapter, I will discuss rape survivors' interactions with legal personnel during the investigative phase of legal cases. The patterns I presented in this chapter suggest some questions to consider as we continue to explore how women negotiate the criminal justice process:

- Are differences among rape survivors sustained through the prosecution process?
- Do women who had difficulty defining what they experienced or debated about involvement continue to behave differently than women for whom reporting was an obvious choice? Specifically, do they show less commitment to the process of prosecution?
- Do women for whom others made reports behave differently than women who were able or allowed to act for themselves?
- How do rape survivors involve others in their legal lives as they progress beyond reporting?
- How are rape survivors responsive to legal personnel?
- How do cultural messages shape rape survivors' negotiation of the investigative stage of the process?

CHAPTER 3

"IT HAD TO BE DONE": RAPE SURVIVORS' PARTICIPATION IN INVESTIGATION

When I asked survivors what further contacts they had in the days, weeks, and months after reporting, their answers varied.

Two days after Mimi survived rape, reported to police, and went through a forensic medical examination, detectives asked her to come to the station to identify her missing car and to construct a composite drawing of the stranger rapist. On the fourth and fifth following day, detectives asked her to return to make sure they "had their facts straight." Six weeks of silence followed. Then, the Assistant District Attorney (ADA) asked Mimi to come to the courthouse to identify a suspect in a lineup. After the lineup, the ADA held monthly meetings to inform the multiple victims of the now-identified serial rapist about the progress of the case. Eight months after the rape, Mimi went to the ADA's offices to give a deposition. Seven months later, someone from the DA's office called to tell her that the defendant had pled guilty to felony rape. Mimi continued attending the ADA's meetings until the last one for sentencing.

Two days after Gabriella ran off the beach, reported rape to police, and went through a forensic medical examination, police asked her to come to the station to view photographs of potential suspects. The rapist was not among those she examined. Ten days after the attack, police asked Gabriella to return and this time she made an identification. Four days later, she attended an in-person lineup and met with the ADA to discuss the logistics of the case. Gabriella asked that the defendant be tested for HIV/AIDS at this time and called detectives several times in the next weeks to find out the test results. Six weeks postrape, Gabriella met with the ADA, and three days later she testified at the preliminary hearing. Shortly thereafter, the defendant pled guilty to rape.

One day after Anna telephoned police to report that her ex-boyfriend had raped her, detectives asked her to travel to the station to make a detailed statement. In the next week, Anna called detectives to report she had received threatening phone calls from her assailant and to ask questions about the legal process. Anna kept track of dates and times of additional threatening calls at the request of detectives and later gave this information to the ADA. Ten days after Anna made her initial report to police, the ADA asked her to meet him in his office, but canceled at the last minute. He did not reschedule. Anna wanted to confront her ex-boyfriend, so she called the court clerk to learn when his arraignment was scheduled and went to the courthouse. However, she was frightened to see him walk ahead of her into the building and left.[1] The preliminary hearing was rescheduled three times over the next four months. Twice, Anna got word of continuances the day before; the third time, she was told that she was not needed when she arrived. During this four-month period, the case changed ADAs. The new ADA had Anna come to her office and again describe the rape in detail. Six months postrape, Anna testified at the assailant's preliminary hearing. Shortly thereafter, the ADA called Anna to discuss offering a plea of sexual battery. Anna consented to the offer of a reduced charge to avoid prolonging her involvement with the process and to avoid testifying at trial.

One week after Wanda reported the rape and went through a forensic medical examination, police asked her to come to the station to give samples of her saliva and blood. Then, there was silence. Wanda believed that because the rapist broke in through a window, his behavior was consistent with a serial attacker described in the newspaper. Thus, although detectives made no more requests of her, she called them on the two-, four-, and six-month anniversary of the rape, to ask if another woman had suffered a similar attack, or if anything new had been discovered, and to find out what was going on. Seven months postrape, Wanda found beer cans in her yard one morning and worried that the rapist was stalking her. She asked an officer patrolling the neighborhood to watch the house, but the officer told Wanda they had caught a suspect. Surprised, Wanda immediately called police headquarters to confirm this news. One month later, Wanda received a letter informing her that charges had been filed. During the next six months, Wanda regularly called the ADA or witness advocate for information and to verify court dates. She repeatedly tried to confront the defendant, attending his arraignment and his probation hearing, and testifying against his release at his bond hearing. The ADA met twice with Wanda to discuss plea offers. Wanda consented to a prison term of 25 years for the rape plus 5 years for a probation violation. Thirteen months after his attack, the defendant formally entered his guilty plea and received his prison sentence.

The rape survivor, while a resource for police and prosecutors, has an undefined role in the investigative phase. As demonstrated in the synopses above, the police or prosecutor may ask her to provide additional evidence or inform her of the progress of the investigation or they may not. But rape survivors do not all set aside their concerns about justice and about their own and others' safety while legal personnel act. Some women, like Mimi, adopt primarily a responsive stance, directing their action toward criminal justice personnel in response to specific requests. Others, like Wanda, assert a right

to know and a right to be involved and even contest police and prosecutors'
right to exclusive control over legal decisions. The specific actions a rape
survivor takes reflect her knowledge of the legal process, how she interprets
the contact she does or does not have with detectives and prosecutor, the
kinds of supports others provide her, and safety concerns like AIDS and suspect's threats. I will turn to these issues after I explain the key decisions that
police and prosecutors make during the investigative phase.

When an injury is reported to police, officers must determine whether its
features meet the legal definition of a crime. They may rely on details in the
initial report made to a patrolling officer, but usually they collect additional
physical evidence and conduct additional interviews. If they determine a crime
has occurred, they "found" the report and pass the case file on to the prosecutor. If they "unfound" a report, no additional criminal legal action follows. In
conjunction with founding, police seek to identify and arrest a suspect. This
process involves using witnesses' descriptions, videotapes, composite drawings,
fingerprints, DNA, and so forth to create a suspect profile. When they associate a specific individual with the profile, investigators will look for physical
and social connections between him and the crime scene (which, in the case of
rape, includes the survivor's body). However, it is generally expected that a
crime victim should be able to identify her assailant. Thus, at this stage, crime
victims will often be asked to select their assailant from a pool of similar-
looking individuals—a lineup—in photographs or in person.

When officers determine a case of founded rape and pass it on to the prosecutor, they reasonably believe a woman's rape claim is credible: that is, she
experienced some sort of sexual penetration without her consent. When police
transmit a founded rape to a prosecutor, she or he may seek an indictment for
a felony charge of rape, another less-serious sexual assault charge, a nonsexual charge, or let the matter drop.[2] When a prosecutor files a criminal complaint, police detectives may pursue additional investigation under his or her
direction in preparation for a hearing to establish probable cause—a grand
jury hearing or preliminary hearing before a judge. Up through the probable
cause hearing, the detectives and the prosecutor may interact further with a
crime victim to develop the body of evidence.[3]

The Demands of Investigation

Investigator Requests

I found legal personnel made four general kinds of requests of rape survivors before they fully committed government resources to prosecute assailants. Type 1 requests were *directed toward accumulating evidence* that would
help police and prosecutors develop a more comprehensive understanding of
the assault event. Police asked rape survivors to again recount the attack in
lengthy face-to-face meetings and to answer detail-oriented questions in telephone interviews. They asked survivors to bring items of clothing worn

during the rape to the station, to submit to be photographed, to give blood, to be fingerprinted, and to identify physical evidence collected from the crime scene (belongings, a car, or clothes). This body of material could establish the criminal character of the sexual assault and, possibly, the identity of a suspect.

Type 2 requests were made of survivors to *facilitate apprehending a suspect.* Detectives asked survivors to construct a drawing of the suspect from a composite kit or with an artist, to view photo arrays and physical lineups to positively identify a suspect, and to ride in a car with officers to find the physical location of the rape.

Type 3 requests were those directed toward *establishing the rape survivor's credibility*—the truth of her account of the rape event. Officers asked women to take polygraphs, to make sworn statements *before* court events, and to make taped phone calls to known suspects in search of admissions of guilt.

Type 4 requests were used to *establish an evidentiary basis for a suspect's detention and/or high bail,* and involved asking survivors to speak at bond hearings.

Police sometimes conducted follow-up interviews and identification of photographs in the women's homes, but other requests required the rape survivor to travel to police headquarters, a detention facility, the courthouse, an impound yard, or another location. For women who lived outside urban centers the commute was well over an hour. Police provided transportation to some, but not all, women. The survivors had little control over the timing of their involvement in physical lineups, which involved detained suspects, but officers were flexible within normal working hours for most other activities.

Detectives made the majority of telephone and face-to-face contacts during the investigative phase. Slightly less than one-quarter of the survivors recalled meeting the prosecutor before charges were filed. Still, in this chapter, I will frequently refer to contacts made by "legal personnel," rather than "police," because prosecutors directed some actions of the police detectives.

The Burden of Requests

In general, police and prosecutors did not place many demands on survivors between their initial reports and preliminary or grand jury hearings. Legal personnel made a total of 91 requests in these 47 cases, an average of less than two per survivor. Accumulating evidence (56 percent) accounted for the largest proportion of requests legal personnel made, then facilitating the apprehension of a suspect (32 percent), establishing a victim's credibility (10 percent), or determining ability to serve in a witness capacity (2 percent). When I compared how often legal personnel made each of the types of requests with how often they could have made them, I found lower percentages, but the same general pattern. In short, examining the cases together suggests that detectives and prosecutors were more focused on engaging women to collect evidence and apprehend suspects than on subjecting their claims to evaluation and scrutiny.

I separated the sample on the basis of the relationship between the victim and assailant—stranger versus known—to determine if women received different treatment on this basis. The frequency of requests directed toward accumulating evidence followed the representation of subgroups in the sample. However, almost all requests for assistance with apprehension were made in cases involving strangers and more than three-quarters of requests related to credibility were made in cases involving known assailants. Thus, strictly on the basis of counting requests, legal personnel appeared primarily to engage survivors of stranger rape in the process of pursuing their assailant, but required survivors of rape by known assailants mainly to substantiate their claims.

The most requests made of any survivor was six; the least was zero. On average, detectives seeking to apprehend or establish the identity of stranger rapists demanded more of survivors than detectives who were dealing with known assailants.[4] The stranger-known pattern did not hold, however, for cases in which detectives made Type 3 requests, directed at interrogating survivors' credibility. These cases, selected for the most scrutiny, all had multiple inconsistencies with stereotypes of rape. Four of the six the women subject to credibility-focused requests and multiple interviews by legal personnel were younger (late teens or early 20s), had been in prior intimate relationships with their assailants, were attacked after inviting their rapist into their residence, and were not seriously injured—at least physically. Other people had helped five of these six women define the acts as criminal and make reports, a fact known to police.

Detectives actually asked nothing of six women, who knew their assailant, before the probable cause hearing or plea. Police apprehended a suspect at the scene of the crime or immediately afterward in only 3 of the 27 stranger cases. Thus, they needed assistance from survivors to help construct the image of a suspect to find him. Prosecutors charged many known assailants on the basis of information gained through survivors' initial police reports and, in most of these cases, they later allowed defendants to plead guilty to lesser charges. Detectives may have been wary of devoting time and effort to investigate cases that they expected to be resolved short of trial.

As previously noted, less than one-quarter of survivors met with prosecutors before charges were filed. Yet, the stranger versus known differences carried over to this aspect of the prosecution experience for those who did meet with prosecutors. Survivors attacked by men they knew were asked to extend themselves to prosecutors, while prosecutors extended themselves to women attacked by strangers when the opportunity arose. Prosecutors asked all the women attacked by men they knew to make a special trip to their office for a face-to-face meeting. These women reported feeling "checked out." In contrast, prosecutors met with women attacked by strangers when they were fulfilling other investigative requests; these women felt "encouraged."

Other than the relationship between survivor and rapist, I found no other survivor attribute (age, reporting delay, or race) or case attribute (use of weapons, injury, place of assault) to be associated with obvious differences in the distribution of kinds of requests made by detectives. Legal personnel had little direct contact with minor survivors residing at home. They spoke with these survivors' parents when they telephoned and the parents dealt with scheduling conflicts, conveyed the requests for legal participation to their children, and provided transportation.

Given legal personnel's varied orientations toward different kinds of cases, survivors' experiences with investigation also varied. As women raped by strangers met repeated requests, legal personnel conveyed the message that their participation was vital to the success of prosecution and fostered a sense of case ownership. These women became familiar with the detectives, often being told "inside" details about the case as the investigation unfolded. In contrast, despite the same or a greater amount of contact, legal personnel did not verbally convey a message of partnership to women raped by known assailants. Instead, they were asked repeatedly to give accounts of the rape and to establish their credibility in other ways. Legal personnel also did not offer women of whom they made no requests a meaningful place in the investigative phase.

Survivor Initiatives

The Scope of Initiatives

Survivors of rape often temporarily or permanently move after attacks or change their telephone numbers to ensure their safety. As time passes, they move on with their lives, following job opportunities and taking scheduled vacations. These geographic shifts present a problem for legal personnel, because rape survivors rarely are able to predict their future whereabouts at the time they make a report or even at a follow-up interview.[5] If legal personnel do not maintain contact with rape survivors during the investigative phase, they may not be able to reach them when testimony is needed. Thus, rape survivors' unsolicited attempts to ensure their continued availability to legal personnel are supportive of the legal agenda. Fifteen percent of the survivors asserted their importance to the legal process by ensuring that legal personnel knew their whereabouts. They called to convey changes in their residential status, new telephone numbers, and travel plans, or to explain their lack of availability.

In an effort to integrate their testifying obligations with their other responsibilities, 17 percent of the survivors initiated contact with legal personnel to learn when and where formal depositions and court events were scheduled and how to get there. Some called many times to reach a reliable source of information.

Thirty-seven percent of the survivors telephoned legal personnel to share details they recollected about the rape event or about their assailant, to provide names of witnesses willing to testify for the state, to express a realization that a suspect featured on television news resembled their attacker, or to relay a message an assailant left on a telephone answering machine.[6] They acted to facilitate apprehension of their assailant and, when legal personnel had questioned their credibility, to ensure that sexual assault charges would be founded and filed. In an effort to provide better evidence to legal personnel, two women also paid to undergo hypnosis. Unfortunately, neither was able to improve her recall of details about the assailant and assault.

Forty-seven percent of the survivors called to ask the detective or prosecutor "What is going on?" They raised questions about the development of new leads, identification of a suspect, his arrest, his bail/custody status, or whether charges had been filed. At a minimum, this questioning represents women's belief that they had a right—as the crime victim—to be informed of legal personnel's progress in apprehending suspects and building a legal case. Some viewed their questioning as instrumental, even pushing legal personnel to act, or as an outlet for their growing frustration. Sandra falls in the category of "right to know." She explained that her perception that more was needed from her as a victim and her lack of knowledge about the custody/bail process led her to call the detective repeatedly.

> I kept thinking, [...] don't they want to talk to me or something? I was feeling very confused, and overwhelmed, like God, is this the way it goes? I don't understand. And um, those first few weeks were basically like, is he out of jail, is he not? [I was] calling T— [the detective] asking: What's going on? How does this work? How does he get out of jail? Is this going to trial? Do I meet with...? You know, things like that. He always talked to me, um, he always called me [back].

Rachel also made numerous calls to detectives and prosecutors to find out "what's going on" and characterized herself as a nuisance. But, the telephone conversations she initiated with legal personnel were important for two reasons. First, they allowed Rachel to see momentum in the case, however small, affirming for her that officials were responding to her claim. Second, calling gave Rachel a feeling of taking action, apart from the impact she may have had on criminal justice personnel. Calling allowed her to nurture the anger that she had finally been able to summon against her ex-husband. Calling was a simple means to "stand my ground" and it "kept [her] going." To the degree that making calls helped survivors sustain a sense of place in the process, it helped maintain their commitment to prosecution and thus served the needs of legal personnel.

Without direction from legal personnel, four women attended arraignments, bail hearings, or other motions.[7] Their purposes were twofold. One was investigative and tied to the belief that they would eventually testify in preliminary hearings or trials. They went to observe the courtroom setting or to study the defense attorney, with whom they expected to interact. Second, they conceptualized these court events as opportunities to work through some of the feelings they had about the defendant. They placed themselves in their assailant's presence in hopes of reducing their fear of him or to realize a reversal in the power dynamic of the rape. In short, Francine explained that she wanted to let the defendant see her as powerful and to watch his attorney in action. She was so determined to achieve her objectives that she ignored an instruction of the court officer to leave the courtroom:

> I wanted to see if he was as frightening as I remembered him being. Um, I wanted him to see me with no bruises, no cuts, no bleeding, not scared, strong, determined, angry. I wanted him to see me standing there alive, well and going on with my life, while he is standing there in chains. I also wanted to see his attorney. [...] So I went over [to the courthouse] with a couple of friends, and um, [...] the prisoners took up one half of the courtroom. The spectators could only be on the other side, so the other side filled up and people were standing in the aisles. One of the court officers said, "any one who is not here appearing on a case has to leave." And my friends looked at me and I said, "I have a right to be here, I'm the victim, I'm not going anywhere. They will have to drag me out of here. I've been told that I can be at all the court appearances—that's where I'm going to be. And they can't make me leave."

Jennifer explained that she was concerned about her ability to testify in the presence of the rapist, having been reduced to tears during the time he held her against her will.

> I was shaky as to whether I could actually see him again, I'd talked to him [in a blind phone call from the police department], but I didn't know whether I could see him.... He was going to be there the whole time I was talking about what happened, and [I didn't know] what my reaction was going to be.

She decided to attend his arraignment to test her reactions. She believed that appearing at the arraignment showed her commitment to the criminal justice process and unwillingness to "back down," which might persuade the defendant to plead guilty and save her from having to testify.

When facing their assailants and seeing courtrooms decreased individuals' anxiety before they testified, it helped them fulfill their witness role. Feeling able to use the criminal justice process to overcome the emotional toll of the rape increased their commitment to the process—also an outcome desired by legal personnel.

Influences on Individual Initiative

Survivors' knowledge of the criminal justice process and expectations of criminal justice personnel had the most significant effect on their initiative. Women who assessed their knowledge of the criminal justice process—garnered from prior participation in the criminal or civil systems, employment, formal education, or media—as satisfactory or better, initiated contacts with criminal justice personnel during the investigative phase. Lauren, a white law student, who characterized her legal knowledge as "pretty good" and attributed it to "some things in school and then working around lawyers and being around court-houses all the time," was particularly articulate about how knowledge shaped her actions. Her confidence led her to try to protect the case when she noted that police behavior was jeopardizing the photo lineup.

> They had six pictures or whatever it was and one person which was my rapist I had pushed aside. I said "Oh, he looks too old," and I pushed that picture aside. Then [the detective] said, "Well you know, people sometimes look older in pho-tographs than they really are." And I knew right away that's who they wanted me to pick. Also ... his picture did not have a staple through it, meaning it was a new picture. The other pictures had staples and they had been attached to some records and I noticed his didn't have a staple through it. I didn't want to do a bad photo lineup so I picked two people, him and another person.

Survivors who negatively appraised their legal knowledge initiated the few-est contacts with legal personnel. Those who assessed it as "poor" made one or no efforts to contribute to the investigation. Anna reported, "I didn't know anything, what it was going to be like. All I'd seen was things on TV and I knew it couldn't be like that. I didn't know anything." She contacted the police only when she feared for her safety. Janice also recounted that she had no knowledge of the general legal process or courtroom dynamics when she reported the rape.

> I didn't know what was gonna happen, I didn't know there was gonna be a preliminary hearing. If the DA hadn't have told me exactly what goes on, then I wouldn't have known anything. [...] I had only been to court for a traffic viola-tion. So, and at that point [the preliminary hearing], I thought there were going to be a group of people in there, just massive, like on Perry Mason or something! (laughs) So I didn't know what to expect going in.

As a result, Janice did not contact legal personnel before the preliminary hearing.

Prior personal *contact* with the criminal or civil justice processes gave survi-vors specific knowledge about the length of the process and its erratic pace, legal personnel's roles, legal terminology, and steps of the process. Women whose prior experiences demonstrated the efficacy of the criminal justice process approached interaction with legal personnel from that standpoint. Women who previously witnessed problems in the criminal justice process sought to intervene, especially when dealing with the same county organiza-tions. The ways in which women sought to avert problems varied in relation to the specifics of their concerns.

Theresa's prior experience with the prosecution of her son's molester taught her that she could not rely on county prosecutors to keep her informed.

They chose not to prosecute and they didn't even have the decency to call us and tell us they had chosen not to prosecute. I called them, probably about five months later and said could you tell me what's going on with this case, and they said oh, the case has been dropped. And it's like gee, thanks for letting us know.

Through the rape investigation and beyond, Theresa regularly contacted the victim-witness advocate to learn about the status of the case. Crystal had to pressure the police department to bring about a follow-up investigation of an intruder that she had reported several months before the rape. Dealing with the same law enforcement unit, it seemed logical to her to make frequent contact during their investigation of the rape.

Overall, other people affected survivors' behavior in the investigative phase less than they affected their reporting. The varied nature of social bonds predating the rape shaped the extent and nature of other involvement. Close friends, partners, and parents of several women strongly encouraged them to stick with the process after making the report. Both older and younger survivors said such emotional support helped them remain committed when the investigation seemed stalled. The parents and spouses of several survivors also placed calls to legal personnel when the women had difficulty getting information.

Some adult survivors asked friends who were lawyers or in elected office for assistance. These legal minds explained the process, encouraged them to place demands on detectives and prosecutors, and guided their responses to requests made by legal personnel. Their effect on cases was not trivial. For example, Bernice refused to examine a photo lineup presented to her by the investigator on the advice of a legally informed individual. Her friend, who was a former prosecutor, warned her that a bad identification could damage the case. Bernice also brought this friend to the in-person lineup and reported that his presence emboldened her to speak up and ask for better conditions for observation.

Frida ultimately asked a U.S. congressman who was a family friend for assistance in engaging the resources of the FBI. The fact that Frida was building on existing relationships and on her repertoire of skills, led her to see her actions as neither unique or heroic. She explained,

I mean I didn't think that I was being incredible, I just thought it . . . had to be done and how do you do it. I mean I just grabbed . . . I kind of just pick a wall and keep running my head into it until I break it down.

Providing only assistance, these legal advisors did not independently interact with criminal justice personnel on the survivors' behalf.

During the investigative phase, survivors also contacted a limited number of rape-related specialists for assistance—victim-witness advocates, counselors, rape crisis advocates, and mental health personnel—when they did not get what they wanted from legal personnel. For example, Candace turned to a victim-witness advocate when the detective couldn't or wouldn't be clear about her likely testifying obligations.

> *Candace:* I got a letter from Sherry [the victim-witness advocate] about AIDS things, you know, and I called Sherry, you know. [...] So Sherry has been very good help, every time I called her she tried to find all the information that I need. I've never heard from the DA. I saw the DA the day, in the court there [at the preliminary hearing], that was it.
>
> *Amanda:* What kinds of calls have you made to Sherry, what have you been trying to find out?
>
> *Candace:* Well, when do we go to court, you know, what's going on with him, when does he go to court, what you know, what ... what's going on, because I mean, I'm blind! I didn't even know the DA's name till last week!

In contrast, Marlene turned to a rape crisis advocate to avert further feelings of guilt and degradation. Her initial response to combative and humiliating interactions with police was withdrawal, yet she wished to see the prosecutor file charges. Thus, when she joined a support group to address the emotional trauma of the rape and the justice process, she asked the advocate who led it to help her get information.

> I was scared of the police. I didn't want anything to do with them, I was just so disgusted with everything. I didn't want to do this case anymore, I didn't want anything to do with it, but I didn't want to take away my ... my press charges against [him.] [...] Then I started going to a crisis center here in [city] because I ... I just ... I was just losing it. [...] Through their help, um, I've had some contact with the county attorney. [The rape crisis advocate] would call for me, and would ask what's going on with the case, uh, and stuff like that.

The length of time women were in the investigative process had no obvious impact on their level of activity, but it appears that the passage of time *was* eventually a catalyst to act. Seven months after the rape occurred, all but two of the survivors had contacted legal personnel at least once. After half a year had passed, these women apparently felt entitled to know something about official progress.[8]

The Dynamic of Survivor: Legal Personnel Interaction

Survivors formed impressions of legal personnel from their first contacts, usually when police responded to take a report. These impressions were later revised or verified as they considered gaps in contact as well as what legal personnel said and how they said it. The interviews revealed three broad categories of concern for survivors: competence, commitment, and caring.

Capability and Competence

Survivors noted police officers' ability to follow through and their apparent working relationship with the prosecutor. Lack of effort on the part of police or apparent miscommunication or disagreement between them and the prosecutor motivated action. For example, Francine noted that officers failed to transmit documents that she gave them to the prosecutor and that they seemed slow to process all physical evidence. She ultimately demanded a meeting with the unit leader in the DA's office to ensure that appropriate investigative actions were taken to enable prosecution. She described their conversation as follows:

> I said, "I was told by the detective that the sheet off the bed that had blood on it and the shirt they found of his, that had blood on it, hadn't gone through the lab!" I said, "The detective told me this, and I said 'Why not?' And he said, 'Maybe the DA feels that we don't need them'." And I said [to the unit leader] "I hope that's not the case, you know, I hope that whatever evidence that was gathered will be processed." And she said "It will be, at the right time."

Francine believed the problems she observed occurred because the criminal justice system was strapped for time and resources. Some cases were simply going to be neglected, but she was going to do what was necessary to keep *her* rape investigation on course.

Commitment

Survivors concluded police and prosecutors were "on my side" or fully committed when they spent lengthy periods of time with the survivor, communicated their outrage at the rapist, wrote a lengthy and detailed report, kept the survivor informed, or assured the survivor they would "get" the rapist. Some who were wary of police at the point of reporting shifted their stance when further contact demonstrated commitment. Survivors interpreted police and prosecutors' displays or statements of disgust, direct questions about their recall or truthfulness, and comments about potential structural obstacles to apprehension or prosecution—flight across state lines, lack of physical evidence, prior insanity pleas, pending prosecution against the suspect—as a lack of full commitment to prosecution.

Survivors acted to address this lack of commitment by correcting obstacles to apprehension or prosecution. Those who were knowledgeable about the legal process were most aggressive. They complied with requests made by legal personnel and also asked for face-to-face meetings and additional kinds of investigative action. Less knowledgeable women restricted themselves to telephoning to urge on the investigators. As described in the opening segment of the chapter, Wanda pressured police officers who displayed a lack of commitment to investigate until a suspect was apprehended: "Basically I (laughing) hounded the police department for eight months until he was caught." Julianne also repeatedly called to urge on the detective after the prosecutor told her he couldn't decide about charging her boyfriend until he received the typed police report.

Julianne: I remember calling the detective, have you finished this? Does he have it in his hands? It was like, I couldn't go through that rejection of saying there's not enough evidence, you know, you lose. I mean to me that would have just been the worst feeling in the world.

Amanda: How many times did you call the detective between seeing him and finally getting the confirmation?

Julianne: I probably called ... called (laughs) five times. [...] I kept on top of things, I ... I kept calling, I ... my biggest fear was that if that DA didn't take that case, I would just be sitting here torn apart. I mean, to me that would just have been the worst slap in the face. So to me, I would have done *everything* I could to have gotten um, to have gotten that case in court.

A period of silence following the initial report was acceptable to women who were fearful of their assailant or ambivalent about involvement in the criminal justice process, but positive about their initial contacts with police. When legal personnel demanded little or nothing of them, it allowed them to adopt a desired passive role. Likewise, women who were involved by legal personnel in multiple apprehension activities were comfortable with a period of silence after a suspect's arrest. They saw legal personnel as committed, felt involved, and expected that further contact would be forthcoming.

When survivors expected regular contact, but it was not forthcoming, some interpreted the silence as a lack of commitment. For example, Theresa was deeply troubled by a short period of time in which the detective did not call her. She had entered the criminal justice process with memories of the failed prosecution of her son's molester, and she read lack of contact by legal personnel as indicative of their disbelief in her. She sought to bolster her credibility when the detective presented her with an opportunity to talk to him.

I told the detective, "I can fill your courtroom with character witnesses of my friends," because I do have good friends, um, there's people that would come not even knowing what happened, they would just be there for me.

Thus, without experiencing overt scrutiny from any legal actor, Theresa put forward evidence to obviate disbelief and to ensure the commitment of legal personnel.

Silence also motivated action when women were unable to integrate their presumed court involvement into their lives. As discussed above, Candace sought out a victim–witness advocate when she felt a need to organize her life.

Caring about Injured People

Survivors described a range of acts of compassion and sensitivity that were responsive to their emotional and physical pain and their fears. For example, Frida felt cared for because the detective was sympathetic, clinical, willing to work with her time table, and attentive to her needs.

[He asked] a lot of . . . graphic questions, but he was . . . he was apologetic and he was also very clinical, uh, so it didn't give you the feeling that um, he . . . anything that he asked was so he could have some fun. [. . .] [He said,] "I have to ask these things of you and if you need to stop in the middle of the question, we'll stop, we've got all day," and he made that . . . as . . . as awful as he knew that it is, he made it easy, uh, or as easy as he could make it.

Demonstrations of compassion increased women's trust in particular legal personnel and strengthened their personal commitment to prosecution.

Survivors' responses to legal personnel's uncaring or insensitive behavior depended on what they believed caused it. When they attributed lack of sensitivity to the character of the legal actor in question, women expressed anger, but generally did not respond. When they believed the lack of caring and insensitivity was a response to themselves or the rape, they felt blamed and sought to challenge or dispel perceived disbelief.

When the police detective first entered Marlene's apartment, his facial expression and body language appeared to indicate disgust and she worried about his commitment to the case. His behavior during a midnight follow-up interview at the police station confirmed her fears. Not only did he demand her participation at an inconvenient time, but he also asked her questions that made her feel guilty, requested that she prove her story through a polygraph, threatened to countercharge her with making false claims, and attacked her personally, challenging her religious faith. Marlene attempted to cooperate, but also pointed out that further interviewing was a waste of time if the detective could not accept that she and the rapist were not intimately involved. When he concluded the interview at two in the morning, she felt abused and was fearful the case against her ex-boyfriend would be dropped. Her fear generated action: She compiled the names and addresses of witnesses who could support her claims about the status of her relationship with the rapist and called to give the information to detectives.[9]

The Impact of Survivors' Assessments of Competence, Commitment, and Caring

Some survivors who found the police to be competent, committed, and caring felt well informed and perceived no need to initiate interaction. Barbara recalled the criminal justice process "kind of had its own momentum." Gabriella said that her involvement felt orchestrated, "the whole thing for me, just flowed very nicely, ya know, up until the outcome. Everything kinda went as the score was laid out at the beginning."

Frequent contact and demonstrations of ability and commitment by police also led Megan to be passive, despite feeing uncomfortable. The detective was in daily contact with her during the first two weeks after the rape, then weekly through the preliminary hearing. He built a rapport with her, but moreover, built in her a feeling of obligation toward him and the other legal personnel. Recognizing the investments that others had made in the case, she came to see the process as unstoppable, even though it made her uncomfortable.

> It just seemed like so many things were happening that were out of my control, like once I said yes, I want to do this, things just *went*, and at times where I felt like I wanted to say no, I was kinda like too scared to say no, just because everyone had done so much, and then to say no would make it seem like a big waste. [...] I feel like the initial push I gave, but after that ... there was just no stopping it. Or at least *I* didn't do anything.

Megan's youth and lack of legal knowledge contributed to her passivity and lack of assertiveness.

> I mean, I know that there are a lot of times where I could have asked questions or I could have said things but I just felt like why listen to me? I'm just 17, you know, a little girl practically.

Alternatively, when police exhibited commitment and competence, some survivors increased their initiative. Thus, women who warily entered the process, describing themselves initially as poorly informed, later became active. For example, police made many requests of Twyla as they worked to apprehend the stranger who raped her. Responding to them made her feel like part of a team and she called them when she discovered that she could identify the suspect. Her action was clearly motivated by her positive assessment of police and, despite taking initiative, she conceptualized her action as responsive: "Um, I'm not aware that I did anything but cooperate in the criminal case and I assume that kept it moving forward."

Interaction with criminal justice personnel also motivated Arlene. Overwhelmed by trauma immediately after the assault, she was not oriented toward prosecution, but supportive friends and family helped her find stability and she became committed. Six face-to-face interactions with detectives offered her an opportunity to influence them. She explained the evolution of her contributions to the investigation:

> Um, but I pretty quickly decided that this was my only shot at ... at getting back at this asshole, and getting something back and getting the power, and decided that not only was I going to cooperate with the police, I was gonna push them. They were gonna find him. [...] I was contacted by the detectives, who wanted me to look at mug shots. [...] I told them that I would fully cooperate, that I was really gung-ho to get this guy caught. And uh, and they said great. [...] You know, I was just saying, "I'll do whatever, you know, whatever you want me to do I'll do. What else can I do?" And he'd say, "Well, I guess you could get an artist to do a sketch." [I'd say,] "Okay, let's do it!" [...] Six weeks after the rape he called me at work and told me that they had picked somebody up.

Some police detectives and prosecutors encouraged survivors to accept responsibility for holding the rapist accountable. They also conveyed, in a broad way, a sense of the type of evidence necessary to accomplish it. I found that only women who legal personnel involved in the postreport investigation called to supply "new information" to assist with prosecution. Those who had no contact with legal personnel apparently lacked the framework to identify information as relevant or a sense that is was their place to present unsolicited material.

Although survivors had concerns about the success of the investigation, they also worried about being further injured as a result of participating in prosecution. Some of their actions were oriented to limit personal damage. One source of concern was retaliation by the defendant. Some women received threats from the defendant after the rape was reported; others deduced dangers. These deductions were based on threats made during the assault or prior experience with the defendant's violence. Deduced threats generally led survivors to restrict their level of involvement. They responded to requests, but did not make them. In contrast, survivors who experienced direct threats sought the help of legal personnel.

A second source of concern was that participation would prove to be too emotionally costly and damaging to the self. While survivors reported that fulfilling investigative requests was emotionally draining, they did not hold caring legal personnel accountable for their exhaustion. They also tolerated all kinds of requests when legal personnel presented them as part of a specific investigative strategy directed at the suspect. For example, several women described feeling humiliated as they were fingerprinted or photographed, because the procedure evoked images of being processed as a defendant. These feelings did not lead to corrective action, however, because they did not feel blamed by the personnel performing the procedures. Likewise, Donna reacted to a polygraph—a credibility focused request—matter-of-factly, because she had a good rapport with the officer who made the request, and he confirmed the defendant would be required to take one as well. On the other hand, when such requests suggested disbelief in survivors' narratives, raised questions about matters far removed from the assault, or challenged their motivation, survivors felt that legal personnel denied their victimization. They responded to perceived disbelief and the feelings of guilt they evoked by challenging legal personnel. When survivors like Marlene thought displays of disbelief indicated a lack of commitment, they often did things to support their claims.

Conclusions and Questions for Further Consideration

My interviews showed that during the investigation survivors initiated interaction with legal personnel to ensure that suspects were apprehended, charges were filed, and they were protected. But women exhibited a wide range of agency, a fact attributable to the varied interactions they had with legal personnel, their legal knowledge and experience, their support systems, and their concerns about use of the criminal justice process.

Wayne Kerstetter[10] has argued that police officers are engaged in two fundamentally different founding projects when investigating cases with strangers and known rapists: establishing a credible identification and establishing the credibility of survivors' claims of nonconsent. He believes that the more easily police can achieve these two ends, the more likely they are to found cases. Thus, we would expect to find more frequent founding when strangers are in custody and when evidence corroborates the accounts of women raped by men they know. Kerstetter's research is consistent with some of my findings.

Several researchers have suggested that rape survivors' "willingness" to prosecute influences police efforts to make arrests. However, others argue that "willingness" is fundamentally malleable, and legal personnel actively seek to influence some women to reject and others to pursue prosecution.[11] These survivors' accounts support this second argument. Women who had face-to-face meetings with prosecutors came away from them with the distinct perception of being encouraged or "checked out." The positive sense of being a team member, which survivors developed as a result of extensive involvement in apprehending the suspect, resulted from direct encouragement. Some women, however, believed that police detectives wanted to discourage their interest in prosecution by conducting repetitive interviews, demanding objective proof of their claims, and, in two cases, threatening to take legal action against them for making false claims. If the purpose of these behaviors was to decrease survivors' willingness to prosecute, they were not fully effective. The women did come to doubt the commitment of legal personnel, but they sought to protect their access to the power of the criminal justice process by providing evidence of their claim rather than dropping it.

Legal personnel offered some women fewer opportunities for face-to-face interaction than others. In doing so, they provided them with less access to information about the progress of the investigation and fewer opportunities to ask questions or to otherwise conveniently present their perspectives and concerns. Although objectively less taxed by demands during the investigation, some of these women felt left out of the process and uninformed. Their continued commitment to the victim-witness role required greater personal effort and involved greater frustration than others who were objectively more taxed. Minors and young women bear special mention. Legal personnel worked through minors' parents and appeared to avoid contact with some young women, and thus these survivors had to engage the help of others—parents and rape crisis personnel—to gain information about the status of the case.

The depiction of rape and the criminal justice process found in public media affected the reporting behavior of many women. A number of survivors talked about courtroom scenes in television shows and movies—*Perry Mason, LA Law, The Accused*—or print and video coverage of real trials—William Kennedy Smith and Mike Tyson. In these trial-focused media representations, rape victims had a clear role as testifying witness and a clear adversary in the defense attorney. In comparison, media representations of crime investigation, whether factual or fictional, focus almost exclusively on legal actors. Newspapers and magazines generally report what legal personnel are doing to find and prosecute suspects. Very rarely do they cover the efforts of an aggressive victim to speed up the process or influence charges. In television dramas, crime victims appear when they are objects of legal personnel's action: in interviews and occasionally when viewing lineups or identifying evidence. In short, the available cultural frames that crime victims have for thinking about their place in the investigative stage of the legal process offer only a passive role. Thus, it follows logically that the women in this study who said their legal knowledge was poor and came from television and movies adopted a passive role, initiating little, in comparison to women who reported a satisfactory or better grasp of the criminal justice process.

In the investigative phase, no survivors talked about rape stereotypes when explaining their motivation to respond to legal personnel's requests or decisions to initiate action independent of requests. This was unlike the ways in which stereotypes featured in their discussion of reporting decisions. However, rape stereotypes clearly framed some women's interpretive processes and actions in the investigative phase. Several survivors inferred blame from the behavior of legal personnel and from periods of silence. A key difference exists between the reporting and investigative phases, however. While survivors debated reporting, they conceptualized a general social audience who thought in terms of stereotypes. During the investigation, they narrowed their attention to what they believed individual legal personnel—detectives or prosecutors—thought about *them*. That is, survivors considered whether legal personnel held *them* accountable to stereotypes.

Chapter 2 described how fear of the defendant, need for social support, and concerns about rejecting rapists with preexisting social ties resulted in reporting delays. For some women, I found that these concerns carried well into the investigative phase. For example, Maria, who was fearful of her husband and reluctant to use the criminal justice process against him, took a passive role despite telling me that she had wanted to be better informed. Conversely, involvement in the investigative phase catalyzed other women's commitment. For example, Julianne, who was cautious about using the criminal justice process against her boyfriend, developed her interest in prosecution through her involvement in the investigative phase.

Survivors' accounts of their investigative involvement highlight the continued importance of rape professionals—rape crisis personnel and victim-witness advocates—at this stage in the process. Overall, a minority of survivors made contacts with such individuals at this stage, but for some they filled an information void and reduced the frustration associated with playing telephone tag with legal personnel. The rape professionals positively endorsed women's interest in their witness role and the process.

Higher class status appeared to contribute to involvement in the investigation of others who had a formal legal education. Several older, middle-class,
professional women drew from informal networks that were not available to
working-class and poor women. These findings that class background lead
witnesses to enact different kinds of behavior are consistent with anthropological research about the approach of middle- and working-class individuals to
the civil justice system.[12]

I did not find that survivors' racial or ethnic backgrounds were independently associated with the number or kinds of initiatives they took. White
women and women of color were both active and passive.

Survivors' accounts of their reporting decisions generally emphasize the
power of the criminal justice process to hold their assailants legally accountable for their actions. Their accounts of involvement in the investigative phase
suggest at least one alternative end: using the process to stand up to or confront the defendant. If new goals or motivations for participation evolve from
engagement with the criminal justice process, they are likely to shape both
rape survivors' levels of satisfaction with the treatment they receive and their
future strategies of involvement.[13] It is an important finding that rape survivors did what legal personnel asked and acted to achieve what they perceived
legal personnel wanted and needed. It is essential to consider the potential
impact of survivors' initiative.

For example, did survivors' initiatives shape the legal outcome of the
case—whether it was founded or charged? Survivors' self-initiated contacts,
no matter how intrusive, indicated their continued interest and willingness to
be involved in prosecution, particularly when legal personnel asked little of
them or challenged them. It is my strong impression that the actions taken by
Theresa, Marlene, and Julianne (and the involvement of Julianne's father)
influenced police and prosecutors' decisions to arrest the suspects and file
initial sexual assault charges. Such initiatives contradict expectations of
passivity and concretely opposed the hesitancy these three women displayed
immediately following rape.

Another aspect of the exercise of agency is the resulting impact on the
actor. Did exercising initiative increase survivors' commitment to their role
and the process of prosecution in which they were involved? Did it increase
their feelings of capability? When women viewed themselves as members of a
team, opportunities to take action seemed to inspire self-confidence and a
deeper commitment to the team. It did not, however, appear to increase their
feelings of power relative to legal personnel. The women who contributed
information or successfully pressured legal personnel into expanding the
scope of the investigation described their actions as "important" only in
response to my retrospective questions. When survivors initiated contact with
legal personnel to fill a silence or an information void, the cycle of calling necessary to produce results sent them a message of their inferior status in the
process. For some, this raised questions about the desirability of persisting

with prosecution. Even though I believe that Theresa, Marlene, and Julianne, who acted to challenge perceptions of blame, affected the legal personnel's willingness to charge, their actions did not alter their social relations with the legal personnel and they *did not* experience a boost in their confidence.

After the investigative phase, legal personnel pursue cases through grand jury hearings and on to trials. If the ways in which legal personnel investigate cases are patterned, it is reasonable to ask several questions:

- Are there patterns in the ways that legal personnel invest in preparing rape survivors for the victim-witness role?
- And, if the lack of contact between legal personnel and survivors in the investigative phase results in negative appraisals of legal personnel and activity on the part of survivors, how do rape survivors assess the preparation they receive?
- Do they find fault with legal personnel?
- Do they initiate their own preparation efforts?
- If they act on their own initiative, do they do so to protect themselves or to aid legal personnel in some way?

The answers to these questions are explored in the next two chapters.

CHAPTER 4

Too Little, Too Late: Prosecutors' Precourt Preparation

"Please tell me about the interactions you had with the prosecutor," I asked.

Theresa described a rushed and perfunctory meeting with a DA in Urban County, California, held minutes before the preliminary hearing.

> We got down there [to the municipal courthouse] about 1:00 ... and we were sitting on one bench and there was a woman sitting on the other bench, and um, we looked at the court calendar that's on the outside of the door, and all of the sudden the lady asked me if I was Theresa, and I said "yes," and she introduced herself as the DA. And she took us into the witness room. And then she started telling me kind of what was going to happen, and I was going to have to identify him and um, that the defense attorney would get to cross-examine me, and that um, then the judge would decide if it was going to trial or not.

Natalie reported a different kind of interaction with a Louisiana prosecutor before trial. He prescheduled a meeting, and during a detailed accounting of the court event, encouraged her to interact with him from the witness stand.

> To prepare me for my day on the stand, he [the prosecutor] even brought me into the courtroom and told me where I would be walkin' in, and he let me sit on the witness stand while he was tellin' me everythin' that was gonna happen, which I was very comfortable with. And I think that really helped me out a lot, just sitting on the witness stand and just knowing where he would be sittin' and where the defense would be.

Theresa and Natalie described vastly different experiences. Does it matter?

I submit that it does. Although a part of U.S. culture, the courtroom functions as a unique symbolic world. Few rape survivors have had previous courtroom experience or extensive formal knowledge of courtroom dynamics. As a result, they are often unaware of the scope of their witness role; the roles the prosecutor, defense attorney, judge, clerk, and others play; or the rules that govern interaction during testimony. At the time of their entry into the criminal justice system, many survivors are anxious about testifying because they feel like ignorant outsiders. Whether or not prosecutors prepare them for court appearances determines, in part, how comfortable they will be performing their witness role. This chapter examines the preparation of survivors for preliminary and grand jury hearings and trials.

Information and Advice Given to Survivors

Survivors received 20 unique sorts of information or directives from prosecutors before court events that may be grouped according to how they help sustain the case:

- Group 1: six modes of preparation oriented survivors to the scope of the witness role.
- Group 2: nine modes of preparation enhanced the credibility of survivors' testimony to support the prosecutor's version of events.
- Group 3: five modes of preparation enhanced the credibility of a survivor's self-presentations to ensure that she looked and acted the part of a victim of rape.[1]

Nondirective forms of preparation supplied rape survivors with information about how the process worked or what they could expect but did not require specific actions from them. *Directive* forms of preparation guided rape survivors to behave in particular ways, either to comply with the law or to accrue some substantial benefit for the prosecution.

Preparation to Orient Rape Survivors to the Court Situation and the Witness Role

Prosecutors *oriented most survivors to the broad parameters of the courtroom situation.*[2] Prosecutors told women what role each person in the courtroom would play: the defense attorney would ask questions to protect the defendant's rights; the court reporter would take notes to preserve a record of the event; the judge would primarily listen and rule on procedures; the defendant had a right to be present and probably would be sitting with his attorney; spectators might also be present. Then, prosecutors described the order of events involving the rape survivor: swearing in, direct examination, cross-examination, re-direct, and re-cross. Typically, prosecutors depicted the witness role as a responsive one; the rape survivor was to give information when questions were asked and to fit her behavior into the ongoing patterns of interaction. Finally, some prosecutors explained the legal purpose of nontrial events.

Laws pertaining to criminal procedure set parameters for interaction in the courtroom. They specify who can be present, how attorneys can ask questions, what information can legitimately be sought through questions, and so forth. Many prosecutors gave women what appeared to be standard descriptions of rules of procedure. These brief conversations, some conducted by telephone, did not address the legal scope of cross-examination or explain rape shield legislation unless survivors asked questions that required it: Can the defense attorney yell at me? Are they going to show me my underwear? Are they going to ask me about my previous relationships? Because prosecutors answered when women asked such questions, more assertive and knowledgeable women obtained more complete court process information and took up more of prosecutors' time.

Some prosecutors emphasized that the survivor's witness role prohibited her from hearing others testify. Underscoring their witness status also set the stage for the prosecutor to make other requests concerning participation. Two survivors reported that the prosecutor told them that they would have to *point out their assailant* in court. Women who greatly fear physically confronting their attacker benefit from this information because it enables them to mentally prepare.

Courtroom tours familiarized rape survivors with the physical context for the court proceeding and gave prosecutors an opportunity to show them where other people would be seated or standing. Julianne said that when she saw the defendant's seat she calculated how close she would have to pass in front of him to get to the witness stand. Natalie evaluated where to tell her family and friends to sit. Arranging and carrying out a court tour required prosecutors to plan ahead and make a significant time commitment to survivors.

When rape survivors are nervous and agitated about their role in the question-answer interaction or about appearing in the public venue of the courtroom, they may blurt out hasty answers to questions asked by the defense attorney or even the prosecutor. Likewise, when pressed with rapid-fire questions from a defense attorney, they may attempt to keep pace and shorten their responses to fit within the minimal space allotted, not fully articulating their thoughts. A few prosecutors gave survivors a number of suggestions about ways they could *manage themselves in the question-answer interaction* to avoid producing answers that might be misconstrued. Specifically, they told survivors to take time to think through questions after they were asked, to carefully formulate responses that said exactly what they meant, and to pause after each question to leave the prosecutor room to make an objection. Such "how to" instructions gave recipients a way to approach formulating answers and supported the notion that they could exert some control in the question-answer interaction.

Several prosecutors also *told survivors what they knew about the defense attorney* to prepare them for interaction with a person with specific traits. For example, the prosecutor alerted Rosanne to expect the defense attorney to attack her personally during the cross-examination sequence of the trial: "He [the DA] told me, he said that the [defense] lawyer that had been assigned to this case can be very cruel." The prosecutor told Cindy that the defense attorney was an experienced trial lawyer, was an ex-prosecutor, and knew his profession well. Cindy interpreted this information as a warning to construct her answers carefully.

Preparation Oriented to Enhance the Credibility of a Rape Survivor's Story

In preliminary hearings, rape survivors must testify in enough detail about the sexual assault to sustain the charges filed by the prosecutor. In trials, rape survivors' testimony must remain detailed enough to convince a jury that the event happened. Furthermore, at trial, a rape survivor's testimony needs to be consistent enough with what she said in previous court events that it is not vulnerable to the defense attorney's attacks on her credibility, *and* it must match the version of the assault that the prosecutor constructs. On the whole, prosecutors directed more effort to enhancing the credibility of survivors' stories than orienting them to court procedures and rules of interaction.

At a minimum, prosecutors gave a brief *description of the kinds of questions that they intended to ask* during direct-examination to enhance survivors' credibility.[3] Telling rape survivors the kinds of questions that they could expect gave them a sense of the order and scope of direct-examination and alerted them to how quickly after taking the witness stand they would have to give an account of the assault. Prosecutors' descriptions of questions assured survivors that some personal issues were beyond the scope of direct examination, easing their worries.

To secure detailed and consistent testimony during direct examination, prosecutors asked some survivors to *read through police reports and transcripts of previous court proceedings* to refresh their memories. If survivors informed prosecutors of inaccuracies in a report before probable cause hearings, prosecutors could file a motion to amend the complaint against the defendant (adding new charges) and craft their questions appropriately to draw the necessary information from the rape survivor.

Prosecutors asked some survivors to *recite part or all of their account of the sexual assault or to examine and name physical evidence* that would be introduced in court—photographs, clothing—as part of the preparation process. Complying gave rape survivors an opportunity to collect and organize their memories in a coherent narrative. It also allowed prosecutors to gently guide them to embellish or tailor aspects of the accounts that were vague or disjointed in reports or transcripts.

The opportunity to recite an account of the assault or see photographs and other material evidence before court seems to help rape survivors gauge the emotional difficulty of providing a narrative of sufficient legal detail. Likewise, seeing physical evidence of the rape, which may also cause vivid memories to surface, allows the survivor to prepare herself to maintain emotional control when she testifies.

Some prosecutors admonished survivors to *tell the truth in the courtroom.* They appear to focus on this obligation for several reasons. First, reminding a rape survivor to "tell the truth" is an effort to maintain her credibility. "Tell the truth" is a warning to her to stick with one version, the true version, of the rape event that she has given before and not to change it or knowingly leave anything out. Second, telling a rape survivor that *her* responsibility is to "tell the truth" narrowly defines the scope of her obligation in the courtroom. It implicitly directs her not to concern herself with winning the case and, possibly, working at cross-purposes with the prosecutor's strategy of swaying the judge or jury. Third, when a prosecutor emphasizes that a rape survivor should "tell the truth," she or he conveys a belief that the survivor's version of events is the reality of what happened. Thus, instructions to "tell the truth" provide the rape survivor with moral support as she enters a situation in which her reality will be publicly challenged.

Directing a rape survivor to "tell the truth" does not require much time. However, if a prosecutor explains why she or he is making such a request, it could become a more prolonged conversation. Only Jennifer recalled that the prosecutor discussed what he meant by "tell the truth." His admonition came with an explanation that oriented her to the issue of credibility. He wanted her to be prepared to tell a *new* version of the assault that was "true" as she presently recalled it, three years later. It was reasonable that she would no longer recollect all the details of the assault event, and being honest about what she did not remember would enhance her credibility with the jury.

Although survivors may give a truthful account of the rape, some prosecutors recognize that the way women feel most natural describing sexual attacks may get in the way of meeting legal requirements of proof as well as jurors' expectations. Prosecutors told some women that they *needed to describe the assailant's behavior in detail and use explicit language* that would convey how the assailant penetrated their body in some sexual way. For example, before a preliminary hearing in California, the prosecutor told Trudy to "be clinical."

> He didn't so much tell me what to say as he told me to be clinical about it, and not be embarrassed about it, and he gave me some terms you know. [. . .] Instead of saying "he raped me," to say, "he put his penis in my vagina," and be clear about it.

Prosecutors also alerted women they felt had not testified effectively in their initial court appearances to problems of vagueness or inappropriate language before they testified again. For example, before trial, Virginia prosecutors informed Joanna that the large number of "ums" and pauses in her preliminary hearing testimony could be interpreted by jurors as confusion about what happened: "[the DA] said, 'It's gonna appear to a jury that you don't know what you're talking about even though we know that's just the way you speak'." In this case, it was vital that Joanna be clear because her assailant, who raped her in his home, claimed that she seduced him and then cried rape.

Some prosecutors directed survivors to avoid providing much detail at preliminary hearings—for example, to give "short answers" or "one-word responses" to all questions and to "be concise." Having rape survivors leave out information about the periods of time before and after the act of sexual penetration gave the defense attorney a limited amount of information on which to base a defense for trial.

Talking to survivors about how to discuss their experience encourages survivors to see their witness role as an integral part of the prosecution and themselves in league with the prosecution against the defense. To do this effectively, prosecutors must evaluate any existing prior testimony and its potential impact on judge or jury and spend some time with their witness in conversation. Thus, it is a fairly labor-intensive method for prosecutors to protect the credibility of a rape survivor's story.

Prosecutors *told some survivors the stories that defendants had related to police* when they were arrested for allegedly committing rape. These stories presented all sexual activity as mutually agreed upon and often provided some explanation for why the rape survivor might falsely accuse the defendant. For example, the prosecutor told Monica, a white teenager, what the much older black defendant said:

> I was supposed to be a prostitute, he said. And he said that I just did this [reported a rape] because I didn't want to have a black baby. So that was the whole reason I had called the police 'cause I had gotten mad about that. And so he [the DA] told me about that.

Telling survivors known defendants' stories was a nondirective form of preparation that required little planning. It provided a context for prosecutors' direct requests that rape survivors craft their testimony in particular ways, specifically including or emphasizing some information. It also alerted women to the possibility that the defense attorney might veer off into questions that were inconsistent with their own accounts of the rape. Thus, telling survivors about statements made by defendants served a similar warning purpose as alerting them to possible defense questions. Unlike an actual description of questions, however, knowledge of these stories did not prepare rape survivors for the way the defense attorney might broach the subject.

Prosecutors wanted witnesses to substantiate the charges that were filed; moreover, they wanted to protect the state's version of events from defense critiques. Thus, some prosecutors instructed survivors to *include particular information in their testimony to emphasize certain aspects of the rape event.* For example, before trial, a Montana prosecutor gave Isabel information about the defense strategy and instructions to shape her testimony to fit the charges against the defendant. The prosecutor strongly encouraged her to describe aspects of the defendant's behavior following the rape that would contradict his claim that he was insane at the time of the crime, and therefore not responsible for his actions: "You have to make sure that you tell the jury and tell the defense that he sat on that couch and said he was sorry, because mental people or insane people have no remorse." The prosecutor also asked Isabel to be sure to include the information that she never removed her tampon, telling her: "It's a sign of rape—that you didn't consent to sex."

The prosecutor sat down with Janice some time before trial and asked her to respond to the substance of statements made to police by defense witnesses. Together, they identified what she could add to her testimony to contradict the expected defense claims that she was drunk, consented to sex with the defendant, and reported rape because she felt guilty for being intimate with a black man.

> I was told [by the prosecutor that what the defense attorney was trying to do] was make a black-white issue out of the whole trial. [. . .] [The prosecutor] said, "I want your background on everything. The club that you were going to. Was it uh, was it basically an all black club?" I said "yes, it was," and she said, "Now, do you have friends who are black?" I said, "Yes, I do." And I said, "If this would help, my children are half-black." [. . .] She said what the public defender's office had gotten was that I was falling down drunk, but my blood alcohol level was um, was way under the legal limit, basically. And um, I said, "well, I don't remember drinking all that much that evening." [. . .] I said, "But, I was coming down the stairs and um, the stairwell is not well lit and my heels are . . . are very high-spike heels . . ." I said, "I did fall once because my heel caught on the edge and it slipped down, so I slid and I was holding onto the rail and one of the bouncers came over and helped me up, and I was kind of embarrassed" (laughing). She goes, "you're gonna have to bring that up."

Asking survivors to tailor their accounts of the rape is no small request; it potentially requires them to substitute the prosecutor's understandings of the rape experience for their own. Thus, it is not surprising that the exchanges in the above quotations reflect a well-developed rapport between the rape survivors and prosecutors. The prosecutors who prepared survivors in this way had previously met with them and established trust.

The above statements from Monica and Janice demonstrate that race and gender shaped prosecutors' concerns about credibility and decisions about preparation. With reference to these two cases, it was the survivor's race in relation to that of her alleged assailant that was cause for concern. He was African American; she was not. In Urban County, where race infused politics and juries were frequently racially mixed, an allegation that a crime victim was motivated by racial prejudice could not be ignored. Minimally, the prosecutor needed to warn the prime witness of defense allegations of racism, as Monica was, so that she did not inadvertently behave in a manner that lent support to the claim. In Janice's case, the prosecutor went a step further to offset the allegation of prejudice, probably because she admitted to willingly accepting a ride from her assailant after leaving a bar. Establishing some direct counterevidence of racial tolerance would negate or at least limit jurors from concluding there was merit to the claim that she retracted her consent to sex after the fact.

Some prosecutors *described potential questions* the defense attorney might ask. This prepared rape survivors for the type of scrutiny they might encounter in cross-examination and undermined the potential shock value of specific queries, As part of Natalie's preparation for trial, the Louisiana prosecutor explained that the defense attorney could not refute that the rape had taken place, so he would attempt to show it was less serious than charged. The prosecutor suggested several questions the defense attorney might ask to achieve this end.

> He [the prosecutor] said [...] , "if I was in [the defense attorney's] shoes, [...] I would just try to lessen the aggravated part of everything," You know, like "Natalie, oh, when he was beatin' you, you really didn't think he was gonna kill you huh?" You know, and then I replied, [...] "yes, I did, there was blood everywhere, you know, I really did think he would kill me." And he told me that was a good answer.

Telling survivors what they might be asked was a nondirective mode of preparation that required forethought about the specifics of the case, but that took little time to relay unless, like Natalie, the rape survivor engaged the prosecutor in dialogue.

Only two prosecutors actually asked several survivors to *pose answers to defense-type questions* before hearings for probable cause. By doing this they ensured that their prime witness could support the criminal charges that had been filed and could maintain a consistent story. Additionally, rehearsing defense-type questions helped these survivors gain confidence in discussing information that made them uncomfortable. Because these prosecutors established a good rapport with the women before cross-examining them, this type of preparation required a significant commitment of their time.

Preparation to Increase the Credibility of a Survivor Self-Presentation

Prosecutors instructed many survivors in *how to dress and make themselves up for their testimony* to ensure that their key witness' appearance did not contradict her narrative of victimization or the image they built of her during opening statements (in her absence). Specifically, prosecutors directed women to wear conservative clothing to fulfill the cultural stereotype of a true victim of rape and to appear deferential to the court's authority. Brian, a prosecutor from Urban County, explained this concern:

> The main thing that I do is get them to dress appropriately for court, to not wear makeup or tone down the dress so they won't look like a hussy. I guess that's the main coaching I do.... Actually, the worst quality [for a victim] would be sexual promiscuity, 'cause that doesn't sell well, ... if you look and act like you're sexually promiscuous, then um, the juries just hate that.

Some prosecutors directly conveyed their desires by linking court to a specific nonsexual setting with which survivors were familiar. They told women to "dress as you would for church" or "wear what you wear to work." Other prosecutors provided similar information indirectly or through negation. For example, when Joanna asked what she should wear to a preliminary hearing, she was told, "don't wear fishnets or anything like that."

Through this preparation, prosecutors communicated that being a good witness was more than simply describing "what happened." The survivor as witness had the responsibility to visually reinforce her credibility as a victim of rape. Some prosecutors' discussions of attire became lessons about the importance of meeting the expectations of the jury. The prosecutor and the detective gave Lauren a long, detailed set of instructions before trial.

> They said think of these people as your grandparents or something like that, and [think about] how would your grandparents want you to dress. [....] They said not to wear anything short, mostly not to be revealing. Don't um, don't look like a um, I guess prostitute or anything. [...] And they said don't try to be, so that anybody might dislike you for any reason: like don't wear big jewelry, don't wear lots of makeup, try to be average, don't um, get frou-froued up, don't have your hair all dolled up.

In spite of the fact that some women were displeased that prosecutors asked them to project an image inconsistent with their personal sense of self, all who received appearance directives said that they followed them.

In several cases involving minor survivors, prosecutors elected to file statutory rape charges.[4] Thus, they primarily needed to establish that it was unreasonable for the perpetrator to assume that his victim was old enough to consent to intercourse. Prosecutors encouraged these younger survivors to emphasize their youth (and sexual innocence) through their clothing in stereotypical ways. Seventeen-year-old Nellie was told to wear a dress and tights to a preliminary hearing, clothing she characterized as "an Easter dress." Sixteen-year-old Monica, who dressed like a business woman for the preliminary hearing, was told to appear more feminine and youthful at trial.

> I had gotten some black pants and a blazer and a white shirt under it and he's all, "you don't look 16 year-old enough." [...] He [the DA] told me I should wear a silly dress because that's what 16 year-olds do, so I went out and I got a silly dress. [...] He said it should be frilly and maybe flowery.

In addition to making Monica look more adult than child, hampering a conviction for statutory rape, the professional outfit also implied self-assurance. Wearing a frilly flowery dress was more consistent with her childish story of making a bad decision and being raped by the "nice" man who stopped to offer her a ride home from the bus stop.

Conveying appearance directives to rape survivors does not require a time commitment from prosecutors. However, if the survivor questions the stereotypes that the prosecutor is working against, a more lengthy explanation may be required. The more detailed the directives, the more time-consuming they are for the prosecutor.

In addition to being associated with specific types of attire, social roles are encumbered with feeling rules. These rules lay out the scope of permissible emotions that may be expressed by individuals who inhabit the role. To play one's part effectively, one must display emotions that are consistent with the role. For example, a funeral requires displays of sadness consistent with mourning from next-of-kin. The bereaved son or daughter is expected to suppress the urge to giggle at a eulogy that glosses over legendary poor character traits of the deceased. The act of suppressing giggles or making an attempt to shed tears, without an accompanying feeling of sadness, is a willful effort.[5]

Prosecutors directed survivors to *display a narrow range of emotions in the courtroom* to enhance the likelihood that judges and jurors would accept them as legitimate representatives of the victim-witness role.[6] They told survivors that tears or other visible indications of fear or pain would reinforce their credibility as rape victims. A straight face (flat affect), while usually associated with rationality, was open to the interpretation that the alleged sexual attack had little or no impact—that the witness testifying was not seriously victimized by the defendant or that no victimization occurred at all. The prosecutor gave Lauren instructions to appear frightened as well as speak about her fear.

> They [the prosecutor and assistant] asked [. . .] what I thought would be good to bring up into the case and things like that, like um, just to show that I was frightened and to make sure that we could make an aggravated rape charge stick. Once again they started telling me I needed to get emotional, [even] if it meant staying up all night [the night before trial], and they said, "jurors like to see people get emotional," things like that.

Prosecutors also indirectly conveyed their desire for survivors' emotion management. The prosecutor did not tell Janice that she must cry, but strongly suggested that she not testify in an inexpressive way, because a previous case had been lost when the survivor had suppressed her emotions while on the witness stand.

> So she goes . . . "What I'm telling you is that if you want to get emotional, get emotional." She said, "don't let anybody stop you, if you want to cry, go ahead and cry." She said, "What you're trying to do is, you know what happened, you know it to be true, these people don't know what's going on." [. . .] "All I'm telling you is *don't sit there.*"

Several prosecutors also commented on the need for survivors to display emotions. Brian, an Urban County ADA, argued that a rape survivor's emotional display in front of the jury, her visible suffering, was the key element of her court performance:

> I think that sexual assault cases are not complicated and the most important thing
> is the victim's emotional reaction in front of the jury. To some extent, I don't want
> them to be prepared. I want them to, when they get in front of the jury in essence
> to be really shocked and to show that. I want them to suffer for the jury.

Steve's reflections about the performance of a survivor-witness in an Urban
County case in which there *was* significant corroborating evidence underscore
this concern with having emotion on display at trial when the jury is present:

> She [the survivor-witness] was great at the prelim[inary hearing], she had all
> that anger. She didn't try to justify, but she zinged a few things in here and
> there.... She lost all that by the time she was in trial.... There was nothing left,
> she was really flat and stale at trial, which presents a difficult problem for me:
> because ... you want them to be angry, you want them to relive it, you want
> them to show emotion.

Steve's statements that the survivor-witness should have been more emotional at trial are all the more noteworthy because he made them *after* the jury
found the defendant guilty of multiple counts of aggravated rape.

But not all emotion is acceptable for a rape survivor-witness to display.
Expressions of anger or frustration are open to two negative interpretations.
Jurors may infer that the survivor is overly concerned about being questioned
and has something to hide or that she is inappropriately vindictive. Thus, it is
not surprising that prosecutors asked survivors to suppress expressions of
anger or frustration during cross-examination.

When the prosecutor told Rosanne that he expected the defense attorney to
accuse her of "putting out" for anyone because she was a divorced woman, he
immediately cautioned her to "stay calm." Prosecutors also gave Joanna directions to repress her feelings during cross-examination: "They're like, 'he's
[the defense attorney] gonna be mean, you know, he might ... he might
intimidate you in some way, but don't get defensive'."

Prosecutors spent more time talking about the need for survivors to manage their emotions than talking about their clothing. While carefully considering dress for an occasion is regarded as normal behavior, our society is more
apt to view emotions as emerging from situations rather than as being under
a person's control. Prosecutors seemed to realize that telling survivors to
maintain control over a specific emotion needed to be followed by an explanation about what the expression of that emotion might mean to observers. Furthermore, some prosecutors seemed to acknowledge that rape survivors might
feel entitled to express their true feelings of anger because that emotion con-
tinually verified their personal reality of violation. To do otherwise, the survivors needed a very good reason.

Prosecutors instructed three women to *speak to the jury,* rather than direct
their answers to the attorney asking questions. When witnesses physically
turn toward jurors, they make their faces and emotional states available for

scrutiny. In addition, turning toward jurors makes the act of testifying an act of direct communication with them. This is open to the positive interpretation that the rape survivor-witness has nothing to hide, and it can work against any preconceptions they may have that women lie about their sexual activity.

If, as a result of emotional stress, a rape survivor cannot maintain her composure and complete her testimony, or the way the defense attorney asks questions makes her incapable of providing clear answers, the prosecution's case may be jeopardized. Thus, prosecutors depend on rape survivors being able to manage the intensity of emotions that they experienced while testifying. With this in mind, some prosecutors went beyond telling survivors that testifying would be "tough" or the case might not go the way they wanted. They told the women how they could handle or *manage aspects of the court proceedings that made them uncomfortable.*

Before a preliminary hearing in California, the prosecutor told Arlene that she could exert some control over the scope of questioning by the defense attorney, thereby limiting his ability to embarrass her: "She [the prosecutor] told me, 'If they ask you anything that you really don't want to answer, just look at me and I'll, if I can, I'll do something about it'." The suggestions that Emily reported receiving before a preliminary hearing in Urban County are striking in their concern for her emotional presence in the courtroom and the specific management techniques relayed.

> He [the prosecutor] also gave me some clues as to um, if I was having trouble during the testimony, if I was getting too upset, that I could ask for a break. Um, if things were being too overwhelming or something like that. He told me that I don't have to look at the defendant, uh, that they would ask me if he was in the courtroom, and to point him out and that I could just, you know—I already knew what color he was gonna be in, jail color clothes—and that I could just glance over that way and say, that's him there with this or that on, you know. Um, I didn't actually have to look at him [the defendant]. He told me that uh, that if I was having trouble with the defendant being there, and stuff, that you know, I could keep my eyes on *him* [the prosecutor]. And when the defense attorney was asking me questions, to keep my eyes right on him [the prosecutor], you know. That also, that you know, the woman from rape crisis would be right there so I could you know, be making eye contact with her.

Although prosecutors suggested particular modes of behavior to rape survivors, this form of preparation was nondirective, because the choice to carry out the behavior was left to the women. Like going over testimony with a rape survivor, telling her about managing the question-answer interaction required that the prosecutor devote substantial time to preparation.

Finally, some prosecutors requested that *survivors not attend parts of the trial they were legally entitled to attend:* jury selection, opening statements, closing statements, or charges to the jury. Prosecutors explained or implied that what was at issue was how the jury would interpret the survivors' presence. Urban

County prosecutor Al acknowledged strongly discouraging survivor-witnesses from attending closing statements because he feared jurors would perceive the women as vindictive.

> She should be able to express herself, express whatever interest she has in the case, from the witness stand, and interest in the case should ideally be less about retribution and more about simply telling the story. The less it appears the witness is out to get the accused, the better it is for the prosecution to succeed, because bias against the defendant is something which only works in his favor.

Urban County prosecutor Brian suggested also that jurors could see a survivor's stoicism during closing remarks as inconsistent with the emotional fragility of a real rape victim: "I, as a general rule, forbid them to come back in [after they testify] because I don't want the jury feeling [...] that the victim is hard enough that they can sit through and listen to the closing." Survivors' absence from court, before and after their testimony, was neutral or open to the more positive interpretation that the trauma of the rape made it too unpleasant to be in the presence of the defendant.

Several prosecutors told me that they also spoke about witnesses in unflattering terms if they thought it would help the case. Urban County prosecutor Steve's comments about excluding rape survivors from closing statements take up this issue: "There are good reasons why, maybe, I wouldn't want them there. Sometimes I don't say particularly nice things about my victims in closing: "Yes, she made a mistake; yes, the defendant's a jerk; she never should have gone out with him," that type of thing. She needn't hear that." Thus, while survivors' expressions are an issue because they may be misread by the jury, prosecutors own discomfort with survivors' feelings, reactions, and emotions contributed to their decisions to limit survivors' involvement in court proceedings. A Rural County prosecutor directly told Jennifer that it was easier for him to focus on speaking to the jury when he did not have to worry about her response to what he was saying.

The Patterning of Prosecutors' Preparation Behavior

The amount of preparation prosecutors gave survivors was not extensive, regardless of the court event. Of the 20 types of information or direction discussed above, no individual received more than 13 and more than half of all court events were preceded by fewer than five such pointers from prosecutors. In general, survivors were given fewer pointers before hearings to establish probable cause—preliminaries and grand juries—than before trials. All eight women who participated in preliminary hearings and trials received more preparation before trials. For example, prosecutors gave Lauren six pieces of information and directives before the preliminary and 13 before trial, and prosecutors gave Jennifer four pieces of information and directives before the preliminary and seven before trial.

Prosecutors also prepared survivors in different ways before and after defendants were bound over for trial. Before probable cause hearings, they gave the majority of women orienting information that was general and could be conveyed quickly and did not focus on their specific testifying responsibilities. They did little to ready women to help protect the case from defense attacks before preliminary hearings, telling fewer than a quarter of them about the defense story and possible defense questions, or asking them to include specific information in their testimony. Before trial, prosecutors prepared more than twice as many survivors in these ways. Prosecutors also directed much more attention to survivors constructing credible self-presentations before trials than preliminary hearings.

Rape Survivor Satisfaction with Received Preparation

Limiting preparation before court appearances, in particular survivors' first appearances, is not without consequences. Close to a third of the women in this study said the prosecuting attorney did not adequately prepare them to testify or was not sufficiently supportive before their first court event.[7] Barbara, who received three types of preparation before a preliminary hearing,[8] said she had wanted to know more about the process that she was entering and the possible outcomes she could expect. She believed that the lack of information the prosecutor gave her indicated his lack of interest in her case. Jennifer had a face-to-face meeting with the prosecutor before her appearance at the preliminary hearing, but she remained confused about her role and the legal process. The prosecutor's brusque manner coupled with Jennifer's lack of legal knowledge resulted in a less-than-satisfactory interaction, and Jennifer did not learn what she really wanted to know. Jennifer had a great deal of praise for a second prosecutor who took the case to trial, because he engaged with her and provided more information.

Joanna had difficulty negotiating her role in court as a result of lack of preparation. While the prosecutor told her not to express frustration or anger, he did not tell her how she might manage conditions that would be frustrating. Thus, she was left to hold back her emotions during cross-examination to the point where she felt physically nauseated. Although her physical discomfort was actually brought on by the defense attorney, she held the prosecutor accountable for her bad experience because he failed to prepare her adequately.

When and how survivors learned about being excluded from court was a source of discomfort for some. When prosecutors spoke to them ahead of their court appearances and gave them legal and cultural rationales to justify their absence from court, they were able to accept their exclusion. However, five women were told that they could not listen to others testify just before the trial and were surprised and upset. They felt the prosecutor had changed the rules of the game, restricting them from fully participating in a long-anticipated event. Sandra's comments capture her frustration about learning the limits of her witness role on the same day that she was scheduled to testify.

> But [the prosecutor] you know, took me [into the witness room when I arrived at court] to talk to me about like, who's going to go on first, and *then* I found out that I couldn't be in the courtroom. [...] I was really sick to my stomach, and I was like, "Why can't I be in the courtroom?" Because I'm the—that was when the witness part came [in]. "You're a witness, this is not your case." [...] I'm nobody, um, I'm *just a witness* to what happened. [...] I wanted to hear what this jerk had to say.

Survivors who received early warning of exclusion, but were not given reasons for it, also were frustrated.

It bears mentioning that women's negative assessments of prosecutors' preparation activities were not tied to the outcome of cases. Women expressed dissatisfaction when assailants were convicted and when they were acquitted. Among the survivors mentioned above, Jennifer's and Barbara's assailants were convicted and Sandra's and Joanna's were not.

Conclusions and Questions for Further Consideration

Like Holmstrom and Burgess,[9] I found that the preparation rape survivors reported receiving from legal personnel was not extensive. Similarly, my finding of differences in preparation between preliminary hearings and trials was consistent with the different quantities of information they observed that prosecuting attorneys provide to survivors before their appearances in district and superior court. My results suggest that the two women quoted at the opening of this paper were both typical. Theresa did not meet the prosecuting attorney until the day of the court event—quite predictable given that she was being prepared for a preliminary hearing in a jurisdiction in which prosecutors reported they were short-staffed. On the other hand, Natalie, who was being prepared to testify in a trial by a prosecutor who had handled all aspects of the case, received significantly more information and directives.

As a result of the lack of preparation, the typical survivor-witness is unprepared to comfortably perform her role before the majority of probable cause hearings and a large minority of trials. She is not knowledgeable about the situation she will enter or about her ability to control the question-answer interaction and, as such, is open to attack by the defense attorney. Additionally, lack of discussion about how to manage the discomforting aspects of testifying leaves her exposed.[10] Before trials, more rape survivors are knowledgeable about the courtroom situation because they have previously testified and because prosecutors go over more procedural rules. However, prosecutors may request significant psychological work from rape survivors to sustain the state's case. Producing some emotions to appear victimized, suppressing others to avoid the appearance of defensiveness or vindictiveness, and testifying with a particular emphasis can all involve substituting another reality for one's own. Denying their own reality is stressful for some rape survivors and leads them to feel guilty and angry with themselves. When prosecutors provide little preparation or primarily focus on rape survivors' self-presentations, they can unintentionally contribute to the second assault on and re-victimization of rape survivors.

Lisa Frohmann[11] has demonstrated that race and class feature in prosecutors' thinking about rape when they decide whether or not to file charges. It is logical that they would also shape prosecutors' later handling of the case. Racial differences among the survivors in this study did not in themselves appear to lead prosecutors to give white women and women of color different kinds or more or less preparation. On the other hand, prosecutors were attentive to possible defenses, including allegations of racism and vindictiveness on the part of white women raped by black men. Before trials, they worked closely with several white women to enhance the credibility of their stories. These women, who received more intensive preparation, may have a better testifying experience than other white and nonwhite rape survivors. It is probable that race shapes preparation in other more subtle ways. It is likely that some prosecutors feel it necessary to defend African American women against stereotypes of hypersexuality, regardless of the race of their assailants.[12]

If survivors receive little in the way of information from prosecutors about their testifying obligations and how the court process works before court dates, it is reasonable to ask several questions:

- What might they do for themselves? Do they take action to learn about the court process?
- Do they act to increase the success of the case, as they see it?
- If so, does the level of preparation they receive from prosecutors shape the intensity or types of self-preparation?

Rape survivors' greater investment in investigation as a result of being asked to meet requests by police, as described in chapter 3, suggests this result. The answers to these questions are explored in chapter 5.

CHAPTER 5

"I Wanted There to Be No Question": Survivors' Self-Preparation for Court

"Please tell me about getting ready for your court appearances," I said. Julianne focused on meeting observers' presentation expectations.

> I remember when I was home I went shopping to make sure I had an appropriate outfit for court: something um, conservative, something um, something very presentable, um, nice, a dress, a skirt, a blazer. I remember even shopping and thinking I have to get clothes just to present myself. [...] [On the day of court [I] definitely wore waterproof mascara, that was like necessity item, and I had two different outfits and put them both on to see which one my parents thought was better.

Arlene prepared to deliver her testimony confidently and clearly.

> Well that thing about falling apart on the stand was [a problem]. I was very worried about it beforehand, but in the actual experience I had no question that I would do that. I had rehearsed it, I knew what I was going to say, and I had rehearsed the hard questions and how to say them. And [I] practiced it, and I knew that I wouldn't.

Joanna selected a team of people who could provide her with unconditional support in the courtroom.

> So right before trial time, we had ... we kind of had it out. I said [to my parents], "I don't want you there. I don't want you there at all." In fact, I said, "I feel like I need to be strong on that day, and I don't need to feel like I'm hurting your feelings by anything I might be saying on the stand."

Sandra worked to fill in the gaps in her legal knowledge.

> I was on this rampage of having this information, you know. (sighs) So I got a lot of information just from reading. I went to the library, and found out about laws um, the laws and what the defense attorneys could do, I mean, I read it in the

[California Penal Code] . . . I went to the library. It's like I felt I couldn't get any information [from court personnel]. Like, I had to go and read about it myself, and so that's what I did. I tried to read a lot about it, although it didn't [give me all I needed].

These stories show that before their court appearances, rape survivors act in a variety of ways and without the direction of legal personnel to enhance their capacity to perform their victim roles effectively. They also demonstrate that women whose reports are delayed by trauma responses (Arlene and Sandra), or debate about whether a public legal response is appropriate (Julianne), or debate about whether their experience meets the definition of rape (Joanna) deepen their commitment and investment in prosecution as they progress further into the criminal justice process. This chapter examines the full scope of what rape survivors do to prepare themselves to fulfill their witness roles and why.

Modes of Survivor Preparation

Appearance Work

Survivors purposefully selected clothing and made themselves up to demonstrate respect for the court and to conform to visual standards separating rape victims from women "who asked for it." These were their intentional efforts to shape how jurors and judges would view them. Some women crafted their appearances without outside influence; prosecutors' requests motivated others.

Survivors who attended to their appearance consistently sought to project conservative, businesslike, and nonsexual personas. Some went to extra effort to choose clothes that hid their bodies and to keep their makeup subtle. Despite Northern California's mild weather, Megan selected "a long, black floral dress, buttons down the front, about down to here [indicating her calf], and I wore boots. " She laughed when she recalled, "You couldn't see any of my body!"

Theresa explained that a person who did not present herself in court in a businesslike way might not be believable to others.

Well, I kind of had thought of what I wanted to wear, you know, something that was . . . something that I would normally just wear to work, you know, because I dress business-like when I go to work and so I thought you know, that that's the way it should be. I mean, you know, you're not gonna go to court in a miniskirt and be believable.

Because she and Connie similarly viewed the court as business, they both selected clothes from their work wardrobes to testify. However, as Connie was an executive and Theresa a clerical worker, they appeared for their respective attackers' preliminary hearings in different attire. Connie wore a business suit and pumps, while Theresa came to court in a light pink short-sleeved blouse, a pair of black crop pants sprinkled with pink flowers, and flat shoes. The way these two white women of comparable age implemented their common understanding reflected their occupational status and class position.

Although survivors often based their court personas on an existing role and aspect of their self-conception, they selectively revealed aspects of their identity. Connie consciously avoided presenting the aspect of herself that she associated with backpacking, a dimension of her persona that would, perhaps, appear to be too self-reliant. On the other hand, Arlene created a court persona that bore little resemblance to her sense of self, because she thought that court personnel might question her character. She became in appearance and manner what she hoped was the embodiment of a stereotypical rape victim.

> I dressed in a . . . in a very uncharacteristic way for me. I wore, you know, a skirt and a blouse and a jacket and hose and heels and all that stuff, I mean I looked the part that I wanted the court to think I was. [. . .] I have always been the kind of person that runs around in jeans and t-shirts as much as I can, and that's essentially what I was dressed in when I was raped, and I was very clear that I wanted there to be no question on the part of the court about my character, that I was going to play every game that I thought that they expected me to play. [. . .] It was not about who I was or who he was or what could have happened, it was about my objective that this fucker was going to jail, that's what was on my mind.

Some survivors even purchased new clothes to create their desired appearance for court. This activity cut across class lines, suggesting that to live up to cultural expectations of victims, working-class and poor women may take on a comparatively greater financial burden.

Rehearsal

Most survivors believed that they needed to give detailed accounts of the rape to judges and juries. This was problematic for two reasons. Some were unsure that they would be able to remember the specific details of what had happened months or even years before and they worried a great deal about cross-examination. Others knew that giving a detailed account would require them to get close to the experience of the rape and were worried about the prospect of being overwhelmed with tears on the witness stand. These two kinds of concerns prompted the preparation strategy of "rehearsal."

A quarter of the survivors reported rehearsing all or parts of their expected testimony to ensure an accurate portrayal of the rape and to keep their emotions under control. Some women, like Natalie, prepared themselves by telling their stories to supportive friends or relatives. She enlisted her husband to be an audience for her testimony the night before she was due in court. She explained why:

I have to know that I'm ready and that's how I was feelin'. I had to be certain that I could get up there and say everything that happened to me, and I didn't want to forget anything. [...] I wanted to say everything that he [the rapist] ... that he had did to me. [...] I said, "Sam"—my husband—"I know this is hard, but what I really need instead of just readin' my statement is to say it, to say what happened, and for you [to listen]." And he did [...] and I got through it all and I didn't forget anything and I felt better.

Natalie learned through rehearsal that she could rely on her memory, thereby resolving one aspect of her anxiety and gaining confidence.

Other survivors rehearsed for their court appearances alone. Jennifer was troubled about conveying the sexual nature of the attack to a public court audience. Thus, before the preliminary hearing she sat down and thought out statements to most comfortably describe how her assailant threatened and coerced her to orally copulate him. Arlene considered the account that she had given police from the perspective of the defense attorney. As described in one of the quotations that open this chapter, she composed answers to the hardest questions that she could imagine him asking her, and then she practiced reciting them. On the day she went to court, Arlene knew that she would not "fall apart on the stand." The final rehearsal activity involved visualization. To overcome her intense feelings and the tendency she had to cry uncontrollably when discussing the rape, Julianne imagined successfully carrying out the role of witness, sitting on the witness stand testifying steadily and with conviction.

Emotion Work

Survivors prepared themselves to achieve courtroom demeanors that were consistent with social expectations of witnesses and victims. Recognizing that the ideal "witness" was polite and composed, indicating honesty and an appropriate deference to the court's authority, some women sought to repress displays of obvious anger or pain, which would result in their loss of emotional control or make their truthfulness suspect. Others prepared themselves to lose emotional control and cry on the witness stand, living up to the expectation that they be truly overcome by memories of the assault.

In the following series of comments, Donna, who testified in two trials, explains how she went about achieving different emotional states as her analysis of what was required to convince a jury changed. Before the first trial, Donna sought to achieve an inner calm and to preclude any show of emotion.

So I had gone to one of the elders in my church and I said I want a blessing before I go to court. [...] So um, they got all together and they gave me a blessing, and it was like the day before, and I was totally calm when I went through that first trial. [...] I felt that I had done everything that I was supposed to do and I was determined I was not gonna cry.

After the first jury was unable to reach a verdict, Donna decided to become a stereotypical rape victim. She chose not to receive religious solace and turned away emotional supports before the second trial.

> I had gone over the testimony that I knew I was gonna give, and I figured that ... there was a part I was just gonna have to lose it on. [...] But I figured that I was gonna have to, 'cause otherwise they weren't gonna believe anything.... Uh, CASA [a rape support service] offered to come and go with us to trial, but I said no, I didn't need anybody. I'd already made up my mind I was not gonna get a blessing this time, 'cause I was not gonna be calm, cool, and collected. If they [the jury] wanted somebody hysterical on the stand, they were gonna get one. And all I had to do was wait for [the prosecutor] to push the right buttons 'cause I was sure he was gonna do that.

Donna's preparation had the desired effect; she fell apart on the witness stand. Other survivors simply wished to keep their emotions private and sought counseling or cried freely before the court event to work out undesired feelings.

Team-Building

More than two-thirds of survivors recruited specific people to attend court events with them. Many felt that they needed others to support them emotionally on the days they were called to testify, to endure the seemingly endless waiting in hallways and usually windowless victim-witness rooms with them, and to provide a friendly face in the courtroom during their testimony. They carefully selected from among those who were available to most enhance their ability to achieve credible courtroom performances.

Theresa described a carefully considered support plan. Sometime before the scheduled preliminary hearing, she evaluated her emotional and physical needs and asked two women to fill specific roles that she considered necessary to sustain a successful performance. She recruited a third team member to ensure that her friend, who had been subpoenaed, would have company and support as well.

> *Theresa:* Well, I set up someone [#1] to sit with me on the stand, and um, I had one friend sit in the courtroom that I could look at and talk to [#2, the only person who had been told the details of the assault]. And also I had one other person come who could be in the witness room [#3] with the other witness while I was on the stand so the other witness wouldn't be alone, and get all nervous. So, and the person I chose to sit with me [#1] was from um, the rape crisis center. [...] What her purpose there was, was to breathe loudly so I could hear her, because what I tend to do is [Theresa holds her breath in an exaggerated way] (laughs).
>
> *Amanda:* Hold your breath?
>
> *Theresa:* Yeah, so that was her main purpose there, and to see that I constantly had water, 'cause I'm on anti-depressants, and my mouth feels really dry.

Survivors weighed the investments of others against their own needs and excluded from team membership those whose attention might be elsewhere, who could not fully support them, and whose feelings might be hurt by hearing their testimony. The result was that individuals who were close to the rape survivor, and may have been involved in reporting decisions, were occasionally ruled out as courtroom team members. Joanna, quoted in the opening of the chapter, asked her parents not to attend the preliminary hearing because they had not demonstrated unqualified support for her when she first told them about the rape. Arlene chose not to involve several sympathetic women friends who she believed were emotionally distressed by the rape or a man friend whose inability to control his anger about the rape made her uncomfortable. Candace recruited her 20-something daughter to be her main support through the preliminary hearing and the trial that followed. In contrast, she did not tell her adult son the details of the rape or when the preliminary hearing would be held, fearing the consequences of him hearing her describe the attack.

A third of the survivors asked personnel from RCCs or victim-witness advocacy programs to attend court events with them.[1] Many women selected such staff because they would provide unconditional sympathy and emotional support, but would not expect or need anyone to protect their feelings. Anna chose a victim-witness advocate to be in court with her to protect her mother and her boyfriend from details of the assault that would be revealed through her testimony. If an advocate was not available, she had planned to go through the preliminary hearing alone. Candace explained that she recruited a victim-witness advocate to join her daughter and herself for the preliminary hearing and trial, because she felt that she could not risk involving her friends in the proceedings. She was unsure of their beliefs about rape and feared that they might reject her after learning the extent of her degradation or possibly hold her accountable for being raped.

When several survivors found that would-be supporters were unwilling to respect their standards for team membership, they experienced a difficult situation. At the least, they felt annoyed. Sandra fled the courthouse when her boyfriend, whom she had asked not to come, appeared anyway. Members of the team that she had assembled went after her and brought her back. Her boyfriend realized that he was jeopardizing her participation in the case, and he left the courthouse.

Survivors who relied on victim-witness advocates generally found them to be well informed about legal process and procedure. However, several women reported that their advocate sometimes seemed to withhold information specific to the case.[2] Survivors universally found that rape crisis volunteers provided good moral support, but often had a minimal grasp of the workings of the legal process.

When survivors received little education about the process from prosecutors and were not comfortable contacting RCCs or victim-witness organizations, they sought individuals with prior court experience as team members.

The quality of the information and support they received was relative to the personal contacts they had. For example, Janice asked a coworker who had recently been involved in a criminal proceeding to accompany her, while Bernice was able to invite an attorney friend who had previously prosecuted criminal cases.

Finally, survivors strategically encouraged other people to be present in the courtroom to influence the jury. Most encouraged family members and friends to attend to show that they were believed by a large number of people. Cindy invited her black friends to be in the courtroom during the trial, because they visibly contradicted the race bias argument that she expected the defense attorney to make. It was her intent that these friends and the book that she openly carried about, would dispel any perception that she was a white bigot with a vendetta against all black men.

> The [trial was on the] Tuesday after the Saturday after the gubernatorial elections, so ... needless to say, things are a little strange between blacks and whites at this point because David Duke [former Grand Wizard of the Ku Klux Klan] is running [for governor], you know. I mean that whole thing was the topic of conversation in Louisiana for the previous month. [...] It made things very strange between black people and white people. Um, and I ... you know, he [the defense attorney] was smart enough to kind of take advantage of all that. I think, he really set it up. So I found myself really consciously trying to um, dispel that, you know. I had black friends in the courtroom with me, I was reading a book by J. California Cooper, who is a black woman writer, and I made sure that I was seen reading that book, you know what I mean? Um, you know, I did everything I could to try and dispel the whole kind of racial thing by manner and stuff.

Role Research

Survivors engaged in library research and sought the guidance of people with legal knowledge to better understand rape law, the legal process, and the possible interactions that they might have when appearing in court. Unlike the activities of appearance work, emotion work, or case enhancement, such "role research" was not directed toward meeting cultural expectations of rape victims. Survivors hoped to gain knowledge and skills that would help them participate more effectively in a foreign "legal" space and produce legally appropriate responses to questions they might be asked.[3]

Sandra and Joanna, both college students when they were raped, described trying to find relevant information in their university libraries. They looked up legal terms and legal codes that defined "rape" as well as general court process information. As Sandra described in a quotation that opens this chapter, she put a lot of work into researching information. Unfortunately, she was not successful in obtaining all that she felt she needed. Joanna was more satisfied with the research effort she conducted and indicated that what she discovered guided her word choice while testifying. Specifically, Joanna reported that she learned that the state of Virginia differentiated between forced vaginal intercourse (rape) and sexual assault (forced sexual contact short of penetration), and that she needed to say "rape" while testifying rather than "sexual assault," the term she used when reporting the incident to police. Megan, another college student, went to the university counsel's office for information. The fact that all three college students undertook role research suggests that their presence in institutions *for* research and education shaped their response to the criminal justice system.

Other women called therapists and lawyers for information when it was not forthcoming from prosecutors and their assistants. Rachel explained that she received detailed guidelines about how to answer questions from her therapist:

> He basically told me how the questions are asked, to think very clearly before I answer anything, and how to try to, um, direct my answers and that they will try to trick me. [...] "His lawyer will try to prevent you from saying what you really have to say. So say, Well there's two parts to that. It's um, the yes part of it is (pause) and the no part of it is (pause). Whatever you want to say, say that first. That way, um, you're more than likely to get in what, what you have to say, otherwise they cut you off."

Case Enhancement

Of their own volition, nine survivors brought documents that corroborated their version of the assault event to the attention of legal personnel either before court events or as they went to court. Their behavior reflected an understanding that the courtroom is a place where proof is required and that their testimony alone was not sufficient evidence that a rape took place. Theresa supplied a telephone bill that supported her claim that she called a particular friend immediately after the defendant left her home.

> I keep my phone bills, and I dug it out, and there it was, 1:03 [A.M.] on that night, I was on the phone with her for over 20 minutes. [...] You know it's like, anything I can do to prove my case. I know that any documentation is that much better for me.

The phone bill provided evidence of a "fresh complaint," although Theresa did not report the assault to the police until several weeks later. Recognizing it as useful evidence, the prosecuting attorney asked Theresa to provide a copy when the hearing was over.

Rachel brought her daily diary to the attention of the prosecuting attorney several weeks before the scheduled hearing for probable cause because she thought it might help the prosecutor understand the history of her relationship with her assailant, her ex-husband. At the hearing, Rachel used her diary for reference and it was entered as evidence.

While physical evidence of rape is collected by hospital personnel and police investigators, information regarding a rape survivor's mental state that may account for her behavior during or after a sexual assault is not. The materials supplied by survivors quoted above provided support for their claims that they did not consent to intercourse with the men with whom they chose to associate. Their case enhancement efforts, like appearance work and emotion work, indicate that they were aware of and trying to accommodate stereotypes of rape.

When prosecutors told survivors about known defense strategies, a few produced evidence to counter them. For example, Natalie brought eight years of excellent employment evaluations to the prosecuting attorney after learning that the defense attorney was planning to argue that she had precipitated the assault during a drug deal. Although, Natalie assessed the argument as "totally ridiculous," she felt compelled to take personal responsibility for the successful outcome of prosecution and counter it.

The woman who took the greatest responsibility for the outcome of her case actually prepared it for the prosecution. After the defendant was brought to trial once and the jury failed to reach a verdict, the prosecutor approached Donna about participating in a retrial. Dissatisfied with his initial efforts, she and her husband took action to construct a stronger case.

> Well, let's see ... they [the prosecutor's office] called me after [the first trial], and I said, "If you do it again it's gonna be first degree rape and that's it." And I said, "you have to call witnesses." I said, "we need to get character witnesses for me." And I remember that we [Donna and her husband] sat down and drew a map showing the distance from the house to the bar [where Donna's husband worked]. I remember that we took pictures to show where the house was in relationship to the bar, and my path [from the house to the bar after the rape], and we took pictures inside the house. [...] My husband and me, we basically built their case for them.

In the cases that I have discussed thus far, survivors provided concrete pieces of evidence to back up their claims, and they found that their efforts were accepted and incorporated by the prosecuting attorneys. However, other women's efforts to shape prosecution strategy with their ideas were not as well received. Julianne's experience provides a straightforward example of this point. Several weeks before the scheduled preliminary hearing, she learned specifics of the defense attorney's strategy from a mutual friend to whom her rapist boyfriend had spoken.

> *Julianne:* [The defendant's friend called and] said, "I want you to know, they're gonna bring up this and they're gonna bring up this, you know," [...] He was giving me ideas about [what] they'd bring up for me to be prepared with an answer.
>
> *Amanda:* Can you remember any of those specifically right now?

Julianne: Um, he uh, past history about our intimate times together, um, a time that I ... I ... said "no, no," and ... and ended up going ahead and giving in. [...] So I went back and called the DA. [I said,] "I want you to know I found out this, this, and this."

Julianne communicated the information to the prosecutor hoping that a rebuttal of some sort would be planned. Instead, he told her not to worry, brushing off her concerns without addressing their validity. Unfortunately, Julianne's information was accurate and the case resolution reflected this.[4]

Prosecutors' acceptance of evidence and their rejection of ideas speaks to a boundary issue. Witnesses who provide strategy challenge the prosecutor's right to determine whether and how prosecution will proceed; those who provide tangible corroborative evidence do not. I suspect that Donna's efforts would have been dismissed as overly intrusive had the prosecutor not failed to convict the defendant on his first attempt.

Explaining the Patterns in Survivor Self-Preparation

Survivors, as a group, did some preparatory activities more than others. More than two-thirds built courtroom teams, slightly more than half crafted their appearances, nearly a third prepared themselves to manage their emotions or enhanced their case, about a quarter rehearsed, and close to a fifth researched their witness roles. Some individuals also prepared more than others. One-tenth of the survivors did nothing, a bit more than a third prepared in one way, nearly half did two to four kinds of activities, and one-tenth prepared in five or six ways.

Survivors' Preassault Knowledge of Legal Processes and Courtroom Procedure

Survivors who worked for or in close contact with the criminal justice system, or who had been involved in civil or criminal proceedings before being raped, had a fairly good working knowledge of legal process and procedure. Such knowledge made them less anxious than others about whether the system was working properly. First, their experience gave them a sense of the often lengthy time frame of legal matters and of the possibility of continuances that would delay the prosecution of their assailants and alter known court dates. Second, having been in courtrooms, they had an idea of the physical layout (where various actors stood or sat), and they had some idea of the range of behaviors of various players, including attorneys, judges, and witnesses. A sense of the layout and roles made the situation they would enter somewhat predictable and they were not highly motivated to prepare themselves. In some sense, these survivors already knew what others sought to learn.

Many women who lacked firsthand knowledge about legal process and procedures, in contrast, viewed the courtroom as alien and unpredictable. They were not confident that they could walk into the witness role, and several women described themselves as "fearful" of the courtroom. Their lack of understanding about the courtroom situation that they would be entering was, thus, an incentive to prepare for court, and they researched their roles to fill in perceived knowledge gaps. Their class background, age, and access to expert knowledge influenced where and how they sought information. In the absence of good knowledge, some built teams that included friends who had some sort of prior court experiences.

Not all survivors who lacked knowledge about the criminal justice process sought to educate themselves, however. Those who perceived the witness role to be primarily responsive waited for direction and guidance from the prosecuting attorney. Such passive perceptions of the witness role were more common among the women who traced their legal knowledge to television serials, in which attorneys come to the rescue of helpless victims week after week.

Survivors' Evaluation of the Fit Between Attacks and Rape Stereotypes

All the survivors were aware of the common cultural notions that (1) rape is an exceedingly violent assault carried out by a stranger, and (2) an overwhelmed woman, despite her mental and physical anguish, reports to police just as soon as she is out of harm's way. Thus, it is not surprising that another obvious difference among those who prepared extensively and those who prepared little or not at all was the extent to which the assault they experienced and their postassault behavior matched such stereotypes. Thirteen of the 19 survivors who did none or but one preparation activity were raped by strangers. Given the consistency of their experience with what they knew to be rape, they were quite sure that what had happened to them was not their fault and would not be perceived as such by a judge or jury. Lauren, a law student, did nothing to prepare herself before her grand jury performance. Because she believed that she would not be directly attacked by the defense attorney, she prepared for the trial only at the behest of the prosecutor.

> I knew I wasn't to blame. It's like I'm in my home, I don't even know this person. I never invited him any place. I felt justified and I never had a fear that I would be attacked, I mean by the system, and I think that's what motivated me. I didn't have the fear that date rapes have, date rape *victims* have.

Likewise, 16-year-old Nan, who did not prepare on her own, was quite aware of how well she matched with cultural stereotypes of rape victims: "I was aware at the time [...] that being a virgin, being soft spoken, not having a history of any wild behavior was really helpful."

Four low-preparing survivors, raped by someone they knew, were overcome with great violence or a weapon and, thus, had many attributes of stranger assaults. They also did not perceive a great need to offset victim stereotypes.

In contrast, eight of the 13 women who prepared in three or more ways knew their assailants and did not make immediate reports to police. These survivors were aware of the mismatch between their experience and the behavior and stereotypes associated with rape. Friends and family of several women openly questioned their labeling of the attack as rape. Doubting and doubted women, like Rachel, expressed serious concerns about the nature of the cross-examination that they would experience.

> In the beginning, all I could remember thinking was that they were going to eat me alive in court. He's your ex-husband, um, you know they're gonna use every-thing they could possibly use against me. They are gonna make me seem like this ... horrible person, you know, that's just out for revenge or something.

Rachel consequently prepared in four ways.

Megan had entered the rapist's room willingly and accepted alcohol from him before being attacked, and she was well aware that her behavior deviated from cultural stereotypes of "real rape" and "real victims." She greatly feared cross-examination and prepared in four ways to ready herself for a defense assault on her character despite the fact that she was a virgin with essentially no sexual experience.

Some women who took action believed cultural stereotypes were valid. They considered themselves legitimate victims, but thought that other women precipi-tated assaults by leading men on or cried rape after "bad sex." Other survivors acknowledged that jury members and judges might well believe stereotypes, even though they personally did not. The strategies that believers and non-believers used to prepare themselves were similar, however, because all were intent on proving that they were legitimate victims in the courtroom forum. Thus, appearance work, emotion work, case enhancement, and team-building did not challenge the validity of common cultural frameworks for understanding rape, and some women were engaged in the affirmation of the belief systems that they found oppressive. This was a paradox a few painfully acknowledged.

Survivor Self-Confidence

Generally inexperienced with bureaucracies, minors did not see themselves as independently capable of shaping or changing the legal environment. They were more oriented to meeting the demands of persons in authority, like police and prosecutors, rather than making demands of them. Furthermore, as I dis-covered with the investigation, they did not have much contact with legal personnel, who tended to call their parents.

Sixteen-year-old Monica's concern about going against the wishes of her parents kept her from building the courtroom team that she desired. She wanted to exclude everyone from the courtroom except her boyfriend; how-ever, she "felt pressured" and accepted the presence of a victim-witness advo-cate whom her parents felt she needed. Nan, also 16 years old, was aware that others were not necessarily acting on her behalf, yet she was unable to formulate a plan of action of her own or even tell the prosecutor what she felt she needed.

> I do remember, I think this was just reality, just the perception that they are not here with me. They have their own business, and their own agenda might be different from mine. I didn't even know what my agenda was.... [My greatest difficulty was] telling them what my needs were.... My father was really taking care of that [dealing with the criminal justice system] for the most part.

Ultimately, Nan responded to the prosecutor's request that she work on her appearance.

Several survivors who lived hundreds of miles from the jurisdiction in which the case was being tried did not actively prepare for court events. They were removed from the relevant rape crisis and victim-witness organizations, written information they could obtain in their local libraries did not apply to the jurisdiction in which the case was being tried, and their family and friends were not available to be drafted onto their teams. They also believed that prosecutors, who had chosen to go forward when they could have dropped the case with few negative repercussions, would give them strong support.

The Quality of Interactions between Survivors and Legal Personnel

Rape survivors' early encounters with legal personnel shaped their perceptions of the competency, caring, and commitment of those who are trying their assailant. These encounters also shaped their understanding of their victim-witness role and their efforts to influence the process through preparation. Survivors attributed competence to legal personnel who regularly contacted them. They perceived as good follow through the calls that detectives made to determine if they could remember more about the assault. They identified calls from prosecutors that were made for just about any reason as a serious commitment to the case and as warrant for their trust.

Some prosecutors who had precourt contact with survivors said or indicated that their role was only to testify; others encouraged women to participate in other ways. Because survivors generally responded to direction from prosecutors, their preparation efforts reflected these opposing messages.

Most women who were involved in the investigation before a suspect was apprehended came to see their witness role as active and themselves as part of a team. They got to know the detective, and at times the prosecutor, through repeated interaction. They perceived that their participation mattered and sought ways to contribute to the prosecution's effort as the case moved forward, including preparing themselves for court. Likewise, survivors who were told their courtroom participation was vital to the case sought ways to make their performances as believable as possible.

Cindy and Rachel provide good examples of contact-facilitated preparation. The stereotypical qualities of the rape and Cindy's immediate report would suggest her lack of involvement in the legal process. However, with her assailant at large, legal personnel drew her into the investigation. During this time, she was asked to construct a composite drawing, and later, when a suspect was apprehended, she was asked to identify him in a photo lineup. Following a grand jury hearing, she left town for several months to visit family and friends. She returned to discover the DA desperately trying to reach her and found this desire for her contact gratifying. Regular contact between Cindy and the prosecuting attorney continued after this meeting. Cindy ultimately engaged in appearance work, role rehearsal, instrumental and emotional team-building, and case enhancement to prepare for her appearance at her assailant's trial.

Prosecutors gave Rachel positive feedback for providing them with the diary that chronicled her relationship with the defendant, her ex-husband. This positive response, in conjunction with their availability, led her to believe it was important to continue to be a team player and do the work that would make the case stronger.

> What helped me keep going was that I had people around me that were, that I felt were pulling for me. I did a lot of footwork on this case. I went to [the prosecutor], I got paperwork. I did, you know. I brought paperwork to her, I picked paperwork up [the defendant's statements] and went through it line-by-line-by-line, and called her [about] every little [inconsistency]. I mean, I marked everything. I kept immaculate notes on this.

Problems Rachel had with the assailant's family also led to repeated contact with the detective on the case. The detective's ability to halt their harassment was further evidence of the system's support and increased her commitment to the case.

Women who were raped by men they knew and were concerned about how the judge and jury would respond found the absence of prosecutor-initiated preparation to be problematic as court dates loomed closer. They had no idea whether the prosecutor was doing anything to meet their concerns and not knowing made them feel that they had to preempt all the possible problems they perceived. They tried to inform themselves about the court process and form themselves into viable witnesses, and some made it their project to obtain or pass on information, assuming that silence indicated the prosecutor's lack of investment in their case.

Conclusions and Questions for Further Consideration

Studies of real and hypothetical rape reporting have found that women who are raped by men they know, without the use of weapons, and who experience few injuries in addition to the rape are less likely to report their violation to police.[5] A likely extrapolation from this is that late reporters will be less-willing witnesses and less committed to the prosecution process. These results show, however, that lack of consistency between a participant's experience and rape stereotypes does not affect her preparation in such a way. Women in this study whose experiences were the least consistent with stereotypes and who delayed the longest in making reports to police were among the most active in working toward prosecution. This counterintuitive finding is important. It suggests that the documented practices of not bringing charges against suspects or plea-bargaining when rape survivors delay in making police reports, or when they experienced something other than stereotypical rapes, exclude women from the prosecution process who would be committed to it. Specifically, it excludes women who are willing to devote time, energy, and personal funds to have the opportunity to see their assailant held accountable for his actions.

I found that white women and women of color carried out each of the six preparation strategies, indicating that racial and ethnic background does not limit the kind of preparation in which survivors engage. On the other hand, I discovered that racial stereotypes shaped some survivors' involvement in prosecution. Some of the white women in this study who were raped by black men thought about stereotypes of the "black rapist" during the early stages of the process and several concluded that their assailants' race relative to their own could make the prosecution's case more convincing to a jury. It is possible that such assessments could have translated into less motivation to self-prepare, although none stated this. On the other hand, Cindy's comments about building a courtroom team including black friends, because she expected a predominately black jury and was aware of heightened racial tension in her city, show a rape survivor thinking through the race relations in her immediate geographic context. When rape survivors are knowledgeable that jury pools are drawn from specific geographic jurisdictions, preparation such as Cindy's would seem likely. Information provided by police or prosecutors also made survivors attentive to their assailant's race or the expected race of jurors, and shaped their self-preparation. For example, as discussed in chapter 4, prosecutors informed Monica and Janice that race would play a role in the trial.

I did not find that survivors' education levels, reported incomes, or occupational statuses were associated with substantial variation in preparatory behavior, suggesting that working-class and middle-class women perceived their witness role similarly. On the other hand, these attributes did appear to contribute to the specific nature of team-building and role research in which survivors engaged as well as what they wore. Women of all socioeconomic backgrounds used rape crisis hotlines and drew victim-witness advocates onto their teams, but only middle-class professional women were able to ask friends who worked as lawyers to accompany them to court. Young women attending college had access to extensive libraries and the university counsel to conduct role research; others relied on consulting "experts" by telephone. These findings that socioeconomic difference lead witnesses to enact similar strategies in different ways are consistent with John Conley and William O'Barr's[6] discoveries about middle- and working-class witnesses in the civil justice system.

Differences in survivors' understandings of the causes of rape and personal acceptance of rape stereotypes did not substantially differentiate their preparation efforts. Feminists prepared similarly to those who identified in other ways. However, the personal costs of carrying out behaviors consistent with rape stereotypes may have been greater for feminists. Their ideological opposition to rape stereotypes may have required them to engage in more emotion work to carry out their activities. Clearly, acting in a way that was not in accord with their personal values underscores their serious commitment to successful prosecution.

Entering the courtroom knowing that they were presenting themselves as stereotypically credible victims helped rape survivors put aside any doubts that they were not. Thus, doing precourt appearance work and emotion work helped make performing the role of witness an easier task. With their doubts decreased, survivors were better able to concentrate on the business of testifying. In addition, their selection of businesslike and modest clothing tended to restrict them to businesslike and modest posture, thus producing a physical performance befitting a stereotypical victim.

Women who rehearsed their testimony in some fashion gained confidence that they could successfully talk about their assaults. They also took the witness stand with a sense of what they wanted to say, not just a general expectation that they would talk about the rape. This made them feel less defensive.

Through team-building, rape survivors constructed a sympathetic audience they trusted and by whom they felt believed and to whom they could direct their testimony. This reduced the anxiety associated with the task of telling their stories. The orienting information their supporters supplied, in the absence of preparation from legal personnel, eased their worry about testifying. When survivors brought people into the courtroom who symbolically underscored the validity of their claims of victimization, this also contributed to the prosecution effort.

Through role research, survivors gained information to successfully perform their witness role and enabled them to be productively involved in the legal process. What they learned eased the worry of some, thus boosting their confidence. It may also have helped them formulate testimony in ways that supported the prosecution effort or made them better able to comprehend the logic of requests made by prosecutors. On the other hand, role research was a frustrating experience for the women who came to realize their ability to obtain knowledge fell short of gaining a complete picture of the witness role. In spite of their effort, they did not gain confidence about testifying.

Case enhancement efforts that brought to light material corroborating survivors' stories generally supported prosecutors' efforts. Having something credible on paper to which they could refer during a hearing also boosted their confidence. To the degree that survivors could limit their testimony to these documents, they supported prosecutors' efforts to keep the scope of key witnesses' testimony within narrow bounds.

Did survivors' acts of self-preparation improve their prosecution experience? Yes, when self-preparation made them feel more confident and capable in their witness roles. However, when prosecutors narrowly circumscribed the courtroom participation of women who had already prepared themselves, some had increased feelings of frustration and anger. In a sense, being thwarted in their effort to participate fully in prosecution increased the emotional difficulty of the trial process.

The heightened confidence several women had about their abilities to fulfill the witness role increased their willingness to put themselves through testifying in preliminary hearings and, tangentially, increased prosecutors' abilities to obtain guilty pleas from defendants. It is not possible to determine the full impact of survivors' case-enhancement initiatives, but several women who supplied prosecutors with concrete evidence appear to have influenced the prosecution strategy. But what women do for themselves may not always support prosecutors' interests. For example, a survivor's effort to prepare statements to defend her postrape actions could work against a prosecutor's plan to present her as unintelligent or easily tricked by her assailant.

Whatever the kinds and amount of preparation rape survivors engage in or receive from legal personnel, they must appear at court if prosecution of their assailants is to go forward. For most, testifying from the witness stand is their first occasion to make a public statement about the rape experience.

- How do survivors manage the emotional aspects of testifying?
- How do they negotiate interaction with prosecutors and defense attorneys?
- How do they actually put their thoughts into words?
- How does their construction of emotion work, case enhancement, appearance work, rehearsal, team-building, and role research help them?
- How do prosecutors' efforts to orient them, improve their credibility, and shape their performances impact them?

These questions are the focus of the next two chapters.

CHAPTER 6

"I Don't Have to Be Afraid of You!": Rape Survivors' Emotion Management in Court

When I asked survivors to tell me about going to court, many emphasized their efforts to control their emotions.

Joanna suppressed her tears to deny the defendant the satisfaction of seeing her continued discomfort.

> I felt like it [cross examination] was very demeaning the entire time um, and I felt awful on top of it, but I told myself that I wasn't gonna let myself break down in front of them [the defendant and his attorney]. [...] I guess I felt like he had seen me vulnerable too much before, and I was vulnerable before, and he hurt me, and that I wasn't gonna let this attorney intimidate me to the point that I would break down and cry. [...] As soon as (of course) he [the defendant] walked out the courtroom I lost it. (laughs)

Donna allowed herself to fall apart while testifying to make the pain of the rape visible to the jury.

> I cried on the stand and told them what he had said, and [I] broke down every time I had to say "fuck." [...] I had gone over the testimony that I knew I was gonna give, and I figured that I was ... there was a part I was just gonna have to lose it on, and I figured that was gonna be it, and that's about the part that I did start to cry, and they called a recess and ... and handed me some water and calmed me down and then went on from there. But I figured that I was gonna have to 'cause otherwise they weren't gonna believe anything.

And, Lauren harnessed her growing anger so that she could reject her fear of the defendant.

> I stopped crying and started gettin' mad, and [I] wanted to look at [the defendant] so I did. [...] They asked me to identify him in court, and asked me if I was sure that was him. And I was able to look at him, and say yes it was, I felt that it was him. Then it started feeling exhilarating, 'cause I saw that I'd won the jurors over, um, that they believed me. [...] Knowing that I was in control, I

think that was where it went exhilarating. [...] It's like, "I don't have to be afraid of you!"

Whatever the kinds and amount of preparation rape survivors engage in or receive from legal personnel, they must appear at court if prosecution of their assailants is to go forward. In rare cases, a rape survivor's presence at the courthouse and apparent willingness to testify is in itself enough to convince a wavering defendant to accept a plea offer before a scheduled preliminary hearing. When this happens, the rape survivor's courtroom participation consists of watching the defendant enter his plea and waive his rights. In many other cases, however, survivors must take the witness stand or enter the grand jury chamber and testify about the rape event. If an indictment is obtained and the case is not later dropped or resolved by plea, they must return and testify again at the defendant's trial.

This chapter documents survivors' incentives to manage their feelings and expressions of specific emotions and shows the social origins of their individual strategies for deflecting, suppressing, and cultivating emotion. Because organizational contexts frame emotional experiences, I will preface my discussion with some background information about formal characteristics of U.S. criminal trial process, the question-answer format used in courtrooms, and the questioning strategies used by defense attorneys.

Preliminary hearings and trials are formally organized events. The roles that are most central to court proceedings involving rape survivors are judge, state's (prosecuting) attorney, defendant's (defense) attorney, defendant, witness, and juror (if a trial). The periods of interaction in a trial include jury selection, opening statements, introduction of evidence, closing statements, and charges to the jury. The periods may be interrupted by occasional recesses and vary in length from an hour to several days. Evidence is introduced without opening or closing statements in preliminary and grand jury hearings, which are generally completed within hours.

Rape survivors who take part in preliminary hearings and trials enter the role of witness and participate in evidentiary sequences. During these court events, rape survivors interact with both prosecuting and defense attorneys and laws of criminal procedure provide behavioral parameters for all parties. A significant feature of the evidentiary sequence is its division into direct examination and cross-examination. During these segments, the prosecuting attorney and defense attorney alternately question each witness. Rape survivors are brought forward as prosecution witnesses and are directly questioned by the state's prosecuting attorney. Prosecutors usually lead them through an account of the attack to establish that the features of a crime occurred and that they can identify the defendant as the rapist.

During the cross-examination sequence in a preliminary hearing or trial, the defense attorney questions the rape survivor. She or he works to weaken the prosecutor's case by raising doubt about a rape survivor's credibility in the judge's or jurors' minds, asking questions to show that (1) the survivor is wrong about the identity of the defendant, (2) the survivor consented to the sex acts described and has some ulterior motive to fabricate a rape story, or (3) no sexual activity actually took place.

The attorneys shape what survivors will talk about by the focus of their questions: details, generalities, the sexual assault, or other issues. They also establish a tempo to the testimony through the speed of their delivery and control the order in which survivors must address topics by the way they string questions together. To perform their role successfully, witnesses must supply an answer for each question posed by a prosecuting or defense attorney.

Direct and cross-examination are, however, different experiences for most rape survivors. Generally, a prosecutor organizes questions to help a survivor reconstruct a logical account of the rape and adjusts her or his tempo to meet the survivor's needs. Conversely, because the purpose of the cross-examination is to discredit the survivor-witness, the defense attorney constructs questions and shapes his or her delivery to make answering difficult. The prosecuting attorney is not allowed to lead the witness during direct examination; however, during cross-examination, attorneys may ask leading questions. Many use this questioning technique because it gives them more control over a witness's possible response.

When a prosecutor's questions appear to lead a survivor toward a specific response, the defense attorney may object. When a defense attorney asks a survivor questions about her past sexual history, prohibited by law, or raises topics that were not addressed in direct examination, the prosecutor may object. Prosecutors may also object to halt styles of question delivery that go beyond the bounds of what they believe to be acceptable treatment of a witness. When either attorney raises an objection, he or she is temporarily halting the interaction and requesting that the judge invalidate the last question asked. Thus, each objection affects the survivor's performance: She gets a momentary break from being questioned and the judge either sustains the attorney's request, allowing her to remain silent, or overrules it and requires her to respond. The judge may also intervene unsolicited.

Sources of Emotion in the Courtroom

Three-fourths of the survivors described testifying as an intensely emotional experience. At some point in their court appearances they said that they felt extreme fear, anger, embarrassment, frustration, anxiety, or unspecified pain. The most frequently reported sources of intense emotion for survivors were, in declining order, recalling the rape experience, encountering the defendant, and having the defense attorney make interaction difficult. Powerful but less often mentioned contributors were waiting, observing the emotional pain of supporters, speaking before a public audience, and feeling uninformed about the legal process.

Recalling the Rape Experience through the Act of Testifying

The emotional memory of the rape was omnipresent for a few survivors, and talking about the rape in the courtroom was not easily done, as it required remaining seated while experiencing an intense desire to cower or flee. However, the majority of survivors had gained at least some emotional distance from the physical attack by the time they testified. Nevertheless, as they gave accounts of the rape in direct-examination, many recalled beginning to feel as though it were recurring. When they described the defendant overpowering them, threatening them, and abusing them, they indicated that they actually reexperienced terror and lack of control. For example, Cindy felt sudden overwhelming terror when she tried to give a comprehensive account of her experience of the rape. As she described the defendant's threats, trying to make clear to the jury that she was not a willing participant, she suddenly recalled her fear of death.

> I described everything that happened, it was . . . it's hard, you know, especially when I got to the part where he was telling me . . . when I got to the part where I had to tell the jury that I had to give him a blow-job, you know. And I'm telling the jury, "Now remember this guy said to me that this was a test. And I'm still aware that this is a test, you know, and that I can get an A or a B or a C or I can flunk the test." . . . And I said, "if there was ever a test in my life that I ever wanted to pass, it was this one." And then, I lost it, you know. And I just completely lost it.

When this intense emotional recall occurred, survivors agreed that it was vivid and extremely frightening. Why did it happen?

Some women tried to recall aspects of the attack that they had successfully repressed so that they could give details necessary to convince a judge or jury that a rape took place, and this entailed letting down their emotional barriers. When these survivors finally did recall the attack in detail, they abruptly reconnected with their emotional experiences of it. Unlike the rape survivors who entered the courtroom with intense feelings, these women unpredictably experienced rushes of pain, anger, hatred, disgust, and fear, which were not easily ignored.

The introduction of tangible evidence of the rape was another trigger for sudden intense emotion. Stoic survivors were sometimes overcome when presented with police photographs of their bloodied and bruised bodies or with their clothes. Seeing these items provoked feelings and brought back the horror of the assault experience.

Testifying at trial, Janice had distanced herself from the experience of rape and was able to give a detailed account of the attack and the events leading up it without difficulty. Yet when the prosecutor asked her to identify photographs taken at the emergency room, she recalled the rapist's violence. She explained: "I hadn't remembered what my arms and my neck and everything looked like. [. . .] I just kind of freaked out and I started crying." Janice asked to leave the courtroom to compose herself.

I personally observed Candace suddenly break down on the witness stand as the prosecutor asked her to identify photographs of her body. She had described the rape thoroughly earlier that morning and before at the preliminary hearing, without exhibiting much emotion. The prosecutor began by showing Candace pictures of her face and head. He then worked his way down her body to demonstrate the extent of the injuries she had received from being punched repeatedly by the defendant. Her voice was steady as she talked about her blacked eye and bruised breast; however, when the prosecutor got to photographs of her knees, scraped badly from being forced into a submissive kneeling position on a rough concrete, she lost her composure. During our later interview, she said that she started crying because she wondered how she had survived such a close brush with death. Candace remembered much more from the photographs than she had allowed herself to recall while describing the rape. She remembered not just that she was attacked and how, but what it felt like to be powerless: "And I looked at them and I started crying because it was just like, how did I, how did I do it? How did I even survive, you know?"

All the survivors who reported this type of response to photographs and clothing said that they had not seen the particular materials that brought on their intense emotions before court. Natalie, who reviewed pictures of herself in the prosecutor's office the day before trial, described a similar intensity of feeling then. But she had no audience and her husband at her side. When she testified at trial, the pictures were not the main source of her discomfort.

Encountering the Defendant and Reexperiencing Dis-empowerment

Between one-third and one-half of the survivors said that they carried feelings of *great* fear of, anger at, or betrayal by the defendant well beyond the rape. Thus, many of them had intense emotional responses when they encountered him in the courtroom. For Natalie, the physical presence of the stranger who raped and beat her was a visual reminder of what he forced upon her and the serious injuries she suffered. Testifying about being raped in his presence was, for her, tantamount to reexperiencing the assault, and it was emotionally overwhelming.

> I was crying because of fear from him, seeing him again for the first time brought all those memories back, and goin' through the story with him in the room um, it just brought it all back to life again. It was so real, it was happenin' all over again. And also havin' I think, my family and my brothers listenin' to all that again and seein' them upset. But mainly it was just fear of him and, and, and just goin' through the whole thing again, and I think that's why I was cryin' so much.

Other fearful survivors did not report flashbacks, but nonetheless felt irrationally paralyzed in the defendant's presence.

Reports of anger at the defendant capture a similar intensity of feeling.[1] Anna was one of the most closeted survivors I interviewed. She was coaxed to call me by her close friend, and I was among only a handful of people with whom she had discussed the rape. Given her shyness, it is not surprising that she had ambivalent thoughts about testifying in front of people she didn't know and said that it was difficult to make herself leave the waiting area and enter the courtroom. However, fear of exposure is not what Anna recalled most vividly about the hearing for probable cause. Watching her ex-boyfriend sit there at ease was more difficult.

> The hardest part [of the court event] was just him sitting there, just staring at me like, "I'm going to walk away." [...] I'll never forget that look on his face, never. [W]hen I saw him looking at me like, with this look on his face like he was so sure nothing was going to happen, I thought pardon me but, "You son of a bitch! How dare you sit there like you have done nothing wrong!" He was sitting there like he had, I mean he leisurely walked in and had a seat and nothing was wrong.

Although it may be difficult to conceive of the survivor and defendant as engaged in an interaction when they exchange no words, the defendant's object status for the survivor is quite apparent when it gets in the way of her interactions with others. For example, Cindy found that her emotional involvement with the defendant pulled her attention toward him and away from the attorney questioning her.

> It was the first time I'd seen the guy you know, the kid who raped me [...] and I was intimidated by that. I mean he was really very arrogant and was staring at me, you know, and I stared right back. [...] So it was hard for me while I'm testifying, because I'm looking directly at this guy and locked into this mind thing, and then I have [...] the defense attorney acting like this little bulldog, you know.

Focusing on meeting the defendant's gaze, Cindy was less than attentive in formulating answers to questions. This had serious consequences for her because she was involved in cross-examination when it happened.

> So my testimony was a little weird and at one point [...] when um, the defense attorney asked me how good a look I got at the defendant I had said well, "just a glimpse really." Now *that* has come back to haunt me big time, you know, during the trial. He [the defense attorney] brought out that transcript, you know, and said you know, (she laughs), "How can you possibly know that it's him if all you got was just a glimpse?"

Problematic Interaction with the Defense Attorney

Difficult interactions with the defense attorney were the third most significant contributor to intense feelings, particularly those of frustration and anger. Most often, women were disturbed by the defense attorney's attempts to make interaction difficult for them or to cast blame on them.

Survivors reported that defense attorneys' rapid questioning, interruptions, and efforts to limit them to one-word responses undermined their ability to formulate good answers. Survivors identified some questions as illogical or illogically placed within a sequence of questions. They were concerned about their ability to provide a "right" answer and were anxious about being forced into giving an answer they would later regret. Isabel told me, "I remember sitting there being questioned by the defense [attorney, and] a little flag kept coming up that they're trying to trap me. I felt like a victim again, they're trying to trap me."[2] Survivors also believed that defense attorneys repeated some questions simply to wear them out or to confuse them, and that they focused on minute details of the assault event or assault location only to prolong the length of time they were on the stand. This angered them as it wore on them mentally and physically. A few women felt that defense attorneys asked personal questions to embarrass and anger them. They believed that these questions were unrelated to the rape, and they should not have had to answer them. Some also said that the defense attorney appeared to be emotionally invested in the interaction and seemed to enjoy making them uncomfortable. Such investment breached the decorum they expected from a legal actor, and they were not sure how to respond to it. Moreover, it left them feeling that the interrogation had no limits.

Rachel said that she was angry enough to want to slap the man defending her ex-husband—an attorney who appeared to enjoy making her uncomfortable. The defense attorney pushed Rosanne to the point that she became physically incapable of continuing to testify:

> I mean it got totally out of control, I got hysterical, I mean I was shaking so bad that I couldn't even answer him [the defense attorney] because I was so angry and I couldn't believe all this was happening and the judge finally said, "I think that's enough."

In sum, survivors were frustrated and angered by defense attorneys' manipulation of the parameters of the interaction to challenge their self-control and because the defense attorney failed to extend either respect or sympathy to them.

Additional Sources of Intense Feeling

Some survivors with little knowledge of the criminal justice system, and thus little knowledge of the norms of interaction in the courtroom, reported a generalized fear of the unknown that made them anxious. A few felt grief as they observed the pain of family members who sat listening to them speak about the details of the assaults. Gabriella started to cry during the interview when she recalled her parents listening to her testimony at the preliminary hearing.

The public audience observing the court event raised the stress level of other women who felt embarrassed to discuss the sexual activity in which they were forced to participate. Bernice and Trudy, who were both raped by strangers, were particularly disturbed by being a public spectacle.

> *Bernice:* I had no idea it would be that emotional, or that I would be that emotional, because I can talk to you about it now and be calm, but um, in the room with all those people it was scary, stressful, embarrassing, very traumatic.
>
> *Trudy:* I just kept wondering what all these people were doing here, you know, I couldn't imagine that they were all involved with the case, they were just there to watch, I was their entertainment for the day (laughs). That *bothered* me.

Finally, Rachel, who was angry enough at her ex-husband's attorney to want to slap him, explained that the stress of waiting was more emotionally taxing than answering questions. Like a few others, she reached a state of mental and emotional turmoil that caused her to become physically ill:

> I had such knots in my stomach. I mean, I was just sick over it. I actually went down to the ladies' room several times and got sick [vomited], because I was just so upset. And every time they would call break, even though I was tired, I would just dread these breaks. [On] one hand I was looking forward to them, but towards the end I was beginning to realize that these breaks were killing me. [...] I'm like waiting in this room for me to be called back into the courtroom, and that time that I'm waiting, it's like waiting for the guillotine. [...] That was the hardest part about the court.

In sum, survivors confronted feelings in the courtroom that emerged from interaction with the defense attorneys (in which they were explicitly engaged); from interactions with the defendants, their families, and the public (in which they were tacitly engaged); and from their recollections of past interaction with the defendant. Most women reported more than one source of intense emotion during their testimony and sometimes multiple causes and multiple emotions overlapped. For example, a survivor might experience fear as a result of seeing the defendant and recalling the rape. Alternatively, she might painfully view her parents' misery as they listened to her story, while she experienced anger at the defense attorney's efforts to blame her for the rape. The intense feelings brought on by testifying were in themselves problematic for the survivors because they were negative emotions and caused them physical discomfort. The feelings aroused in the courtroom interfered with their ability to concentrate on testifying and maintaining their desired demeanor, conflicting with a successful performance of the witness role.

Prosecutor Abandonment

As discussed in chapter 5, some women felt let down by prosecutors' minimal and late efforts to prepare them before court. None blamed their emotional discomfort in court on prosecutors, but some prosecutors acknowledged manipulating survivors to produce appropriate emotional displays. In particular, prosecutors contributed to rape survivors' feelings of isolation and disempowerment by reducing interaction with them during their testimony.

Brian, an Urban County prosecutor, explained that at trial he reduced his eye contact and limited the supportive facial cues he gave rape survivors in the hopes that they would feel isolated and vulnerable—in essence feel like a victim—and emote accordingly.

> In the prelim I make contact with the victim and smile and try and look reassuring or I try to give them positive feedback. In front of the jury I look away, don't make eye contact with my victim and it's partly so the jury doesn't see me doing that like I'm coaching, but also partly it's all or nothing in front of the jury, and I want the victim to feel isolated and get her emotions, to feel most vulnerable and portray that to a jury, if possible.

Incentives to Control Emotional Expression

When they were intent on formulating answers to questions, women perceived and experienced intense emotions as a general threat to their ability to testify. Unpredictable physical responses that accompanied feelings intruded on their efforts to give the accounts they desired the court to hear. Nausea, as described above by Rachel, inhibited concentration. Unbidden, breath-stealing sobs or tears, running down their faces, smearing their makeup, and dripping onto their clothes, broke their lines of thought. Tears and involuntary gestures also impeded survivors' efforts to exert control over the questioning behavior of defense attorneys. These expressions "given off" let the defense attorney know that his or her line of action was having an emotional impact.

Some survivors also believed that revealing their recalled terror of the assault, their discomfort with the defense attorney's questions, and particularly their fear of the defendant was to lose control to him again, even as they sought to assert themselves and use the legal system against him. Jennifer explained the importance of stifling the tears that invaded her testimony as follows:

> I started crying. [...] I hated it. [...] And at that point everything came back. [...] I wasn't going to give him the satisfaction. [...] 'Cause I cried through the entire night, when I was in the truck with him. And that was the first time I'd ever done something like that. First time I'd actually had a break that *deep* in my control. And I wasn't gonna let *him* do that to me again.

Most survivors were aware that standards of appearance included emotional expression as well as dress and many made an effort to keep their emotional displays in the courtroom within socially approved limits. Typically, survivors believed the courtroom called for a neutral and polite demeanor, which reflected both their respect for the authority of the court and a commitment to the search for truth in the facts presented to the court. Some felt obliged to provide information in a calm, businesslike way, because any display of their felt anger or other intense feelings might appear impolite or even irrational. For example, Gabriella indicated that she "knew" she could not openly display how the defense attorney made her feel:

> But [the defense attorney] was an asshole. I mean, I wanted to kill him. I was so angry with him.... [Gabriella goes on about being cross-examined.] I just wanted to say, "Fuck you, you fucking asshole!" But, I knew that I couldn't say that in court.

Similarly, noted above, Anna described *thinking about* swearing at the defendant, her ex-boyfriend, rather than doing so audibly.

As discussed in previous chapters, survivors and prosecutors were aware of and responsive to stereotypes that women make up allegations of rape to get revenge and are not "really" injured by forced sexual contact. Thus, women were also motivated to avoid appearing angry, deceptive, or hard (that is, unmoved and inexpressive) and living up to the image of a false rape victim. In court, they believed it was socially desirable to appear damaged by rape: visibly afraid, embarrassed, and subject to emotional breakdown. In this regard, several survivors mentioned the televised and tearful testimony of Patricia Bowman, who was involved in the prosecution of William Kennedy Smith in Florida in 1991.

Strategies for Managing Emotions

Limiting Conditions of Discomfort

Many survivors made efforts to limit conditions that would initiate or intensify their anger, embarrassment, fear, and so forth, whether or not the emotions were desirable from the standpoint of feeling rules. Most of the women who made this effort directed their energy at avoiding interaction with the people who would make them the most uncomfortable. As discussed in chapter 5, some women asked would-be supporters who might add to their unease not to come to court. Megan, Theresa, and Joanna, all of whom felt very anxious and embarrassed about testifying before a public audience, asked the prosecuting attorney if the court could be closed or the audience limited. Prosecutors told Megan and Theresa it was not standard legal practice and could not be done. Joanna was successful in this effort, however, because the prosecuting attorney believed she legitimately feared retaliation from potential audience members and argued her concern to the judge.

Women for whom the defendant's presence posed an emotion-management problem described two ways of avoiding interaction with him: putting him out of sight and putting him out of mind. The tactic most used was to avoid looking in the defendant's direction. They averted their eyes except when it was absolutely necessary to look at him, as when making an in-court identification. Theresa took advantage of the position of the judge's bench relative to the witness stand.

> *Theresa:* The judge's name [plate] was set in such a way that I couldn't even see him, which was great, so I couldn't even see the defendant.
> *Amanda:* Except when you had to identify him?
> *Theresa:* Right.
> *Amanda:* Or did you identify him without seeing him?
> *Theresa:* No. I leaned forward, saw him and identified him and then sat back so the name was blocking my view of him, so I didn't have to keep seeing him.

However, the small size and layout of the courtrooms in which preliminary hearings were commonly held made this physical avoidance strategy untenable for many. At the preliminary hearing, Julianne testified six feet in front of the boyfriend who raped her and she had to walk right by him to take the witness stand. His gaze was not something she could easily avoid.

Putting the defendant out of mind, and thus figuratively out of sight, is harder than simply averting your eyes, but it is not limited by the physical environment of the courtroom. Isabel did this successfully. She dismissed the defendant from her scope of concern and, thus, also the emotions associated with him, and enabled herself to focus her attention on the people who would be making a decision: the judge and jury.

> I don't believe I ever even acknowledged him as being a person in that courtroom, my state of mind was he wasn't worth it, it was the other people in that room I had to convince because he already knew the truth and he wasn't worth it.

Survivors also avoided eye contact with spectators in the courtroom who aroused feelings of fear—usually the defendant's supporters and family. Some women, like Sandra, feared the judgment of the jury and avoided their gaze as well. She recalled, "I was scared to look at the jury. I was wondering what they were thinking of me, do they believe me? ... I tried not to look at the jury because I was afraid of them." Even Natalie, who tried to follow the prosecutor's instructions to direct her answers to the jury, ignored them when the content of her testimony required her to minimize strong feelings of embarrassment:

> I was embarrassed with some of the things that I did have to say about um, you know, the oral sex, and ... and the things that he had told me. For those parts, I would just ... I would close my eyes and I would just say it. I couldn't look at the jurors when I was sayin' those things, um, the very personal things. I, I'd just either look down or, or close my eyes and, and got through it. And then when I was finished I would be able to look at them again.

Three survivors tried to avoid eye contact with the defense attorney who aroused their anger. It is possible that others did this as well. However, it would not be surprising if this action is infrequently done, because it goes against the social convention that two people in conversation maintain eye contact. In addition, defense attorneys may challenge those who try, because it is harder for them to manipulate a witness who refuses to look at them. I observed a defense attorney who challenged a survivor in her late teens who deliberately avoided his gaze during the preliminary hearing. With the prosecutor's consent, she had turned her chair and focused her direct-examination testimony on a victim-witness advocate seated to her side. She did not move when the defense attorney stood up to begin cross-examination. His first statement to her made an issue of her potential lack of eye contact with him:

> I am B—— M——, I want to make some comments. You don't have to look at me, but it might be easier. I want to point out for the record that *the witness* is not looking at me. Try to remember please not to guess....

Despite this effort to intimidate her, the young woman maintained her posture and a very controlled, neutral demeanor.

Many survivors experienced embarrassment and found it difficult to put forward a timely answer when a defense attorney initiated a topic that they believed to be illegitimate. Their embarrassment was heightened if they believed that the attorney was trying to place blame for the assault on them. Survivors also felt anger or frustration developing as a result of defense attorneys repeating the same questions or excessively questioning them about minor details. To counteract these negative feelings, some women disengaged from developing a conversation with the defense attorney and focused on answering individual questions. Survivors who used this technique interpreted and answered each question without thinking about the broader meaningful context within which it was asked—how the sequence of questions fit together. In short, they ignored the argument being built by the defense attorney.

Dealing with individual questions broke the cross-examination into a series of discrete tasks and undermined their emotional investment in the subject matter of the questions. Through this strategy, they also protected themselves from becoming confused or pulled into a trap.

Maintaining Control over Emotions and the Physical Manifestations of Feeling

When some survivors felt the intensity of their feelings was growing, they focused on maintaining a calm outward appearance, hoping that it would help them maintain an even temper. By representing themselves in a way that was consistent with ideal notions of witnesses, women tried to alter *what* they were feeling.[3] For example, Anna swallowed her profanity and gritted her teeth in an attempt to turn her anger into something else.

In some cases, survivors' efforts worked and the intensity of their unwanted feelings did not increase. However, many eventually fought an intense urge to yell, cry, vomit, or shake—physical manifestations of their intense emotions. When this happened, they described shifting to surface acting or simply maintaining their demeanor—that is, concentrating on holding or "keeping" their presentation of self intact until they were out of range of the defendant, the judge, and the jury. Once their responsibilities as witnesses were over, they allowed themselves to relax their self-control and vent. Women described explosively releasing their emotion (such as "bursting" into tears, "losing it," or "breaking down"), implying a complete loss of control and an inability to carry on any other activity.

Joanna, quoted at the opening of this chapter, provides a good example of someone who held emotions at bay until the circumstances changed. Toward the end of a strenuous cross-examination she was angry, frustrated, and nauseated with emotional discomfort. However, she fought back tears (which would make her true feelings apparent) to deny the defendant continued power over her. Joanna finally allowed her self-control to dissolve when the defendant and his attorney left the courtroom: "I lost it."

Natalie held herself together while painfully recounting the rape in her direct trial testimony, but broke down when she left the courtroom during a break in the proceedings: "I cried, and cried, and cried." She handled her feelings almost identically during the prior grand jury hearing, suppressing her expression of them until her testimony concluded:

> I told them [the jurors] everything, um, but I didn't cry. You know, I was you know, I wanted to get through this. I mean tears were just comin' down my eyes but ... but I was strong, I didn't cry. [...] [After] I had answered all of their questions [...] And as soon as I walked out that door, I just started burstin' out cryin'.

Natalie's distinction between tearing up and crying is noteworthy. She identified the difference between emotion that was under and out of her self-control. The former did not obstruct her ability to testify; the latter, which involved lack of breath and vocalization, would have made answering questions difficult if not impossible. Several other survivors made similar distinctions between tears and audible crying.

Despite survivors' talk about needing to meet cultural expectations that victims are distraught, there was little indication that they cultivated such displays once testimony was under way. Most were more concerned about the difficulties of recovering from a complete loss of composure associated with their feelings of pain, anger, and fear. However, two women recalled consciously making their feelings available to the court audience to enhance their credibility.

Donna went to trial twice. The first trial ended in a hung jury. During that trial, she maintained full control over her emotions and testified in a calm, almost stoic manner. After her assailant was released, Donna became concerned that her stoicism during her testimony in the first trial was not believable in the eyes of the jury. She concluded that her fear of the defendant and the pain of the rape needed to be visible if the case went to trial again. Thus, Donna decided that she would "have to lose it" when testifying again. As discussed in the previous chapter, before going to court, she prepared herself psychologically to allow her emotions free rein. As she describes in the quotation that opens this chapter, her testimony in the second trial was very tearful.

When Jennifer testified at trial, she recalled that on one occasion she deliberately tried to perform her fear of the defendant for the jury. She differentiated between the part of her emotional display that was responsive to the defendant—the "honest part"—and the part that was a conscious extension:

Jennifer: I had dressed real prim and proper again as they would put it, and I just [tried] not to look at anyone. I didn't want to look at Mr. T. [the defendant]. [...] Just basically [I was] trying to radiate the personality that "you can believe me." I wasn't aware of how I was doing it, I [thought] if I continue telling the truth they'll believe me.

Amanda: Why did you not want to look at him?

Jennifer: Because at that point I was feeling a slip on my control of my emotions, and I also felt that if I didn't look at him, that was also conveying that I can't stand to look at this guy 'cause of what he did to me. So there was [the] honest part of it 'cause I didn't want to look at him, and also the conscious decision that if I could convey that by not looking at him that'll help the case.

Other survivors' concerns about having an appropriate demeanor led them to monitor jurors' and judges' responses to their open expression of feelings of fear and embarrassment, although not in an effort to cultivate emotional displays. When they received a positive response to their tears, several said that they felt believed. Although none of the survivors who evaluated the judge's or jurors' reactions described purposefully trying to extend episodes of crying, receiving positive responses seems to have dissuaded them from further suppressing their tears.

Some survivors nurtured their anger to help displace feelings of fear, anxiety, and embarrassment and concentrate on the business of the court. However, intentionally harboring anger did not necessarily mean expressing it openly to conflict with cultural ideals of credible victims and witnesses.

Arlene described how she let herself experience rage to suppress anxiety about testifying and how, through doing this, she created an emotional space in which *she* had control.

I had a good idea of how to create a kind of space for myself. Not only by what I did, but how [I felt]. I was very nervous and um, found what it was to like [to] let my rage take over. I wasn't like enraged at all, on the stand, I was very clear.

> A couple of times I got angry, but um, I was able to stay very focused on why I was there and very clear about what I was doing and not let my feelings get in the way.

Note that Arlene distinguishes between feeling rage in a controlled way and displaying it to the court—that is, being "enraged." Those who chose to embrace their anger or to let themselves become angry were shielded from defense efforts to arouse other types of emotion in them and to break their self-control.

In one of the opening quotations, Lauren described how "getting mad" allowed her to achieve an intense but controlled emotional position, after repeatedly breaking down in tears. Achieving control in the face of her fear was an exhilarating transformation with ongoing consequences.

> I saw that he was cowering, trying to hide, and then I finished up and I walked out of the courtroom and I was jumping up and down and screaming. It was just, "Yeah!" outside. And my family came out, and everybody said how well I did, and everybody was crying 'cause I'd made it. And then [the other survivor/witness] though was like, "Oh my God, is it good or bad?" I told her, "It was like going to Disneyworld ten times over to feel everything like that. It's the best thing I've ever had in my life, I think, at the end."

Lauren's description highlights the fact that, for some survivors, testifying is part of the healing process, in spite of its draining properties. In facing her attacker in the courtroom, Lauren was able to hold him up against the terrifying image she recalled and reject it. Cowering and trying to hide from her, he was not behaving like a rapist and was not worthy of her fear and tears. This gave her the upper hand in their tacit interaction and led her to dispense with feelings associated with being dominated by him. Had Lauren not taken the stand, it would have been a very long time before she felt like "going to Disneyworld ten times over."

Several other survivors discussed their need to confront the defendant. Angry and unable to retaliate physically for the harm he caused, testifying and visually imposing themselves on him had to suffice. For these women, testifying was a necessary hardship on the road to mental health. For them, the potential costs of experiencing their anger were far outweighed by the personal satisfaction of doing so.

Interpersonal Emotion Management

Several survivors who had supporters in the courtroom engaged in interactions with them to avoid negative emotions or to bring them under control. These family members and friends formed a team invested in maintaining the survivor's presentation of self in her ongoing interaction with the prosecutor and defense attorney. Interactions between women and their teammates did not appear to be noticed by others present in the courtroom, because they were completely nonverbal.

During direct examination, and specifically while giving their descriptions of the assault, initiating eye contact with supporters helped survivors ward off embarrassment, associated with testifying publicly about details of the assault, and fear, associated with relating their rape experience and seeing the defendant. During cross-examination, nonverbal interaction with supporters provided an opportunity for women momentarily to disengage from their troubling interaction with the defense attorney, which had aroused frustration and anger.

Sandra's courtroom team, her sister and two friends, who were rape crisis counselors, were more expressive than most. When the badgering of the defense attorney made Sandra feel that her loss of composure was imminent, she turned her eyes to them. Her sister demonstrated her encouragement with a hand signal as well as through eye contact.

> [During cross-examination] I was looking at [the defense attorney]. I kept eye contact with [the defense attorney], and when I started to get a little upset, I would look at [my sister], and [my sister] would like do this (Sandra makes a fist with one hand over her stomach area). You know, like "Right on Sandra!" and stuff like that.

This helped Sandra regain her focus; suppress her frustration with the interaction, her fear of the jury, and her anger at the attorney; and proceed with her testifying task. When Sandra was finally unable to suppress these emotions and lost her composure, she again looked to her supporters to regain control.

> And so when I started crying, I looked up at [my sister]. And then [the friends] were there [sitting near her], and they were going, you know, doing the breathing thing. (Sandra shows me: breathing slowly and deeply in an exaggerated manner.) And they're doing that, so I started to do that.

By following the nonverbal cues that her supporters gave, Sandra was able to regain physical control, modulate her emotional expression, and resume answering questions.

As these examples show, many survivors were overcome by undesired emotions despite their best efforts to shape what they were feeling and suppress the intensity of their feelings. For the reasons described above, they attempted to recover themselves as quickly as possible when this happened. They looked to their supporters and asked the court for tissues, water, or a break from questioning. Prosecutors and judges met women's requests, and occasionally judges offered them access to a back room where they might retreat for a few minutes. During these short breaks from the courtroom situation, they were able to gather themselves to resume testimony.

Survivors generally perceived the behavior of legal personnel to be displays of kindness in the face of their obvious discomfort.[4] However, closely examining two cases demonstrates that rape survivors' emotion management is essential to the smooth functioning of the court.

Neither Julianne or Janice was able to pull herself together after breaking down in tears and each continued to cry convulsively. Eventually, the judge overseeing Julianne's case and the attorney prosecuting Janice's attacker directed these two women to overcome their tears—to exert control over their emotions. This direct intervention was not typical of the experiences of survivors in this study. However, this intervention is worth examining closely because it sheds light on the instrumental quality of prosecutors' and judges' less-intrusive actions.

When Julianne entered the courtroom for the preliminary hearing, she faced her boyfriend for the first time since he had raped her. She was emotionally overwhelmed with feelings of betrayal, and she found that it was very difficult to respond to even basic questions. Despite her best efforts to suppress her tears, Julianne was unable to complete the direct examination without sobbing uncontrollably. The judge eventually stopped the proceedings, handed her a box of tissues, and spoke directly to her. He redefined the court's activity as a rational encounter, albeit a painful one, and focused on Julianne's obligation to answer questions while also offering words of encouragement:

Um, the judge first time stopped ... stopped and he says, "Do you need some time?" And the judge handed me a box of Kleenex, and he said, "Julianne, I wanna tell you something: I know this sounds easier said than done, but I want you to think of this as a business." And he said, "I want you to think of it as once you get the answers out, ... it's gonna be over. I know," he goes, "I can tell you have that inner strength, and right now, I want you to find that inner strength within yourself and I want you to pull it out of yourself, and rely on it." He goes, "and we're gonna get through this." He goes, "We're gonna make it as easy on you as possible, I know it hurts, but you're gonna be okay." And I thought, okay, then I'm gonna be fine, and um, so they went on.

Julianne responded to the judge's verbal instructions. She accepted the rational, business definition of the situation that he supplied as well as the calm demeanor that it implied, and she was able to pull herself together and continue.

Janice began to cry during the direct-examination sequence of the trial, when she was asked to identify pictures of herself taken by the police. She continued to cry through her testimony after being given a box of tissues and taking several minutes away from the courtroom. When the court recessed for lunch, Janice recalled that the prosecutor asked her to stay in the courtroom and then directed her to bring herself under control:

[She said] that I would be questioned by his [the defense] attorney and it could take however long. She did say a couple of times that, "you have got to get a hold of yourself." [. . .] I said, "Okay."

Janice got the prosecutor's message—control your emotions before you enter cross-examination and deal with the defense attorney—and complied with her directive.

If judges and prosecutors only responded to survivors' tears out of kindness and sympathy, we would not expect the specific directions Julianne and Janice received. I contend that judges and prosecutors are regular, but unacknowledged, participants in survivors' efforts to protect their courtroom performances. Their offers of tissues, water, and breaks that are experienced as acts of kindness by survivors are, in fact, instrumental efforts to preserve the flow of the legal process and the prosecution's case. Their offers of assistance assert their own understanding of what is and should be going on emotionally in the courtroom context.

Judges need to know that witnesses are in control of their faculties in order to believe that the mission of the court is being met. Prosecutors must believe that survivors can understand what is asked and have the capacity to respond. Despite their interest in tearful victim-like performances, prosecutors must have confidence that their key witness can, when appropriate, support the case. This becomes questionable when a woman is in tears and breathing irregularly. Judges further need to avoid lengthy delays that will prolong legal proceedings in backlogged court facilities. Thus, judges and prosecutors both monitor survivors' emotional displays and facilitate recovery from breakdowns that threaten the continuation of interaction. Most of the time, the survivor's own focus on maintaining her self-presentation meets the needs of prosecutors and judges. When intense feelings lead to losses of control, small acts of assistance follow. I suggest that when a survivor is unable to achieve control, prosecutors and judges will do more, as with Julianne and Janice.

Conclusions and Questions for Further Consideration

Ample evidence from this and other studies suggests that emotions are central to rape survivors' experiences in courtrooms, and testifying makes many women feel uncomfortable. However, this study also shows that rape survivors' efforts to control their emotions are an integral part of their court performances. Prosecutors depend on rape survivors' willingness and ability to manage their emotions to support the case they construct against the defendant.

The sources of rape survivors' discomfort in the courtroom found in this study are consistent with, but more extensive than, those documented in previous studies.[5] More important, however, these findings show that survivors respond in reflexive and unreflexive ways[6] (1) to mitigate threats to their selves,[7] (2) to protect their position in interaction and, thus, their ability to perform their role,[8] and (3) to enhance the credibility of the content of their testimony in keeping with feeling and display rules they recognize.[9] The findings underscore the need to rethink victimization.[10]

Rape survivors do not have one essential emotional experience in the courtroom. Differences among them and among case specifics shape the intensity of emotions that they experience as well as their management efforts. If a survivor has emotional difficulty during direct examination because she recalls the assault, and later the defense attorney focuses on her identification of the defendant, cross-examination may actually be emotionally less taxing than direct examination. A survivor who has little difficulty describing the assault during direct examination, however, may run up against a defense attorney who makes it difficult for her to answer questions and fulfill her witness role. She then may expend a great deal more energy managing her feelings and maintaining her self presentation during cross-examination.

This examination of rape survivors' accounts of their emotions and their management efforts reveals how unspoken aspects of interaction affect legal order. It demonstrates that the interactions between witnesses and the attorneys who question them are shaped by other courtroom participants.[11] In addition, these findings suggest that court performances are shaped by pre-court activity and that cross-examination may be shaped by direct examination. This research demonstrates that emotions are resources for prosecutors, defense attorneys, and witnesses and, as such, are a fundamental feature of courtrooms.

This study offers no clear evidence that rape survivors' emotion management influenced whether judges held defendants over for trial or whether juries convicted. Certainly, Donna's efforts to let the jury see her fall apart were an unsuccessful attempt to validate her claim on the role of victim: The defendant was found not guilty. On the other hand, these interviews do provide evidence that survivors' management efforts helped *them* complete the task of testifying successfully. For example, Rachel's suppression of her emotions to remain focused was critical to her successful negotiation of hours of cross-examination during the preliminary hearing. Without her fortitude and ability to provide answers to all the questions that were asked about her prior sexual relationship with her ex-husband, it is doubtful that he would have been bound over for trial. When survivors felt that they had protected themselves from the defendant, conquered their fear, or successfully stood up to the defense attorney's efforts to undermine them, their confidence increased. This confidence made future court events less intimidating and, presumably, helped the women who still faced trials remain committed to seeing the criminal justice process through to completion.

Despite the benefits of emotion management for rape survivors, their efforts to suppress or evoke particular emotions can have a negative side. To the extent that they create a public impression of the rape survivor that is different from the image the prosecutor is attempting to build for a jury, they can create confusion.

Problems of testifying are not just emotional. Defense attorneys' efforts to make answering difficult and to blame women for the defendant's behavior have the potential to undermine her ability to answer questions in a way that conveys truth. So, it makes sense to ask several questions:

- How do rape survivors verbally respond to defense attorneys' behaviors that evoke feelings of anger, frustration, and embarrassment?
- What are the specific problems of testifying that require action?
- What are the variety of solutions that rape survivors use to resolve them?
- How do rape survivors' responses to problems articulate with prosecutors' goals?

These are the concern of chapter 7.

"I'm Only Gonna Tell You Once": Rape Survivors' Interaction and Information Management in Court

When I asked about any troubles they had with testifying, many women said cross-examination was most difficult, because defense attorneys asked them blaming questions then challenged their ability to construct adequate answers. These survivors creatively responded to such abuse.

At trial, Jennifer requested that the defense attorney restate questions, slowing his rapid delivery and giving her more time to think through her answers.

> I knew the answers that I had already given [in direct examination], and I was real careful [to say], "well I don't know," or I asked them to repeat questions. I felt a little more in control of the situation than I did with the preliminaries.

At trial, Sandra paused after the defense attorney asked questions and made room for the prosecutor to insert himself into the cross-examination interaction.

> I never answered because I knew he [the DA] was going to object. I always was just like waiting [sitting still with hands in her lap and looking at me]. I always knew that he [the DA] was going to object. Um, I started to be able to tell what would be objected to and what wouldn't. I'd always look at [the DA] and see. I'd always wait, I started to learn how to wait.

And Megan, who felt the defense attorney was actively impeding her ability to answer questions during the preliminary hearing, challenged his right to do so by halting interaction.

> He [the defense attorney] would ask leading questions and compound questions and she [the prosecutor] would object. He would ask questions in a way where if you answered "yes" you mean "yes to the last questions and no to the four before it." He asked me like three questions in a row, and I finally just said, "Well, what question do you want me to answer?" And everyone in the courtroom just went quiet, and you could hear the court reporter kind of like (Megan made a snickering sound).

Rape Survivors' Interaction Management in Court

Smooth vs. Troubled Interactions

To maintain the flow of interaction and meet the requirements of being a "good" witness, a rape survivor must provide a response for every question asked in direct and cross-examinations. To conform to cultural expectations of credibility, she must also appear to provide her answers without difficulty and avoid extended periods of silence.[1]

Typically, direct examination is untroubled for survivors, because prosecutors support their efforts to provide answers and to convey their perspectives. The open-ended questions they usually ask allow the women to describe the rape as they recall it: in the order and in the degree of detail they choose and at their tempo. Arlene explained: "I was pretty much able to just answer the questions in a way that she didn't have to like lead me through it, and I was able to give them a narrative." Natalie gave her entire direct testimony at her own pace.

> I got on the stand and um, [the prosecutor] just started me out on, you know, where I lived, and my occupation, and if I was married, and how many kids I had, and then just basically asked me if I could say what happened on the mornin' of [date]. And I just took it from there, and I went through the entire day [of the rape]. I kept on talkin' and talkin', and I would say after the hospital we went to the police station, and [the prosecutor] just let me go.

When the prosecuting attorney follows a survivor's lead, she has a ready answer for each question asked. Enabled to tell her story, she can focus on conveying information and, if necessary, channel her energy to deal with the emotional impact of what she is discussing. When survivors feel successful in performing their witness role in direct examination, they gain confidence.

Cross-examination can also be an untroubled interaction when the defense attorney does not undermine the survivor's ability to provide answers or attempt to provoke emotions that impede her concentration. In six preliminary hearings and two trials (22 percent of court events), survivors reported that their cross-examination interactions with defense attorneys were smooth. As Trudy's recollections illustrate, the defense issue central to almost all of these cases was the survivor's identification of the stranger assailant.

> *Amanda:* Tell me about being cross-examined, how did that work for you?
> *Trudy:* Oh, I forgot that, sorry. (She laughs.) It really wasn't much of a cross-examination. He [the defense attorney] asked me a question about the fact that I had said he had freckles and did I see [...] that he didn't really have freckles. And I said, "well, it was a bad complexion, and I was confused about that, I could remember spots on his face." And, that was about it really. He didn't ask much.

In contrast, many defense attorneys do work to undermine survivors' ability to answer questions and to fulfill their role. The remaining 78 percent of the women in this study experienced troubled interaction during cross-examination sequences.[2] Defense attorneys made it difficult for them to convey their perspectives by asking questions quickly, by interrupting them, and by limiting their reply options to yes and no. Defense attorneys also asked illogical questions, presented questions in an illogical order, and focused on minute details of the rape or the environment in which it took place for periods of time that seemed excessive to survivors. A few women believed that defense attorneys asked them personal questions unrelated to the assault and prohibited by law, which they should not have had to answer.

Prosecutors had prepared some survivors by telling them that cross-examination might be "difficult," but informed few of the specific nature of the problems they might face. Thus, most survivors entered court anticipating that defense attorneys would ask them personal questions but not challenge their ability to answer. Mostly, through trial and error, they developed ways to assert themselves.

Strategies for Negotiating Troubled Interaction

Survivors used three strategies to negotiate occasions when defense attorneys' questioning became problematic. First, unable to answer the way they would prefer, they adjusted how they approached the answering task to accommodate the defense attorney's disruptive behavior. This involved exerting self-control to fit answers into the minimal space that the defense attorney left for them. Second, without naming the problem or disrupting the flow of interaction, survivors tried to force the defense attorney to alter his or her questioning strategy. Third, survivors drew interaction to a halt and called attention to the fact that the defense attorney was making answering difficult.

Exerting Self-Control to Manage Problems

When they did not feel their testimony was seriously threatened, survivors tended to accommodate defense attorneys' troubling questioning by exercising greater self-control. They used two opposite techniques of analysis and disengagement. Some switched between them as the content of topics changed or as they felt more or less tired or susceptible to confusion; others adopted only one technique.

When questions were repetitive, confusing, or brought on strong emotional responses, some survivors focused on discovering the meaningful connections between them. Uncovering the defense attorney's logic helped them to anticipate probable next questions and begin to formulate answers before they were asked. Survivors described this activity as "out-thinking," "out-smarting," and "figuring out" what the defense attorney was up to.

One particularly thorough description of why analyzing the defense attorney's questioning is useful came from Rachel. Because the defendant was her ex-husband, with whom she had had a prior sexual relationship, she was not legally protected from questions about her past sexual history. At the preliminary hearing, the defense attorney asked her to answer a particularly wide range of uncomfortable questions.

> Um, I remember feeling embarrassed, I remember feeling angry, and scared, um, and I remember thinking why is he asking me this? I mean, he asked me about past work experiences, you know, things I didn't even feel were . . . was relevant! You know, I remember thinking well, why? (Rachel sighs.) You know, where is he going with his questioning? I tried to out think him. [. . .] If I knew where he was going with his questioning, then I could pretty much answer the questions ahead of time. And you know, in my head, I'd pretty much know what I was gonna say and have it all worded out. And um, and he did a couple times try to switch his line of questioning on me very abruptly and try to throw me off. And it does for a few seconds, it throws you off. So I tried to out think where he's going with *this* line of questioning. Whether it's gonna be something I'll feel comfortable with, I guess that's it. Whether it was going to be something to feel comfortable with or whether it's gonna be something where I'll have to grin and bear it.

By anticipating questions ahead of time, Rachel was able to prepare carefully worded answers that she might otherwise not have had time to develop. In addition, by thinking ahead to topics that might make her uncomfortable, she defused the defense attorney's ability to evoke emotional responses that would distract her and make it difficult to produce an answer.

Logical analysis requires that a witness be able to juggle the actual question-answer interaction in which she is engaged with an imagined interaction in her head. Thus, when a witness does not have the mental discipline to engage in these two activities at once, this is not a useful strategy. Logical analysis requires the witness to focus completely on the interaction between herself and the defense attorney and tune out the other aspects of the courtroom. When rape survivors are attentive to supporters or the defendant, focusing only on the defense attorney may be difficult.

Survivors who analyzed questions assumed that or acted "as if" courtroom interaction shared a regular feature of conversation: topics of conversation are followed through to conclusions. When the defense attorney shifted lines of questioning quickly, analysis ceased to be a productive strategy. Sometimes, women did not immediately realize this, and their coping strategy threatened to contribute to their interaction problems.

Survivors used a nearly opposite technique to deal with excessive questions about details or repetition of questions that aroused anxiety, narrowing their focus to consider individual questions separately. They focused on interpreting and answering each question without thinking about the broader meaningful context within which it was asked, the argument being built by the defense attorney, or the questions that preceded it and would follow it. Through this strategy, women felt they protected themselves from becoming confused or pulled into a trap.

Attending to individual questions may become an important strategy as rape survivors become physically and emotionally worn down. Rachel, who spent the bulk of a day on the witness stand trying to "out-think" the defense attorney, explained how she focused mainly on producing complete and precise answers as she concluded her testimony.

> I was thinking ... kept thinking about OK, um, get this over with. Um, try to be as honest and complete about your answers, think about it. Even when I was starting to get really tired, I just kept ... kept thinking OK, don't just blurt. Because that was ... I was just getting to the point of just say anything. And it ... this will make you or break you. Don't just blurt anything out, think about the question, I know you're tired, it's almost over.

While focusing on individual questions may not appear to be an active negotiation of interaction, the self-control exerted to carry out this strategy should not be underestimated. It takes a concerted effort not to attend to the context of questions, because doing so is so central to making sense of utterances in regular social interaction. Furthermore, rape survivors are invested in the way they are represented to friends, family members, jurors, and judges, who sit and listen in the courtroom. Not addressing the overarching picture painted by a defense attorney means letting it stand unaltered before them.

Survivors who exert self-control facilitate interaction and do not draw attention to themselves, contributing to a positive assessment of their ability and willingness to answer questions. Thus, as courtroom strategies, analysis and disengagement are well-suited to accomplishing a credible performance. On the other hand, as invisible efforts to gain control, they do not convey to the prosecutor or judge the difficulty the rape survivor has testifying. If these two parties who have a right to step in to alter the defense attorney's questioning behavior remain unaware of problems, they will not do so. Furthermore, while survivors' exertion of self-control may force defense attorneys to work harder to discredit them, neither strategy alters the attorney's structural control over the tempo of the interaction and topics of conversation. Thus, a rape survivor's experience of competence may quickly pass.

Attempting to Alter the Defense Attorney's Questioning Behavior without Naming the Problem

Some survivors sought to alter the balance of control in the question-answer interaction, without openly challenging the defense attorney's authority as a questioner. They usually turned to this approach when their efforts at self-control ceased to make a difference in their ability to answer questions and they continued to feel manipulated.

After finding logic in the questions asked by the defense attorney, some survivors recalled resisting the repetition of the same questions and lines of questioning that made them uncomfortable. They consciously paused before answering or they asked the defense attorney to rephrase or repeat questions just asked. These acts slowed the tempo of questioning that had been established by the defense attorney, and thus, gave the survivor more time to formulate an answer or prepare herself for a topic she knew would be uncomfortable. Additionally, rephrased questions sometimes came in forms that were more easily answered. Recognizing that they had actually had an effect on the defense attorney gave women feelings of satisfaction and renewed their confidence that they could perform their witness role successfully.

Sandra endured a lengthy and difficult cross-examination at trial from a defense attorney who sought to show that she had consented to intercourse with the defendant. He needled her, focused on minute details of the assault, and rapidly repeated questions. Cumulatively, his questioning made her feel as though he was trying to break her psychologically. Through the majority of the cross-examination, Sandra approached answering from the standpoint of analyzing his line of action and exerting control over herself. However, late in the afternoon when his demeanor revealed his lack of full control over her, Sandra began to actively resist him.

> *Sandra:* I think I was smarter than him. He couldn't get me. He couldn't get me in ... in ... catch me in a lie or anything. He could never do it. I always knew that. Toward the end of the day, he was very frustrated. He began to raise his voice, and that's when I started to gain some power. I started to watch him and realize where he was going, and what he was doing, and I started to get something inside me, going, "I'm better than him and he's not going to break me." [...] "I'm smarter than you, and you're not going to get me." He raised his voice, and he started to get angry, and he could not get me to say what he wanted. I could tell he was trying to trick me, like a lot of questions were trick questions. I started to slow down my answers. I started to take a little more time.
>
> *Amanda:* Consciously?
>
> *Sandra:* Yeah. Or, I was always like, "Could you repeat that?" Or, "I don't understand that question." I was really pissing him off.

Taking some control of the pace of the interaction gave Sandra more confidence. Her actions also turned the tables on the defense attorney, apparently making him uncomfortable and less able to challenge her. She noted, "I was doing it on purpose. I think I was really trying to aggravate him. And ... and it worked."

Jennifer regularly asked the defense attorney to repeat questions during her third court appearance—a trial—to ensure her ability to maintain consistency with answers she had given previously. She verified that she had heard clearly and understood exactly what was being asked, and also gained time to phrase her answers carefully.

> I knew the answers that I had already given, and I was real careful as to [saying], "well I don't know," or I asked them to repeat questions, I felt a little more in control of the situation than I did with the preliminaries. [...] I didn't

clearly hear everything they said, and I wanted to make sure I understood *every* question before I answered . . .

Jennifer's previous two courtroom appearances made her feel able to place reciprocal demands on the questioner. Likewise, familiar with the disruptive questioning strategies used by this particular defense attorney, she felt less personally attacked than Sandra. On the other hand, Jennifer was not emotionally disengaged from the proceedings and admitted that, at least once, she demanded that the attorney repeat his question when she did not really need him to do so.

> I did it once to his [the defendant's] attorney [when] he kept repeating questions to me. I heard him, but he wasn't real loud, so I was going to make him repeat himself once. So I got . . . my own satisfaction out of it at the same time.

Only Arlene *began* the cross-examination sequence of the preliminary hearing with the intent to assert control of the pace of the interaction. Her prior testifying experience in two civil proceedings and active involvement with the progress of the rape case best explains her great self-confidence going into court. Other women with more fears and less knowledge of their cases and the legal process simply could not envision claiming a right to control cross-examination.

Attuned to the role the prosecuting attorney could play in the dynamic between themselves and the defense attorney, survivors reported making room for or engaging him or her in the cross-examination. Looking for a legitimate way to avoid answering disturbing questions, some women delayed their answers to allow the prosecutor time to formulate an objection. Recall Sandra's earlier description of how she learned to anticipate the prosecutor's objections and to wait for them. Rachel and Arlene established eye contact with prosecutors to provoke their intervention in the cross-examination. Arlene explained,

> What she [the prosecutor] told me [before court] was if they ask you anything that you really don't want to answer, just look at me, and . . . if I can, [. . .] I'll do something about it. [. . .] I did it once, and she [the prosecutor] objected. It was about the panties, "were you wearing any?" Um, and I . . . I in fact refused to answer that [and waited], you know, I mean, that's absolutely not right. And she objected and the judge upheld that.

Janice felt so unprepared and uncomfortable negotiating the cross-examination sequence of the preliminary exam after just meeting the prosecutor that she fully engaged her in it. Before she answered each question put to her by the defense attorney, Janice turned to the prosecutor and waited for an "okay" signal. Janice turned what is normally a two-way exchange into a three-way interaction.[3]

Rape survivors who use delay tactics and attempt to involve the prosecutor in cross-examination use role-appropriate tools to manage problematic interactions with defense attorneys. As long as their manipulation remains unseen, it does not contradict an otherwise convincing performance. However, if the tactics surface and the judge or jurors perceive a survivor to be stalling or her requests for repetition slide into a generally combative orientation to all questions, her credibility may become suspect. If she undermines her own credibility, her efforts to gain control of interaction work in the defense attorney's favor.

Several of the survivors quoted above described seeking to involve prosecuting attorneys because they were concerned about the appropriateness of the questions they were asked. In their comments, the connection between interaction control and information control is evident. Survivors who cannot protect themselves with a well-worded response face a role problem, that is, how not to answer. Prosecuting attorneys provide one solution; stopping interaction is another.

Halting Interaction and Naming the Problem

The final strategy survivors used to deal with problematic aspects of cross-examination involved breaking off the question-answer interchange. They refused to respond to a question they had been asked or they spoke out of turn. Women openly confronted defense attorneys when they felt pushed to their limits; they were intensely angry and frustrated. For them, the question-answer interaction had completely broken down, their role had been undermined, and they had to do something drastic to regain their footing. By refusing to respond appropriately, they challenged the defense attorney's right to question them in a particular way and asserted that there were boundaries to the cross-examination interaction. Rather than being refusals to participate in cross-examination, confrontations initiated by rape survivors were attempts to shape the interaction into a form in which they felt they could participate.

Several survivors described breaking off interaction when they discovered the defense attorney's delivery no longer gave them space to answer all questions asked. In the final opening quotation in this chapter, Megan explained how she responded to a confusing compound question with one of her own: "Well, what question do you want me to answer?" After Megan questioned the defense attorney, there was a lengthy pause. When he resumed the cross-examination she had no further difficulties.

Rachel, who repeatedly was shut out of her speaking turn by a defense attorney, described halting a barrage of questions by claiming both roles—questioner and answerer—herself.

There was a few times, um, where he [the defense attorney] started badgering me, and [. . .] he started pushing his questions very fast, and very hard, and . . . and she [the prosecutor] objected to that, because he wasn't giving me a chance to answer my questions. And then he'd go on to the next questions and I'd get confused. And um, she objected to that. But um, [the prosecutor] said that she felt it was just better that ... to let him ask um, pretty much [anything]. Actually at this point, I answered before [the prosecutor] could object, and I was angry at this point: [...] "Well if you're asking me this, then the answer is this. If you're asking me this, then the answer is that." You know, it's that simple, it's cut and dry. And I was mad!

The "if" construction Rachel used directed attention to the confusing quality of the defense attorney's questions. Strictly speaking, she did not fail in her responsibility to supply an answer, but her manner was confrontational.

Other survivors found that they could not participate in the interaction because the defense attorney seemed to be posing questions that had a pre-determined answer. If their version of truth was not the answer implied by the question, their role of answer provider was placed in jeopardy. Faced with such questions, Arlene used her speaking turn to assert that the defense attorney's queries about the functioning of her car seat were illogical, and therefore, not answerable.

The defense attorney in the prelim asked me a lot of questions about why I didn't fight. He asked really detailed, ridiculously detailed questions about the lever on the [car] and how this guy had managed to pull it up. And [it] couldn't possibly be that he reached over me and pulled it up, it had to be that I voluntarily pulled this lever up, [and] put the seat down. I finally at one point said something like, "I can't figure out the logic of what you're looking for here and I can't give you the answer you're looking for, and this is ridiculous." And the judge told him to knock it off.

Arlene's refusal to respond to the questions that implied she facilitated sexual activity was a success. It brought the judge into the interaction, and he directed the defense attorney to alter the questioning that posed difficulties for her.

Although a number of survivors sought to stop problematic questioning behavior by stopping the interaction, only Isabel went beyond naming the problem and explicitly tried to limit how the defense attorney cross-examined her in the future.

Isabel: I said "no, you're not gonna do this to me, this is the way it happened, and nothing you can do is going to change it," and I was more argumentative.

Amanda: Did you verbalize what you just told me or was that just what you were thinking?

Isabel: That's basically what I told them, I said, "no, you can't change it [the answer] just because you want to, this is what happened." And you know, I basi-cally I told them, "I'm only gonna tell you once." I was getting mad.

Amanda: And did that change things?

Isabel: Yeah. (pause) After that [...] it was the questions. They got an answer and they would go on to another question. Because before, they would have a question, go on to another question and go right back to the preceding question, like that I was going to trip myself up or something somehow.

Why is Isabel unique in setting out the conditions under which she would hold up her end of the interaction? It is likely that most rape survivors can feel safe claiming a right to clarity—being asked questions that allow for real answers—and time in which to respond, because these claims are directed at protecting their own witness roles. However, setting out conditions puts them in a position of dictating the behavior of the defense attorney. Without prior knowledge of courtroom process, this is something few rape survivors would feel qualified to do. Isabel was not typical. She had received extensive preparation from the prosecuting attorney, she had had previous legal experience, and she had researched her role to prepare for her court appearance. This foundation of knowledge may have given her some confidence that she could make demands.[4]

Like subversive delay tactics, use of speaking turns to name problematic questioning behavior breaks the defense attorney's control over the direction of interaction and gives a survivor some breathing room. Sometimes the prosecuting attorney or the judge makes use of the time and intercedes to validate the survivor's claims. For example, Arlene noted that "the judge told him to knock it off." The following exchange between a rape survivor (RS) and public defender (PD), which occurred during a preliminary exam that I observed, shows how the survivor's refusal to answer a question she considered personal and irrelevant provoked an objection from the prosecuting attorney (PA) and a response from the judge:

PD: What did you say?
RS: I tell him [the defendant] my cousin was leaving, that I was menstruating, anything to get out [of the room], [I'll see you] "later, another day."
PD: Did you use menstruating or did you say you were on your period?
RS: On my period.
PD: What did he [the defendant] say?
RS: Give me an example, put my mouth on it [his penis].
PD: Were you on your period?
RS: Is that any of your business?
PA: Objection!
Judge: Sustained.

When a rape survivor asks a question rather than giving an answer or speaks out of turn, her strategy of gaining control is open and available to all others in the courtroom. It may raise questions for a judge, or among jurors, about her respect for the authority of the court or about what she has to hide. Compared with cultural expectations that rape victims are both passive and helpless, a survivor's act of confrontation is contradictory. Some women expressed awareness of the negative inferences that might be drawn when they brought interaction to a halt.

Information Management

Prosecutor-Requested Information Management

In chapter 4, I discussed the precourt preparation that some rape survivors received from prosecutors and their assistants. In addition to suggesting how survivors should appear and emotionally conduct themselves, some prosecutors told them that testifying in court was not simply a matter of describing what happened to them, like reporting to police, speaking to a grand jury, or talking to the prosecutor. Testifying was about convincing a judge or a jury that a crime happened to them. In court, their responses to questions needed to support the charges against the defendant clearly and head off the defense attorney's challenges.

Prosecutors who prepared survivors for a task of persuasion asked them to use specific terms to describe the sexual assaults against them and to emphasize particular aspects of the attack in order to substantiate the charges filed against the defendant. Some asked women to formulate answers to minimize the information they made available to the defense attorney, and others asked them to include information that countered known or suspected defense arguments, maximizing the data available to decision makers.

Meeting Prosecutors' Requests in Direct Examination

Survivors tried to follow prosecutors' instructions about the content of their answers, because they believed that doing so would provide some personal protection in cross-examination. Julianne's and Emily's recollections illustrate such compliance. During preparation for the preliminary hearing, the prosecutor asked Julianne, ordinarily a very verbal person, to hold back details in her replies to questions he asked in direct examination. Limiting information, he explained, would make it difficult for the defense attorney to interrogate her. She complied, and described her direct testimony as a series of abbreviated responses:

> It [direct examination] was very brief, and I was real careful about what I said because I knew he [the prosecutor] didn't want me to give him [the defense attorney] that much information to have [the defendant]'s attorney come back on me. It was simple answers, I mean "yes" and "no," if I could. And if not, um, "in the room," you know. Just short sentences, one-or-two-sentence things, no detail at all, no description. Just short answers.

In contrast, Emily participated in a prosecutor's strategy of maximizing the information available to the judge in a preliminary hearing. The prosecutor asked her to work with him to introduce the information that she was a convicted prostitute and a drug addict at the time of the rape. This was information that could impugn her credibility and would almost certainly be fodder for the defense attorney to attack her claims to be a victim. However, by leading Emily into disclosure and asking her other questions about her subsequent legitimate work, steady intimate relationship, and continued sobriety, the prosecutor gained the opportunity to frame the debate about her past.

Ordinarily, a survivor's postassault life and relationships would not be considered appropriate material for direct testimony. Having Emily talk about her reformed lifestyle, however, made her a more sympathetic victim. Furthermore, it allowed her some measure of control over the disclosure of embarrassing information. She recalled that publicly acknowledging it in direct examination and talking about the change in her life made the defense attorney's questions less threatening.

> The DA was gonna put anything out in the open that might be (laughs) ammo or whatever for them [the defense]. [...] And I didn't have a problem with that because the DA [...] also ask[ed] me, you know, do you do drugs now? So, he kind of brought out in the open also the change that took place in my life. [...] So I didn't feel too bad about going in there and ... saying ... you know, what had actually happened or anything.

These two examples show that during direct examination, prosecutors can assist survivors in managing information by asking questions that encourage particular types of answers.[5] If they want her to limit the information available, they can ask questions that are answerable with yes or no responses or in brief sentences. Or, they can ask open-ended questions and create openings for women to divulge information not directly related to the sexual attack.

Although prosecutors' information management strategies may offer some protection to rape survivors when they are later cross-examined, fulfilling them in the direct examination requires mental and emotional effort. To produce an appropriately minimalist account of the rape event, a rape survivor must limit her description of the attack and sexual violation to the components the prosecutor thinks are important. This, in some cases, means deemphasizing aspects of the event that are central to her experience of it. Alternatively, to protect themselves and others from the brutality of their experience, rape survivors often use euphemisms and generalities when describing their victimization. (A more complete discussion follows.) Fulfilling a prosecutor's requests to use explicit language to describe the sexual acts perpetrated by the defendant requires the rape survivor to face up to the intimately invasive nature of the attack personally and publicly and to forgo protecting herself and others. For several women, communicating the details of the rape was humiliating and difficult to do.

Most survivors who received information management instructions felt that doing what was asked was difficult but worthwhile. Yet several younger women, like Nellie, felt enacting the witness role in this way was inauthentic:

> It was almost as though I was more like a puppet up there. Um, I had to tell what was true, but um, I had to make sure that I told it in a certain way so it would be believed regardless of what really happened. I felt like it was a big game.

Nellie did comply, but she experienced pronounced discomfort in acquiescing to the prosecutor's wishes.

Pursuing the Prosecutor's Agenda in Cross-Examination

While survivors can induce prosecutors to raise objections in cross-examination sequences, they alone must formulate the answers to defense attorneys' questions. What do survivors do when they confront questions worded to counteract the prosecution strategy? Several women in this study made significant efforts to sustain what they understood to be the prosecution's case. Natalie and Janice spoke about this activity at some length.

Before the trial, the prosecutor took Natalie through the evidence available to sustain the state's case and the probable arguments of the defense attorney. Among the instructions he gave her was a directive not to commit herself to the identity of the particular weapon used to beat her, because she could not make such a claim and remain credible. Recalling the instructions, Natalie chose her words carefully when the defense attorney pressed her in the cross-examination sequence.

> They had five flashlights in the courtroom, they had my husband's flashlight, uh, two or three flashlights that they had found at the defendant's house, and then the flashlight that they had found in his car, his abandoned car or whatever, which was the one that he'd used [to hit my head]. They did have bloodstains on that flashlight, but they couldn't type it out because it had been too long or whatever. He [the defense attorney] had [was holding] one of the flashlights and he wanted me to commit that that was the, *the* flashlight that *he* [the defendant] hit me with. And I told him that it was a flashlight that looked exactly like that, but I didn't know if it was that particular one or not.

Before the trial, the prosecutor took Janice through the recorded statements of potential defense witnesses and pointed out all the possible points of contradiction between their accounts and her preliminary testimony that might be emphasized by the defense. As described in chapter 4, Janice, in response, told the prosecutor additional information that countered most of the potential defense openings. Despite the lack of relevance of some of the new information to the rape, the prosecutor instructed Janice to bring it up in her testimony "somehow, somewhere." When Janice testified, she looked for openings and did so. The defense attorney later questioned Janice about being systematically prepared by the prosecutor.

> She [the defense attorney] wanted to know who had called me, 'cause it sounded like in so many words that I was uh, prepped by the DA: that I was told *what* to say. And she made it sound like I was basically told what to say all during the hearing, and I said "no." I said, um, "The DA's office called me to tell me exactly what would incur [*sic*], what the trial would be about. Uh, how many days it may or may not take, how many days it's gonna take to pick a jury, um, what I would be um, what things were being brought into evidence that I already knew about." I said, "and I also did talk to the public defender's office and give them a statement, and I talked to the uh, investigating officer. And there's nobody else I talked to." Well, she kept asking me specific questions [about] what the DA told me to say. I said, "She didn't tell me to say anything." I said, "I was told to be honest and tell the truth and that's what I'm doing."

Janice was concerned that revealing the prosecutor's role in the content of her testimony would somehow taint it and weaken the case. Her denial that the prosecutor had actually put words in her mouth was factually accurate and the information she introduced about speaking to a defense representative supported a presentation of self that was open and honest and, therefore, credible.

Natalie and Janice's information management efforts made them important partners in sustaining the prosecution's case when it was under defense scrutiny.[6]

Even when prosecutors did not attempt to influence survivors' efforts to construct answers, they had an impact on the content of some survivors' answers. This occurred because the women tried to read prosecutors' facial expressions and body language to gain insight into the efficacy of their testimony. Jennifer explained that she wanted to know "whether I was saying the right things, or helping my case or hurting my case" and that she watched the prosecutor for cues:

> He can't stop a little smug smile when he knows he's doing good. He tries to stop it, but I could read it on that. On the same time, I noticed on some of the answers I gave, he wasn't exactly happy with them. I was going: well, I screwed up this time on that answer so maybe I'd better do better on the next.

Survivor-Initiated Information Management

The majority of women, who did not receive information management instructions from prosecutors, did not try to substantiate specific charges through their testimony. Some were unaware of the specific charges against the defendant; others had been told that the charges were subject to change depending on what they said during preliminary hearings. Most unprepared or poorly prepared survivors tried, during direct-examination, to give a "truthful" or clear description of what the defendant did to them and the extent of their injuries. Some also managed their emotions to produce a demeanor that reinforced their story.

Even without instructions from prosecutors, survivors were strategic in their construction of answers when defense attorneys' questions felt like a personal attack on either their credibility or their key social identities. Some women were troubled by sequences of questions that implied their memories were faulty or that they were lying, or questions that pushed them beyond the scope of their original narrative. For them, the goal of testifying in cross-examination was maintaining a consistent story. Other survivors were troubled by question sequences that implied they were to blame for the assault, through either their failure to resist or provocation. For them, the task was to construct answers that established the reasonability of their behavior given their perception of the circumstances, or the unreasonableness of attributing certain characteristics to themselves. When survivors were motivated by an awareness of stereotypes of rape victims, their efforts to preserve their credibility supported the prosecution's case.

But not all strategic answering behavior was motivated by women's desires to perform their witness role credibly. Some found it degrading to talk about sexual behavior and to use language they considered vulgar. Some were deeply troubled that the public disclosure of particular information might undermine their claims to certain identities outside the courtroom and affect their established relationships. Survivors handled questions that elicited such information defensively. These acts of self-protection were far less consistent with the goals of prosecution.

Maintaining Consistency with Direct Testimony

Some survivors began their cross-examination testimony intending to construct answers that were consistent with the account of rape that they had given during direct examination. They believed that their credibility as witnesses depended on their ability to maintain a steady story. With this goal in mind, a number took care to formulate precise responses, limiting the introduction of extra information in each answer to reduce the possibility of contradicting themselves.

Defense attorneys' repeated questions were implicit arguments that the first answer given by a rape survivor was incorrect or unclear, and they were invitations to clarify by expanding on what was previously said. Survivors who viewed them as a threat to maintaining a consistent story tried not to get drawn into elaborating, while also resisting attributions of dishonesty implied by repetition. Some, like Connie and Isabel, asserted the validity of their perspective and repeated their responses to previous questions. Connie defended her lack of recollection about details of the attack, rather than provide the defense attorney with a guess that was different than her previous testimony.

> She *kept* pressuring me saying, "Put yourself back there, can't you remember?"
> And I said, "No I can't remember, I just don't know. I've thought it through
> many times, and I don't remember whether I opened the car door with a key."

Isabel explained that she pointed out to the defense attorney that his questions were repetitive and that his assumptions were wrong:

> They would ask me two and three times, the same thing, and I would keep telling
> them, "You just asked me that, I already told you that's not what happened," and
> then I would repeat my side of the story.

Survivors who repeated themselves to maintain consistency were also aware
that they could only do this so many times before they began to sound like
they were hiding something. Thus, when defense attorneys went over the
same ground again and again, women eventually reassessed the questions as
an *interaction problem*. Then, they attempted to bring them to a stop by manipulating the defense attorney or halting interaction.

Managing Information to Sustain Credibility as a Victim: Countering Attributions of Blame

Other survivors, raped by strangers and by men they knew, strategically
constructed answers to repel the defense attorney's attempts to hold them
responsible for the rapist's attack. One way they countered blaming was to
choose words carefully to ensure that they were depicted as victims and the
defendants as rapists. To do this, they had to analyze and counter the defense
attorney's evolving line of questioning throughout the process.

After Jennifer determined, through a particular sequence of questions, that
the attorney was trying to establish that she had seduced the defendant, she
countered the accusation by asserting her emotional distance from the defendant and denying that he had any positive characteristics. Jennifer refused to
refer to the defendant as "a gentleman" or affirm that he had ever been
"friendly" toward her. To her, both terms implied a person incapable of violent
assault, of which she knew the defendant culpable.

Theresa, who feared that the opinion of a coworker associated with the
defendant would be weighed too heavily, likewise selected language to imply a
limited relationship existed between them. She replaced the word "friend,"
used by the defense attorney, with "acquaintance." She shifted the time frame
in her answers from the present to past, emphasizing that their contact was
limited to a work situation that no longer existed. She also asserted the only
basis for their relationship was expedience—support in an employment context that made them both minorities.

> He [the defense attorney] said, "Do you *have a friend* named Margaret?" I said,
> "No, I *had an acquaintance* named Margaret." And he says, "Well, isn't she *your
> friend?*" And I said, "Well there *were* three women in the whole company."[7]

Another approach a witness can use to limit the defense attorney's ability to cast her behavior as unreasonable is to move the evolving conversation beyond the bounds circumscribed by questions. That is, the witness can supply new information and introduce new topics for discussion to get outside the narrative embedded in a sequence of defense questions. Three women attempted to expand on the information available to the court at different points during their testimony when they felt the defense attorney was assigning blaming. For example, Joanna believed that the prosecuting attorney had not developed the case fully during direct, and the new information she offered about herself could make it stronger.

> Um, I would wait for an opening, 'cause I never took the liberty just to speak when I wasn't questioned, because I thought that I would only hurt myself by doing that. Um, I would always wait until I was questioned before answering, but then if I felt like I wasn't um, articulating what I wanted to say during the answering of that question I would say, "well, let me, let me make sure you understand what I'm trying to say," and I would go back and explain it.

Survivors also responded to strings of questions that implied they were to blame for the sexual contact with the defendant by challenging the negative comparisons the questions set up between themselves and stereotypical victims. The survivors did not answer directly questions that implied they did not adequately resist the defendant's sexual advances, but used their speaking turns to ask what the defense attorney would do or could do in a similar situation. By focusing on the likelihood the defense attorney would behave similarly in the face of the particular threats they experienced, women suggested that their decisions and behavior were reasonable. For example, Jennifer responded to a repeated question about why she did not try to escape from the defendant's truck by shifting the focus of discussion to what the defense attorney's questions left out—that is, her perception of threat. Yet rather than simply asserting the validity of her fear of retaliation, she put the defense attorney in her place and asked him to justify behaving differently:

> And I finally, I mean I was cordial with him the whole time until I finally just broke down. I go, *"Well if someone had threatened your life and threatened your children would you get out of a truck?"* (Stated emphatically.) And he kind of just sputtered for a little bit and he goes, "That's for the jury to decide." But he didn't ask me that question anymore.[8]

The following question-answer series, taken from a preliminary hearing that I observed, illustrates the same response move. The defense attorney was questioning the survivor about the defendant's behavior in the amusement park bathroom in which he attacked her. The woman interpreted him to be implying that the defendant's behavior was not coercive and her compliance not under duress. She (RS) first questioned a question, seeking affirmation of her interpretation. Then, she suggested that the threat posed by the assailant would be similarly experienced by the public defender (PD).

PD: When he asked, did he use a loud voice?

RS: No.

PD: Was he threatening?

RS: What are you asking me?

PD: Did he appear to be angry?

RS: No.

PD: Did you think he would hurt you if you didn't?

RS: If you mean being locked in a bathroom with someone bigger, [I] *figure you would be scared too.*

Survivors' challenges to implicit comparisons with stereotypes that suggested complicity with assaults were not limited to the threat posed by the assailant. For example, Janice countered the defense attorney's suggestion that she was in search of sexual contact because she had worn provocative clothing on the night that she was raped. The defense attorney suggestively held the skirt Janice wore to the dance club against her own body while she asked Janice questions about how much of her legs it exposed. Janice pointed out the size difference between herself and the attorney to challenge the accusation embedded in the defense attorney's particular display of her clothing. She pointed out that a skirt that looked short and provocative when held up against the defense attorney was neither when she wore it:

And she said, "Is this the skirt you were wearing?" And I had a little miniskirt on that night, but most people don't understand that I am shorter than the average person. So she said, "Where did it hit you?" I said, "It hit me about right, you know, on the lower part of the thigh, maybe an inch and a half above my knee." And she said, "This!?" So she held this [the skirt] up and made sure that [the jury could see.] I said, "It stretches." I said, "Just because you're putting it up to you, doesn't mean I'm your height." I said, "What are you, five foot and four inches, five foot and five inches?" I said, "I am four foot and eleven inches!" "I said, "So it's gonna come longer on me, than it will when you hold it up."

Responses that shift the focus away from implied comparisons protected women from having to acknowledge or affirm a version of reality that would make them culpable. Deflecting a line of questions saved them from having to decide whether or not to give an answer that was factually truthful, but inaccurate in terms of their experience of the rape event. Only Arlene described pursuing a strategy of conveying her reality at the expense of a strictly factual response to all defense questions. She refused to acknowledge information that she knew to be correct at the time of the trial, because it was not true in terms of her experience at the time of the rape.

Arlene recalled sometime after the investigation was under way and after she had given a formal statement to police, that she had seen her assailant once on the street several days before he attacked her. She remembered that he had looked at her and she had nodded. Arlene did not reveal this information to the prosecutor, but asked what impact admitting a prior knowledge of the assailant might have on the case. The prosecutor replied that any admission of a prior awareness of the defendant would raise questions about Arlene's story of being carjacked by a stranger, thus undermining the case. Informed that her credibility was at stake, Arlene made a conscious decision to keep the story she told in court consistent with her report to police: to deny any knowledge of the defendant, because she did not recognize him when he attacked her. The defense attorney did ask Arlene if she had seen the defendant before the rape and she denied it: "I said, 'No, never saw him before'."

Managing Information to Protect Social Identities and Relationships with Others

Describing the experience of being raped was an act of self-degradation for some women who were uncomfortable with open sexual discussion. It felt pornographic to describe the physical act of sexual penetration, even though it was the result of force. How to tell the court "what happened" without experiencing themselves as degraded or deviant was the immediate task of direct examination. Some used vague language and euphemisms to distance themselves from the physicality of the rape event and several gave direct testimony at preliminary hearings that was so inexplicit that prosecutors subsequently told them to use specific clinical terms to support the charges at trial.

While some survivors excluded others from their courtroom teams, knowing they would be disturbed by the rape, not all had social networks large enough to do this. Recall Gabriella's tearful description of watching her parents listen to her testimony in chapter 6. Thus, in addition to protecting themselves, it is likely that survivors also used euphemisms and vaguely described the sexual aspects of assaults to keep potentially painful information from people who were in the courtroom to support them. Consider the worries Natalie expressed about her brothers hearing the details of the rape:[9]

It is just that they [my brothers] have so much anger.... And they told me, you know, "I don't want to know details, I don't have to know details," you know, "I just know that he did this to you." And um, so I am just kind of worried that when I say everything that happened in detail, you know, how they are going to react.

Several survivors also described "forgetting" information they previously knew while they were on the stand, without reference to particular lines of questions. It is quite possible that their lapses in memory were subconscious

or even conscious efforts to shield themselves and others from certain information. Julianne's discussion of her lack of recall during the preliminary hearing is a case in point.

Over a month before the trial was scheduled, Julianne made the prosecutor
aware that the defendant possessed embarrassing photographs of her in bond-
age. She knew they could be used to suggest that she sent mixed messages
about her sexual intentions. The prosecutor told her that the judge was
unlikely to allow the defense attorney to introduce the photographs as evidence and urged her not to worry about them. Julianne reported that she took
him at his word and let herself dismiss this factor that contributed to her
anxiety about testifying. During the cross-examination, she said that she for-
mulated answers to defense questions *as if* the photographic evidence did not
exist, she had "forgotten about it."[10]

Theresa and Candace were clear that they weighed their relationships with
others in deciding how they would answer questions, limiting information that
might prove damaging to the relationship. Theresa described an interaction
with the defense attorney in cross-examination, while Candace described her
answering strategy in direct examination.

Toward the end of the preliminary hearing, the defense attorney asked
Theresa if she knew a man named Jackson. She acknowledged that she was
acquainted with him and the defense attorney did not pursue the matter. Later,
when I interviewed Theresa, I asked about Jackson. She told me that it had
pained her deeply to be asked about him in the context of the hearing, and she
had intentionally minimized the information in her response and the extent of
her relationship with him to protect him and his family.

> And Jackson is just a man who I've known for four years. We've been friends for
> four years, and uh, he's married and I did [work] for him on the side and stuff.
> But I happened to fall in love with him. But nothing [happened]. It's just one of
> those things you know. He's married and that's the way it is, and we're both
> Catholic. [. . .] But because I was going to pursue this [prosecution], I told him
> that it was best that I just not see him or do [work for him] anymore. And that
> was my choice, but I didn't want him dragged into it, I didn't want his family
> hurt because there is nothing [between us]. But they [the defense] could, they
> could try and turn it into something, and I just didn't want that to happen.

Candace, a recovering alcoholic and also a religious Roman Catholic, found
herself torn about giving an accurate account of her activities in the hours
before she was raped and beaten, because she had engaged in a consensual act
of extramarital sex and drank with her lover during that time. To tell the
truth about her preassault activities during trial, Candace would have had to
reveal her sins to the public, but more important, to the daughter who accompanied her to court. In her first day of trial testimony, Candace chose to protect her self-image and her personal relationship with her daughter on whom
she depended for emotional support. She did not supply a complete

chronological account of how she had spent her time, omitting her drinking and sexual liaison.

> Yeah, and I lied to [the prosecutor]. I didn't lie to [the prosecutor intentionally], I just didn't know [how] to put that on the stand! You know, I couldn't because my daughter was there. [...] Because how could I even say I have a boyfriend [and had sexual intercourse] when my daughter is there and she's sitting and listening to, you know? I couldn't say it.

Candace's suppression of information failed, however, because the DA had learned her blood alcohol level from the medical examination documentation and noted the discrepancy between it and her testimony.[11] Aware that the inconsistency in Candace's story provided a fertile ground for the defense attorney to raise reasonable doubts about her credibility, and thus reasonable doubts about the defendant's guilt, he took her into a witness room and challenged her. After a verbal struggle, she agreed to describe all of her activities, if her daughter could be excluded from the courtroom temporarily.

> And I went in there [the courtroom] you know, that day, and Caroline [the victim-witness advocate] was with me, and I went in there [the courtroom] and I said, this is what happened. I ... had a boyfriend and I told him—my daughter was not in there—and I said I had a boyfriend and made love [and we drank].

Telling the public audience about her moral failing shamed Candace: "I feel like a piece of shit, you know?" And it gave her new worries: "if my mom knows [about my extramarital sex], my dad would kill me. You know, I mean everybody would kill me."

Rape survivors enter a new social world of the courts when they become witnesses. This world is unique not only because of its formal roles and rules of interaction, but also because its subject matter is the personal details of the rape survivor's life. To varying degrees, others enter this new court world with rape survivors, providing instrumental and emotional support during hearings and trials. Survivors try to maintain boundaries and exclude specific others from entry into the courts when they anticipate contradictions between what they will be required to reveal and what they want others to know. However, the actual scope of talk in the courtroom can be far broader than what a rape survivor anticipates. Additionally, the need to have a trustworthy support in the courtroom tends to lead women to keep others on their teams who are deeply invested in particular social identities. I believe that Candace's struggle to construct answers that balanced the needs of the prosecution with her need to protect her social identity with her daughter is not unique, but rather a quite common problem.

Friends and family who attend court to provide moral support to survivors also contribute to constructing answers in another way. Rape survivors can and do use these trusted others to gain information about the progress of their testimony during breaks in the proceedings. Based on the feedback they receive about their own testimony and the testimony of others, rape survivors may decide to maximize or minimize information. For example, the information-maximization strategy adopted by Joanna emerged from her private lunchtime conversations with a victim advocate.

> We took, of course, the lunch break ... and um, N—— from CASA [Coalition Against Sexual Assault] told me the things that she thought [were not clear]. She's like, "I'm not your attorney so I can tell you what I think. These are the things that I think are not clear. These are the things that I think are [clear.]" N—— was like, "Joanne, you need to clarify why you said those things, you know." So I went back in, I did you know, and made sure that [I said them].

Conclusions and Questions for Further Consideration

Survivors identified two distinct kinds of problems in testifying: (1) certain restrictive patterns of questioning made it difficult to exercise their speaking turns and (2) certain questions or strings of questions implicitly or explicitly undermined their witness, victim, or extralegal social identities. When survivors perceived problems they actively managed interaction and information. Although, problems of meaning did exist independently of how questions were asked, survivors' efforts to manage interaction and information were closely intertwined.

Survivors focused on analyzing the relationship between questions to make moves to deflect or derail implied comparisons in evolving lines of questions. When used to limit the scope of questions asked by the defense attorney, interaction-management techniques that halted questions or drew the prosecutor into interaction also limited the court's access to specific kinds of information. For example, when Arlene stopped interaction, the judge redirected the defense attorney, and the court never learned whether she was wearing underwear.

These rape survivors used the full range of strategies that researchers have found other witnesses in criminal and civil courts use to maintain their speaking turns and assert their perspectives. Survivors described behaviors that are comparable to the avoidance techniques outlined by Valdez and Rice[12]— delays, requests for repetition, anticipation, and elaboration—that resulted in witnesses derailing some of defense attorney's lines of questions. They hedged answers, provided mitigating responses and nonanswers, and asserted their right not to know information when they felt coerced in cross-examination, similar to witnesses studied by Danet and his colleagues and Rice.[13] These women also followed the moves made by defense attorneys and prepared answers for anticipated questions, particularly those constructed to blame them for failure to take action.[14] Based on results that demonstrate the similarity among rape survivors and other witnesses, we should conclude that neither the experience of sexual victimization nor the practices of domination employed in court render rape survivors collectively passive.

Matoesian is correct that cross-examination is often a three-way interaction in a rape trial,[15] but how often the three-way dynamic dominates may be underestimated by research that focuses on prosecutors' motivations. I found rape survivors *seeking assistance from* prosecutors to control defense attorneys. Survivors' engagement of prosecutors had immediate consequences for defense attorneys' questioning and also increased their confidence.

Women's use of more than one interaction strategy during the course of their testimony, and the varying degrees of success with these strategies, show that their choices are not simply a matter of personality differences. When survivors perceived problems in interaction, their behavioral choices reflected multiple factors: their assessment of the size of the problem and the discomfort it caused; the extent to which it disabled their ability to formulate and articulate answers; their legal knowledge and experience; their investment in conforming to the demeanor of a stereotypical witness or victim; their assessment of the danger posed by being seen to disrupt the interaction; and their perception of their capacity to carry on multiple interactions simultaneously.

Previous research has shown that rape survivors' strategies for constructing answers are responsive to cultural scripts of rape victimization.[16] However, these interviews show that women respond to a broader scope of concerns about the way in which they are portrayed. They acted to preserve their social identities as well as their credibility as witnesses and rape victims while on the stand.

Several survivors snickered or laughed openly after describing how they derailed lines of questions, forced the defense attorney to meet requests, and brought interaction to a halt. From this, I conclude that their apparent success in asserting themselves provided some emotional catharsis. Testifying became in that moment more than an experience of being dominated.

In contrast, survivors seemed to experience no pleasure in resolving the conflict between their need to protect their witness selves and their social selves in favor of the latter. Successfully suppressing information was not associated with any spontaneous expressions of glee. In fact, their talk about the conflict in truth claims was circumspect. Arlene may have "felt fine" when planning to deny that she knew the defendant, because at the time of the rape it was her experiential reality. However, even she assessed her answer as "lying."[17] I believe the need to build a case that draws on the rape survivor's entire life as a resource is fundamentally in conflict with the rape survivor's need to protect her social identity.

In this and the preceding two chapters I examined how rape survivors were involved in preparing themselves for and participating in probable cause hearings as well as trials, although as with the criminal justice process generally, the minority of women in this study sample actually testified in trials. The majority of cases were resolved through plea agreements. Thus, it is necessary to ask questions about rape survivors' involvement and investment in these pleas.

- How often and in what ways do prosecutors involve them in plea-bargaining?
- How do they feel about participating in or being cut out of a decision that determines how the crime committed against them will be labeled and what punishment their assailant will receive?
- What impact do legal knowledge, prior involvement with the investigation, and investment in confronting the defendant or putting one's experience on record through testifying have on whether a rape survivor is satisfied with a plea?

These concerns are the topics of chapter 8.

"He Said He'll Plead Guilty. How Does That Sound to You?": Rape Survivors' Participation in and Satisfaction with Plea Negotiations

Fewer than half of the defendants who were charged with raping survivors in this study were tried by a jury of their peers. Thirty-three percent of the cases were resolved by trial, 8 percent were dropped and 59 percent were resolved by plea. Some of the survivors were satisfied with these negotiated settlements; others were not.

Nan read in the newspaper that prosecutors had dropped the rape charge and allowed the defendant to plead guilty to a single felony count of kidnapping her. She understood their desire to settle the case short of a trial. However, the plea agreement, negotiated without her input, was not consistent with her experience of victimization.

> No (laughs) I wasn't involved in that [determining the plea] at all, I was still a minor. [...] That bothers me because sometimes my thoughts when you hear about a plea-bargain are, it is a bit of a compromise. [...] My first position was *reality.* I was kidnapped and I was raped and I had to give some of that up. That wasn't a negotiating point [for me].

Gwendolyn was not active in the investigative phase and did not want to testify in the probable cause hearing. The prosecutor's decision to bargain down the number of sexual assault counts against her attacker satisfied her, because the sentence still was a substantial prison term. She explained,

> He still got life, which is important to me. So even though it was pled down to a lesser degree, he still got 88.5 years, so he'll die in there. And in Washington State there's no possibility of parole, you serve your sentence.

Marlene cooperated when the prosecutor demanded that she repeatedly describe the rape and take a polygraph before he would file charges. She also provided him with the names of witnesses to offset the blame she felt he placed upon her. When Marlene learned from a rape crisis advocate that the prosecutor had decided to allow the defendant to plead guilty to a nonsexual misdemeanor she was greatly distressed.

He [the prosecutor] didn't want to go for rape anymore, because of our long sexual relationship. [...] We went out for three years prior, so we'd had sex prior to that [the rape]. You know, he [the defendant] had every right then to rape me (laughs) is basically what he was saying. [...] I didn't have an airtight case and he didn't want to go for that. He was gonna try to plea-bargain for burglary, um, nothing else. [...] When I found out about that, and it's like, I asked him [the prosecutor] what [my ex-boyfriend] would actually get if it was plea-bargained, and he said normally it was like two years or $5,000 or something like that. I said, "What's he really gonna get?" and he said, "Probably probation or county time." Um, and so it was really upsetting and it was kind of a bad experience.

If a prosecutor decides to negotiate a settlement rather than take the case all the way through trial, she or he may offer the defendant an opportunity to plead guilty in exchange for (1) reducing the seriousness of the charges in the indictment or complaint or (2) requesting the judge impose less than the maximum allowable sentence. In many states, a Victims' Bill of Rights mandates that prosecutors consult with crime victims before they finalize plea agreements. However, these mandates generally leave the term "consult" undefined and do not grant crime victims legal authority in the plea process. Thus, some prosecutors may discuss making the choice to negotiate on specific charges or penalties with survivors before they work out an agreement with the defense attorney, but not all do.

The few studies conducted of plea-bargaining rape reveal three disturbing trends.[1] First, in exchange for pleas of guilt, prosecutors charge many defendants with lesser sexual assaults, including misdemeanors instead of felonies, with statutory rather than forcible rape, and with nonsexual crimes. Second, defendants that have already been given the benefit of reduced charges also receive sentences at the lowest end of penalty ranges. Third, prosecutors accept pleas to lesser charges and lesser sentences more frequently in cases involving nonstereotypical victims of rape and nonstereotypical rape scenarios than those that conform closely to stereotypes.

In this study sample, 83 percent of all defendants admitted guilt or were convicted of *some* charge. But, in 37 percent of the cases resolved by plea, the charges were for something other than felony sexual assault. Although prosecutors negotiated the same portion of cases involving known and stranger assailants,[2] they secured pleas to felony sexual assault or rape in far fewer cases involving known assailants (10 percent versus 100 percent). This overwhelming difference in plea outcomes suggests strongly that stereotypes played a role in prosecutors' decisions.

Rape activists have challenged prosecutors' decisions to "downgrade" and to "discount" rape, especially those that are not stereotypic, because these practices do not hold rapists accountable for their actions and victims of sexual assault do not receive reasonable justice.[3] This chapter is concerned with rape survivors' perspectives. Given differences in their knowledge and expectations of the criminal justice process and concerns about involvement in prosecution, described in prior chapters, it seems probable that their criteria for satisfaction with the plea process will vary. We must ask: How do opportunities to participate in plea negotiation, the labels formally applied to rapists and their crimes, and the penalties convicted rapists receive matter to them?

What Pleas Mean to Rape Survivors

A finding or plea of guilt legally establishes that a defendant may be punished for committing a particular crime and formally fixes a social meaning on an act experienced as personal violation. The punishment function of the criminal justice process was of variable importance to survivors, because their notions of "justice" were tied to how they viewed the defendant. Women who felt brutalized by men who refused to acknowledge their humanity were oriented toward treating them as animals to be locked in prison as long as possible. However, lengthy imprisonment was not necessary or desirable to survivors who believed the assailant was redeemable. Survivors' orientations toward the labeling function of the criminal justice process also varied. Some wanted a public record made of the full scope of the violence they endured at the hands of the rapist. Others primarily viewed formal charges as tools for the purpose of achieving an acceptable penalty—as means to an end.[4]

When they were aware of them, rape or sexual assault statutes framed survivors' thinking about the fairness of plea negotiations. They used the maximum sentences that state penal codes specified to evaluate the sentences defendants received. However, interstate variations could lead survivors in different areas to respond differently to similar sentences. For example, during the time of the study, survivors in Washington and California compared plea agreements for aggravated rape against, respectively, "life" and eight years.[5]

Most survivors had only vague ideas about how the plea process worked. Their views of the witness's role in plea-bargaining were shaped by their exposure to victim-witness materials and some input from friends and relations, but little by past legal experiences. Survivors' expectations were further developed through their interactions with legal personnel during the investigative phase, through their preparation for court, and through their testifying experiences. Some, who were asked to do much during the investigation or who testified in court, came to expect a high level of involvement in the case, including participating in plea negotiations. Others, who were asked to do less by legal personnel or had not previously made efforts to be involved, did not expect to be consulted.

Some survivors' commitment to participate in the criminal justice process was tied to their personal desire to stand up to the defendant. They sought to confront his violence toward them and his power over them by facing him down in a protected legal setting. Seeing him pushed into and pulled through the public process achieved a sort of retribution apart from official sanctions. Given this, they viewed pleas that stopped cases short of court events as obstacles to achieving reempowerment.

Core Contributors to Survivor Dissatisfaction with Pleas

Denial of Victimization

Some survivors who were oriented toward the labeling function of the criminal justice process felt that the outcomes of plea negotiations, though providing for some punishment, denied their experiential reality—that is, what *they knew to be true* as a result of their experience of victimization. In short, the prosecutor entered a set of charges into the official record that mislabeled the crime and the criminal. When the mislabeling omitted aspects of the event that were key to their experience of violation, it was particularly troubling.

This official mislabeling was socially important because it undermined their public representations as raped women and the credibility of their claims for sympathy and accommodation. It also lent credibility to the defendant's claims that the alleged rape was either a misunderstanding or consensual sex. When women struggled to see themselves as victims and worthy of making legitimate claims on the criminal justice process, official mislabeling again called into question their judgment.

Interviews with Nan and Megan show that dissatisfaction of this type was experienced when prosecutors allowed defendants to plead guilty to something other than felony rape. As described in the opening quotation, Nan learned that the prosecutor had negotiated a guilty plea when she read the outcome in the newspaper. As a minor who had not been involved in any part of the process, she did not expect to be consulted. However, she *was* bothered by the fact that the prosecutor dropped the rape charge in favor of kidnapping (which carried more time). Nan explained that she felt a personal loss, when the prosecutor dropped the charge. She had been subject to both crimes and had to "give some of that up." The denial of her reality produced through the plea-bargain bothered her at 16 and *still* bothered her when she completed the interview as an adult, even though the defendant had been sentenced to a substantial 16 years in prison.

Megan was dismayed with the prosecutor's decision to extend a plea offer of misdemeanor statutory rape to her assailant *after* she voiced her opposition.

Megan: Well my DA said, they're meeting before the pretrial hearing, and she asked me how would you feel about a plea-bargain: "What if he says that he'll give in if we lower the charges?" I said, " NO! [...] I think this: he's getting off easy as it is." You know, it was statutory, that seemed unfair to me. [...] And then they had a pretrial hearing [...] which I didn't even know was going to happen. Basically it was a plea-bargain [meeting]. He [the defendant] said he would plead no-contest if they lowered it to misdemeanor, statutory rape, and they did. [...] Let's see, he got fined $1,200, he has to work at a rape crisis center, and he's on probation for two years.

Amanda: How do you feel about that?

Megan: Really pissed off. The charges are *so* incredibly watered down from forcible rape, which is a felony—you can go to jail for years—to a misdemeanor statutory.

I mean, you're on probation for God's sake. And a little fine. [. . .] And that just really didn't seem fair. [. . .] The charges . . . it's like taking a candy bar. (laughs) You know? I mean, it's just a misdemeanor, no one cares, no one's gonna see that.

Megan felt that the charges to which the defendant pled guilty and the related penalty did not match the gravity of her violation. Symbolically, the down-grading to misdemeanor statutory rape—an age-related offense—denied the importance of *her* lack of consent to the defendant's sexual aggression. Legally it didn't matter that she repeatedly told the defendant "no." The prosecutor's decision to ignore her protest and reduce the charge paralleled the defendant's failure to heed Megan's verbal resistance.

The experience of having one's reality mislabeled can involve the denial of broader aspects of the attack, not just the sexual components. Two weeks after testifying in a preliminary hearing, Arlene learned that the prosecutor had negotiated a plea without consulting her. She was not upset that the case had been resolved short of trial, because she did not wish to testify again and was not concerned about the length of sentence the defendant might receive. She was, on the other hand, quite angry that the bargain involved dropping charges that were central to her experience.

The charges were kidnap, robbery, and rape, and he pled to robbery and rape and they dropped kidnap. [. . .] I was furious about that, but the reason was . . . that because of (laughing) Proposition 13, he couldn't be tried for two felony offenses because he'd be in jail too long and they couldn't deal with that.

Arlene's anger was directed at a formal policy followed by the prosecutor rather than his exercise of discretion. However, she also felt diminished because the official record would not reflect her reality.

Denial of Justice

Some survivors felt that the negotiation process resulted in a sentence that was not severe enough given the type of injury they received. Like Megan and others who felt the sentences that followed from denial of their reality were inadequate, Mary was "pissed off" about the reduction of the sentence that accompanied the plea-bargain. Her assailant pled guilty to seven felony charges, which accurately specified the fury of his attack, but the judge allowed the terms to run together (concurrently). This resulted in Mary's assailant being sentenced to serve "a term of seven years and six months," about one-quarter of the possible time.

Denial of Influence

Dissatisfaction with negotiated resolutions also emanated from being left out of the process or being given a part in name only. In particular, women who entered the investigative phase with strong expectations of being important contributors or developed them as a result of interactions with police and prosecutors, were frustrated not to have a role in a key decision about a case that was built upon their injury. In formal terms, they believed that criminal justice procedure broke down, denying them justice.

Carmela was greatly frustrated with being asked to participate in the plea process in a way that was meaningless. Upon arriving to testify at the preliminary hearing, the prosecutor presented her with a plea offer intended for the defendant.

> They got me into this little side room, she said to me, the assistant state's attorney, she said that he doesn't have any prior convictions. "He said he'll plead guilty and we'll give him twelve month[s'] supervision, how does that sound to you?" And I think I asked her what supervision was, and um, and I got really angry, 'cause I said, "Well, he *does* have a prior conviction." I said, "that battery." [...] Nobody told me that when you go to court to see the judge, you might not see the judge, and you might have to make a deal. [...] It really upset me 'cause they got me in there, [...] and then they just pull this rabbit out of the hat, and it was like, here, you gotta take it.

When Carmela asked to review the terms of the plea in more detail, she was given literally minutes to examine the document. She discovered that the agreement reduced all charges to misdemeanor battery and a term of probation.

> *Carmela:* She said, "Look, you know, um, you have to take this because, this particular judge will uh, find this person not guilty, he finds all of them not guilty." And she said, "If you don't take this then you're not going to get anything." So you know, another great choice again. (laughs) Oh great, you know, I'll take it. But then the thing that really pissed me off too. [...] They brought me back in, and then she said to me, "He said he'll take six months."
> *Amanda:* Down from a year to six?
> *Carmela:* Right, and I said, "Since when is he callin' the shots?" And then I just had a fit. I said, you know, "This guy is dangerous running around, doing this to people." [...] I had a fit so she said, "Here, this is what I'll do." She gave me an order of no contact that if he called, I could have him arrested.

Carmela did not feel that her interests were served by the plea, which overlooked the defendant's prior violence, denied the reality of the sexual assault, and offered her no physical protection from him. Yet, she "accepted" the terms rather than get "nothing" as forecast by the prosecutor. Unfortunately, her "decision"—the exercise of her authority—was rendered moot when the prosecutor went back to the defendant and allowed him to negotiate a further reduction in time. Carmela's lack of legal knowledge and awareness that cases are frequently resolved through pleas comes through clearly in the quotation. She is angry to be surprised by the negotiation effort and is further irritated to be maneuvered into authorizing the prosecutor to pursue the plea.

Satisfaction Achieved through Negotiated Outcomes

Survivors' satisfaction was generally associated with parity between the participatory role they claimed and the opportunities offered by the prosecutor. They were also more satisfied when they and the prosecutor shared a common focus on the outcome of the case.

Some women did not seek out an active role and were not given one by legal personnel. Their lack of desire for involvement followed from fear of further contact with the defendant, concerns about the emotional demands of testifying, or a belief that they had no place in the process. Resolution by plea kept them from penetrating further into a process that would require contact with the defendant or public testimony about the assault event and was, therefore, desirable.

Pamela, who did not discuss the rape in detail with anyone other than police, explained that she feared testifying at the preliminary hearing would force her to recall memories of sexual molestation when she was nine years old. Elisa did not wish to revisit the trauma of the attack, which left her cowering in her home unable to act. Twyla sought to sustain the emotional distance from the rape that she had achieved through limited involvement in the prosecution.

Legal personnel did not involve these women in the investigation, and they did not seek out contact during that phase. Twyla testified at the preliminary hearing, but Pamela and Elisa were not asked to do so and had no desire to do so. None of these women wanted or expected to be involved in the plea negotiation. The convictions for felony rape and the six-year sentences that prosecutors negotiated were satisfactory to Pamela and Elisa. Twyla believed that it was logical the defendant should plead guilty and viewed the prosecutor's efforts to resolve the case short of trial as an extension of other efforts not to burden her. The plea was good because the alternative—another court appearance—might have been more than she could handle.

Other survivors sought an active role and prosecutors gave them opportunities to offer their opinions on pleas under development. Ultimately, these women came to share the prosecutor's view that stopping the process short of trial was advisable. While they might share the prosecutor's logical framework for justifying the plea, this was not necessary to secure their agreement with the terms offered. Alternative logics offered by satisfied survivors included a need to ensure conviction, the adequacy of the penalty, achievement of personal objectives in relation to the defendant, and a need to disengage from a process that had become burdensome.

Wanda, Cindy, and Julianne were involved in the investigation, responding to requests and initiating contact, and they desired to maintain their active role throughout the prosecution, including being involved in plea negotiations. When they were given the opportunity to contribute to the discussion of offers in ways that they felt were meaningful, the women each endorsed a penalty that was significantly less than the statutory maximum, as a reasonable course of action. Each emphasized to me her contribution to the discussion of plea negotiations.

Wanda felt that she had been given ample opportunity to provide input and explained that the final plea offer reflected her desires and the desires of the other victims. The defendant did not receive the statutory maximum—a life term—but Wanda noted that his 30-year sentence would put him in prison well into the twenty-first century. Note how Wanda uses "we" and "us" to include herself and a second victim in a description of how the negotiation unfolded with the defendant.

> *Wanda:* So we were in the court like two or three times for that whole process [during the investigative phase], and um, and then we had had a couple of meetings with [the prosecutor]. She had come up with perhaps a plea-bargain um, arrangement. So [. . .] then we gave him, yeah, we offered him a plea-bargain, but then he had like two weeks to get back to us on it, and he turned that down.
>
> *Amanda:* Tell me about these meetings regarding the plea-bargain. What were you told and what kind of input were you allowed to have?
>
> *Wanda:* Oh, we had as much input as we wanted. Basically she explained what would happen with the plea-bargain and [asked] did we feel comfortable with that. The other woman, [a third victim] her folks were for it. [The second victim] and I were both determined, we wanted to go to court. If the plea-bargain wasn't gonna be sufficient or he wanted less than what we were willing to offer at that point, then we'd go to court. We didn't have any problem with that. [. . .]
>
> *Amanda:* Do you remember what that plea-bargain was?
>
> *Wanda:* Yeah, it was 25 to life, 25 without parole, and he turned it down. Uh, then the DNA came back, (chuckles) and it screamed yes, he was the rapist. And we offered him the same plea-bargain, 25 to life, and then another 5 for probation violation, and he ended up taking it. [. . .] So we felt like he was getting something I suppose. He won't be eligible for parole until 2021.

Cindy and Julianne both felt that the prosecutor's desire to bargain with the defendant served their needs, but they gave different reasons for wanting to avoid a trial. Having participated in one trial that ended in a hung jury, Cindy shared the prosecutor's analysis that a plea-bargain was the only way to ensure that her assailant was convicted of rape.

> They called me on the 7th and said, "Are you willing to go on with this?" And I was, you know. I was really getting um, really feeling like you know, I'm gonna go ... I'm gonna go to trial again, and this guy's not gonna be convicted, you know. He's gonna get off again, you know, he has a good defense lawyer, you know. I think I told you before, he used to prosecute rape cases for the district. I just thought, you know, I have no faith in a jury to be impartial, and to be able to um, render a verdict on something like ... on a case like this, without um, their um, prejudices and their own rationalities and everything else entering into the

process. [...] When they came up with the plea-bargain, I was glad. I even said to the DA, 'cause she said to me, she said, "I'm afraid he might get off." And I said, "So am I, and I'm afraid if he gets off, I'm gonna be the one that ends up in jail." Because, I mean I would'a gone after the motherfucker, you know (laughs).

Although the charges against Cindy's assailant were reduced (downgraded) from aggravated to forcible, the main charge of rape remained intact and she was satisfied with the way her experience had been labeled. Furthermore, she believed the formal reduction of the charge would have little substantive consequence because the parole board, which would determine the time he *actually* served, would have access to the initial complaint that was filed *and* she planned to submit a victim impact statement to them. Cindy also discounted the substantive impact of the charge reduction on grounds that the defendant stood a chance of receiving a far greater penalty in prison—death: "I don't think he's even gonna survive nine years in [prison]. He'll get his just desserts up there."

Julianne admitted being oriented toward a plea from the beginning of her involvement with police, because she could not demonize her boyfriend, and she feared for his safety in any detention facility. She struggled in her decision to report his violent action to police and had maintained her commitment to use the process against him through extensive support from friends and family. Yet, Julianne *was* deeply invested in having her claim of rape taken seriously by legal personnel. During the investigation, she responded to requests and repeatedly called the detective to ensure that he sent his report to the prosecutor. She also carefully prepared herself for her court appearance. Julianne explained how she weighed her concerns about her boyfriend against her need to see him justly punished.

Julianne: I from the beginning didn't want to go all the way, I wanted to go ... I wanted to plea-bargain. I just was scared of the system, basically, and um, my dad was like, "You go full blown, you just take this the whole course." I just ... from the beginning didn't want to ever see [the defendant] go to jail because I knew that he would be a victim in jail, and I couldn't see letting that happen. [...] I didn't want any pain on him, I didn't want him to hurt. [...] In prelim when the judge said let's resolve it here, um, ... and we met with the DA, I said [that it] just didn't [matter] to me as long as I knew he was being punished. I wanted him to be punished and I wanted it to be a year, 'cause I thought a year is pretty brutal time, and plus you know, from what I understood, they could get off on good behavior and this and that. I just ... we just all kind of agreed, basically, and my dad said, you know, "Ultimately it is your decision." The DA said he just would almost put money on it that he [the defendant] would not get jail time, and I was fine with that. I mean, I had no problem with that. My dad said you know, "Hey, as long as we know he's punished BUT the full term," and a year was full term. [...] So we said a year of whatever the judge decides is how we liked it.

Amanda: Do you ultimately know what charge he pled nolo [contendere] to?

Julianne: Yes. He has a felony on his record, a sexual assault and battery, and it's a wobbler, which means that he can go back in 18 months, I believe it is, and ask it to be dropped down to a misdemeanor.

Amanda: And that's fine with you?

Julianne: Yes.

Ultimately, the plea agreement gave Julianne a way out of the criminal justice process that benefited everyone. Her injury was acknowledged through her boyfriend's criminal label, but the term he received allowed him to move beyond what Julianne saw as a mistake of judgment.

Rachel was raped by a man with whom she previously had been intimate and who took advantage of her trust. She felt that reporting the rape and pursuing the case was an act of standing up for herself—rejecting her ex-husband's implied claim on her body. Testifying at the preliminary hearing was extremely difficult for her, but it was a momentous personal achievement. When prosecutors offered her an opportunity to end her involvement in the process through a negotiated settlement, she accepted.

Rachel was active in the investigative phase as a result of requests made by legal personnel as well as her own initiative. She also prepared herself extensively before the preliminary hearing, presenting the prosecutor with material she considered evidence. She reported developing a good rapport with the prosecutor and detective, who intervened when the defendant's family called to harass her.

The prosecutor first approached Rachel about extending a plea offer to her ex-husband before the preliminary hearing. Rachel believed the one-year penalty she suggested was inadequate, "I said no. I didn't feel that was enough. [...] I want to go through the preliminary." The prosecutor accepted Rachel's choice and did not extend the plea. Rachel subsequently testified, establishing grounds for five separate charges against her ex-husband. The prosecutor again broached the subject of offering a plea: rape and assault and a three-year term. This time, the plea offer seemed reasonable to Rachel.

Rachel: What [the prosecutor] told me, is if he didn't plead guilty to the three years, with those charges then they were going to give him ... they were gonna give him everything, and there was like five charges total.

Amanda: So they would go to trial with those five charges?

Rachel: Right. And he decided that it'd be best for him to plead guilty to them [the two].

Amanda: How did you feel about that, a plea as opposed to going to trial?

Rachel: I felt better about it, I really felt better about it. I didn't want to go to trial. And I already made up my mind I was not going to trial. [...] I told [the prosecutor] that. I said, "I'm not going to trial. If he doesn't plead, I'm not going." [...] It was just too hard, I mean, going to trial would have been ...

asking for the nightmare again and I didn't want it. So, I said, "No." *He* [the defendant] didn't know that I wasn't gonna [testify] (laughs) or that I wasn't gonna go to trial, so *he* pleaded guilty.

Because the prosecutor never offered the one-year term, Rachel felt that her testimony at the preliminary hearing added two years to her ex-husband's sentence. Her use of the criminal justice process to right the imbalance of interpersonal power with him comes through in her final remarks. She derived a special satisfaction from knowing that he *must have* considered her tenacity during the preliminary hearing in weighing the three-year term, never knowing that she had already decided not to participate in a trial.

Rachel believed that taking the case through to trial would not offer her enough additional satisfaction to offset the burden of participating. It satisfied her to know that she had brought the criminal justice process to bear on the rapist. Her decision to report the rape and participate through the preliminary hearing stage resulted in his receiving a formal label as a sex offender, and, moreover, gave her the satisfaction that the criminal sanction he received was her handiwork.

Satisfaction Denied through Negotiated Outcomes

Dissatisfaction with pleas was often associated with conflict between the participatory role claimed by the survivor and the opportunities offered by the prosecutor. Some women entered the criminal justice process with the belief that their witness role entitled them to participate in the full scope of decisions related to the case. Others developed high participatory expectations as a result of being involved in the investigation or testifying at a probable cause hearing. When survivors with high participatory expectations were not offered what felt like an *active* and *consequential* role in plea negotiations, they rejected the outcomes as illegitimate. Thus, women whose assailants pled to charges that were downgraded or were sentenced to terms well below the maximum *and* those whose assailants were convicted of felony rape and received substantial prison terms were dissatisfied.

As captured in the third opening quotation, Marlene was distressed when prosecutors negotiated a plea to a lesser nonsexual charge without her input. It is hard to imagine that a raped woman would not find such treatment troubling. Yet dismay at not being consulted was not confined to those whose reality was denied, nor was it solely associated with weak sanctions. Trudy, Susan, and Francine, whose assailants all were convicted of felony rape, were similarly distressed to be marginalized—that is, not included in a decision that was central to the criminal justice process.

Trudy was disturbed by being ignored by the prosecutor, although the rapist received a substantial prison term of 12 years. She had been deeply involved in apprehending him (meeting five requests from legal personnel) and had testified at a probable cause hearing. As a result, she claimed the prosecution as her own and had come to expect that she would have a continued role as the case unfolded. When the prosecutor informed her about the plea agreement after it was finalized, she felt "left out."

> *Trudy:* We heard from the district attorney by telephone that he pled guilty and that they were working on his sentence and that there would be some going back and forth, and he told me what he would probably get [12 years], and then he told me there would be a sentencing and that I would certainly be invited. I guess, it would be okay for me to come.
>
> *Amanda:* How'd you feel about that?
>
> *Trudy:* At that point I started to feel left out. I felt like, well, they didn't ask me what he should get, they didn't ask me if he should be allowed to plead down. They didn't ask me (laughs) if, if it was okay with me. They were telling me, now we'll take over, and we'll put him away for you. [. . .] I thought that it was a little more serious than they were taking it. [. . .] I felt like since it was his second offense as a rapist, and who knows how many offenses as a robber, um, that 12 years, and especially since they told me he'll probably serve 7, it just wasn't enough. [. . .] They'd already decided, that that's what he was gonna get, and everybody agreed to it, not me, but his lawyer and my lawyer and the judge, basically decided.

Notable in Trudy's comments is her use of the phrases "at that point" and "take over." Together, they connote her *displacement* from a role of importance. She feels that she was included but is now marginalized by legal personnel who act for her not with her. In short, Trudy recognizes that she is no longer a part of "everybody," she is legally nobody.

Even though her assailant pled guilty to felony rape and received a six-year prison term, Francine was dissatisfied with the way in which the plea process unfolded. During the investigation, she had aggressively pushed for the case to be prosecuted, meeting with the head of the sexual assault unit and preparing a detailed written account of the rape for detectives. She also attended the arraignment to confront the defendant in court, even refusing to vacate the courtroom when the bailiff asked those without business with the judge to leave. Shortly before the preliminary hearing, the prosecutor told Francine that she already had offered to allow the defendant to plead guilty to a single count of rape in exchange for the midterm sentence of six years. Having made every effort to maintain contact with legal personnel, Francine was astonished to learn they had gone forward without consulting her.

> "Look," I said, "I'm willing to go all the way with this." I said, "I'm not going to disappear on you, I'm not going to fail to show up in court, I'm not going to back out, I'm not going to get scared." I said, "I'm going to be an incredible witness." I said, "What I want in return—I don't want him offered anything anymore." She said, "He won't be." She said, "All deals are off. It's all off at this point." And

she said, "If he wants to plead out, that's fine, but he will plead out guilty to all charges, with no conditions."

Yet still the prosecutor negotiated a plea agreement while Francine sat waiting to testify in the preliminary hearing. Technically, she kept her agreement—the defendant was required to plead guilty to all charges. However, the charges on the criminal complaint that had been filed were minimal, following customary practice of the Urban County sexual assault unit. They captured the fact of sexual penetration, but little else. Had Francine testified in court that afternoon, it is likely that more charges could have been added, increasing the defendant's potential sentence.

Francine commented on the inadequacy of an organizational policy that kept cases moving along through the system by rewarding defendants for making early pleas to minimal charges. She accepted that prosecutors had a right to negotiate pleas, but she believed that pleas could never adequately capture a rape survivor's reality of victimization when the threshold was set low at the beginning.

> I think the way [Urban] County charges is wrong. Um, yeah, the fact that what I was told right from the beginning [...] what he had been charged with was forcible rape and I said, "Wait a minute, how about assault and battery with a deadly weapon, how about kidnapping, how about false imprisonment, how about attempted murder?" You know, how about all the rest of this? Um, and I was given several different explanations. One was, [...] "We charge with our strongest charge. And then as the process goes on after prelim we will add other charges," after the evidence has been brought out in court to show that these other things took place. [...] I think it's a backwards system because what happened in my case when they realized that they were in a no-win situation, the defense decided to plead guilty. It was too late to do anything, it was too late to get those other charges added on now, even for the sake of plea-bargaining. In my opinion, he should have been charged with everything, up front in the beginning.

Theresa and Sara both discussed plea offers with prosecutors before an agreement was finalized with the defendant, but they were deeply dissatisfied with the plea process. They did not believe that the plea terms described by prosecutors served their interests, and they did not feel that their desires to go forward to trial were heard, let alone acknowledged. Like Carmela, quoted earlier, they believed the outcome of their conversation with prosecutors was predetermined before it began, because they felt that prosecutors initiated conversations about pleas only to secure an endorsement for a decision that had already been made. Prosecutors appeared to initiate the conversations to persuade the survivors to change their own view of the case, but they were not open to being persuaded. Not only did these survivors view such conversations about pleas as manipulative, they also were disturbed because the interactions mirrored in uncomfortable ways the experience of being overpowered that they associated with rape. In the end, the prosecutor was able to make her or his own reality the legal reality, no matter how much the survivor objected.

I first interviewed Theresa shortly after she testified at the preliminary hearing. At the time, she had contributed to the investigation and had done a great deal of self-preparation for court, because she was concerned that legal personnel might fail to follow through with the case. The prosecutor had said she would contact Theresa if the defendant decided to plead guilty to the single standing felony charge—forced oral copulation—filed on the basis of the police report, rather than the four charges that could be filed for trial based on Theresa's preliminary testimony. Theresa desired to go to trial and felt certain that her assailant would be found guilty.

> *Theresa:* I would like to see it go to trial. I would like to see it go to trial and him found guilty on all four charges. [...] He's so arrogant. And it's like, he needs to ... to be responsible for what he did, and the only way he's going to be responsible is to have to face up to the charges and stuff. [...] I don't know, maybe it's revenge, I don't think so, but it's just that it would be the just thing to have happen, it would be the right thing. [...]
>
> *Amanda:* Do you expect to be consulted if there is a plea-bargain?
>
> *Theresa:* Yes, she told me she would definitely consult me first. She would not do anything without consulting me. [...] Somebody asked me the other night if uh, what I thought was gonna happen, and I said I have no doubts: he goes to trial, he'll be found guilty. I really have no doubts now.

Several weeks later, Theresa called to tell me that the prosecutor had sent her the preliminary hearing transcripts to review and asked her to come in for a meeting. During the meeting, she informed Theresa that the case was weak and she intended to offer the defendant the opportunity to plead to a misdemeanor sexual battery charge. Theresa was confused and upset at the unexpected turn of events.

> She called me on Tuesday and told me she was going to send me my statements. She wanted me to read them and call her back. We set up an appointment. When I got there, she wanted me to see if I could identify the problems. I said I couldn't see any, and the statement was just like the police report. She said that I didn't say "no" enough. She said that I said "no" four times, at the theater, at my house, but I didn't actually say "no" or put up a struggle after he got on top of me. [...] I don't know how juries work. I don't know how they could hear it and not feel that way [like he is guilty]. [...] What difference will it make if nothing is done, even though I am believable! I've never stuck up for myself before. [...] I have to do this in order to hold my head up! I have to say you can't do this to me. [...] I feel like she took me around in circles. She was worried about making me feel like she didn't believe me, but she was trying to win the case. She couldn't

explain it so that I could get it. I went out of there really confused. By the time I got home half an hour later I had the start of a migraine.

The prosecutor had told Theresa that her preliminary hearing testimony was valuable, because it allowed the addition of four charges. Now the prosecutor discounted her testimony through the application of stereotypical expectations that real victims of rape resist physically. Theresa could not make sense of the prosecutor's characterization of the flaws of the case.

> I don't see how she can go from four charges, that she said that she could take to trial, to *misdemeanor* sexual battery. [. . .] She said that if he is tried for felony sexual assault a judge would probably drop it to a misdemeanor because he had no priors. She said that if he doesn't accept this, she has to decide whether she is going to take it to trial or drop it altogether.

In short, by offering the defendant the opportunity to plead to a misdemeanor, the prosecutor gave him a huge benefit. In comparison, she was curtailing Theresa's effort to stick up for herself and offering her no compensation for the time and emotional energy she had put into prosecution. Theresa felt, "ripped off. I didn't have to do all this, I might as well have not done it." Theresa was deeply troubled that the prosecutor could not explain the logic of the plea offer in a way that she could understand it, yet seemed to want her to endorse it anyway.

Theresa's investment in the criminal justice process was an enactment of her own moral worth. From the beginning of the investigation through her precourt preparation and testimony, she sought to counter blame that she perceived in others and held against herself. To grasp the logic of the prosecutor's decision would have required her to see herself negatively, as the prosecutor believed jurors would see her. Theresa's discomfort stemmed from trying to reconcile the prosecutor's attempts to make her feel believed with an endorsement of an action (the plea-bargain) that was inconsistent with her construction of self. Ultimately, this was not something that Theresa could do.

When Sara appeared at the courthouse to testify, the prosecutor proposed allowing the defendant to plead guilty to sexual battery. This did not sit well with Sara, who was deeply invested in creating a public record of her reality of victimization—the fact that her assailant forcibly raped her. She rejected the idea of reducing the charges and stated her preference for a trial.

> What was most important to me wasn't the amount of time that he served as much as it was for him to stand up in court and say, "I raped her, I did this to her." So I was willing to go through the whole thing, just to have him say that and just to have it on record. [. . .] He was going to plead to that [sexual battery], which means that he touched me in a sexual way without my permission, but that does not mean rape.

But when she objected to the prosecutor's plan, he and the victim advocate began to "work on" her and listed reason after reason for Sara to forgo a trial in favor of a plea.

> I held out and held out [...] and they kept [...] saying, "The judge wants a decision now, the judge wants a decision now." [...] I think I did feel that I *had* made a decision, that was my initial response and I think that that was the response that should have been accepted. But [...] the victim advocate, and the prosecutor just kept, kept it up. It's like look, you know, we're gonna play devil's advocate, and this went on from like, you know, like 9:00 in the morning until about 4:00 in the afternoon. [...] As far as I'm concerned you know, I was willing to take the stand and to go through with this, but I really felt that you know, I was all alone. [...] They kept saying, "Why do you want to put yourself and your family through this? Once you get on the stand of course, you're not gonna be the victim anymore." Then they started talking about the public defender. [...] He had a very, very abrasive style, and was a screamer, and would just rip me to shreds if they got me on the stand. Still, I felt that I could deal with it, and that I was willing to go through it.

Ultimately, over six hours later, when the prosecutor repeatedly emphasized the racial dimensions of the case, Sara relented.

> *Sara:* I think what finally changed my mind was the fact that because it was a black-white issue, and this county is predominantly blue collar um, white. They told me that I [a white woman] was running the risk of going in and going through the whole procedure of a trial and having them still let him go. And if the jury said that he was innocent, then he wouldn't serve a day, and it would be just saying that it was okay. [...]
> *Amanda:* Can you explain how a little bit more ... ?
> *Sara:* Um, the man that I had been involved with for a long time was black, [...] the person that raped me was black, and the man I was living with was black, so how does that look to a middle-class, middle-aged white man from this county? Would he be like, "Hey, this [white] woman deserves this"? [...] So um, I held out until about 4:00, and finally ... they said, "If he agrees to this, if you agree to this, we know for sure that he's gonna get a minimum of two years. And if it doesn't matter to you how much time he serves, then go for this. [...] It's gonna go on his record forever, so just do it." And so I finally said, "Okay, I'll do it." [...] I felt that I was being badgered to um, do it their way, not do what I felt was best, and I really regret it.

The offer was extended, accepted, and the guilty plea was entered before Sara left the building.

The interaction that Sara described occurring between herself and the prosecutor and victim advocate was not a two-way debate about the merits of alternative approaches to the case. She was alone on the defensive being pressured to realign her desire to confront the defendant and her reality of victimization with the prosecutor's desire to secure a certain two-year term. The victim advocate was her adversary here, not her ally. Sara's statement that she was being "badgered" underscores that she was worn down over time rather than persuaded to see the situation through the eyes of the prosecutor and victim advocate. Sara entered the criminal justice process so that she could stand up to an individual who took advantage of his physical access to her. She wanted his sexual violence labeled as wrong. "Winning" by achieving some confirmed minimum term was not reconcilable with this. It was the fear of a "complete loss" that led to Sara's acquiescence.

Had the defendant acknowledged his guilt to the downgraded charge with contrition—enacting his moral failure—Sara might have seen herself as prevailing. But he presented a positive front in court, turning around and smiling and smirking at her, which represented to her the success of his reality claims over hers. His enactment of ease in court was the antithesis of her own inability to stand firm and adequately resist the prosecutor and advocate—the essence of being raped.

In sum, Theresa and Sara felt that the discussions they had with prosecutors were merely for show. They were involved in plea discussions that could serve only to vindicate a position previously taken by the prosecutor. Thus, in spite of their apparent participation, the ownership these women had in the cases was denied.

Maria's dissatisfaction with the prosecutor's handling of the plea is counterintuitive, but follows from the same kind of mismatch between expectations that I just described. Her assailant was her spouse, and she came to understand that he committed "rape" as a result of police labeling her description of his behavior toward her. Because of her feelings of responsibility for her spouse and fear of his retaliation, she was ambivalent about prosecution, and she sought to keep her distance from the legal process when the prosecutor filed charges. The prosecutor held the preliminary hearing without her, using a police officer to testify about her victimization, as allowed by California law. Maria accepted a plea as a reasonable course of action to avoid testifying in the future, and she accepted the prosecutor's right to negotiate the terms. However, when the penalty was reduced because sentences for multiple charges were allowed to run concurrently, and the defendant was given credit for time already served, Maria expressed her disappointment to the prosecutor. She believed that her husband's short imprisonment would not be a deterrent and that he would come after her when he was released. Yet what made Maria *most* angry was the prosecutor's implication that her absence from the sentencing hearing, which followed the plea negotiation, was the cause of the meager term.

> He was like telling me off, like, with this um, holier-than-thou attitude, raising his voice, like he was upset with me because . . . "I told you to be there at the sentencing, that that was gonna affect the judge's ruling." Made me totally feel like

shit, you know? [...] But it's like the DA just made me feel like it was all my fault. I really got upset, because they're the one who pressed charges against him. [...] They took the responsibility of pressing charges against him, they should go follow through with it and not pressure me. [...] He [the prosecutor] wasn't taking into consideration that this was my husband, the only man I ever had sexual contact with ever, you know, that I felt obligated to be loyal to this man in spite of everything he did with ... did to me ... you know.

Maria rejected the prosecutor's assertion that she should have taken a greater role in the prosecution and grounded her reluctance in the nature of her relationship with the rapist. She argued that the prosecutor was hypocritical to hold her up to a standard of participation at sentencing that was inconsistent with her lack of involvement throughout the process—one he had tacitly accepted.

Conclusions and Questions for Further Consideration

I found that how frequently prosecutors consulted survivors varied by victim-assailant relationship and degree of charge reduction. Prosecutors contacted a much larger proportion of the women attacked by men they knew than those attacked by strangers before completing plea deals. They also contacted more survivors before they substantially reduced charges—from felony sexual assault to misdemeanors or nonsexual charges—than when they made small reductions.

During the investigative phase, I found that prosecutors infrequently had face-to-face contact with survivors before charges were filed, and initiated telephone contact only slightly more often. The minority of prosecutors met women before their first court appearances. Given this lack of contact, few gained firsthand knowledge of survivors' investment in prosecution and development of case ownership. These prosecutors who had no awareness of women's investments would see no reason to involve them in plea negotiations. In contrast, when defendants indicated a willingness to plead guilty at the onset of court events, survivors were physically present and could not be ignored. At the very least, prosecutors had to explain why survivors were not being called to testify or why jury selection was not proceeding. I found that when plea negotiations commenced at court, prosecutors engaged all the affected women in some sort of discussion about the terms of the plea before it was finalized.

Prosecutors negotiated more pleas with stranger defendants before probable cause hearings. I believe that prosecutors failed to seek the involvement of many of the women these strangers raped, because the women had not initiated contact or demonstrated an undeniable investment in the case.

When survivors participated in court events, prosecutors were exposed to their investment in and commitment to the case and to some of their desired outcomes. However, when plea negotiations commenced or continued in the period between probable cause hearings and trials, survivors were not physically present, and prosecutors were free to ignore them as they pressed forward to resolve cases. Prosecutors who consulted with women after probable cause hearings did so because they already had a well-established rapport with them, the woman persistently maintained contact, or the prosecutor interpreted victim-witness statutes to require such consultations.

It seems likely that prosecutors who were on the cusp of securing pleas of guilt to felony charges of sexual assault and mid- to high-range prison terms considered these outcomes as successful and assumed that rape survivors would share this view. In particular, this assumption seems likely when they had not met the survivor. It also seems likely that most prosecutors considered the possibility that downgrading felony charges to misdemeanors or nonsexual charges was a possible affront to survivors and a source of anger or other bad feelings. If so, prosecutors may have hoped that they could mitigate expected negativity by leading survivors to see the plea as a benefit. Research on prosecutors' behavior in intake interviews suggests this is likely.[6] The narratives of a number of survivors whose cases were substantially downgraded—Carmela, Sara, and Theresa—indicate that this was the form their plea consultations took. Prosecutors used the time to persuade them to adopt the view that a particular plea agreement was necessary and valuable, a better alternative to a trial or possible dismissal.

Rape survivor satisfaction with pleas reflected their responses to the charges and sanctions that were formalized and the nature of consultation, as well as the way in which the plea fit in with their desires to use the criminal justice process to confront the defendant. Survivors' concerns with the plea terms were focused on the adequacy of penalties—were they fair—and on whether the charges conveyed their experience of the rape event. Consultation was not expected or desired by all women, but it was a particular source of dissatisfaction when it was expected and absent or when it took a form that they found manipulative. The same factors that limited women's interest in investigation at the time of reporting—fear of the defendant and relationship-related concerns—depressed their interest in being involved in plea negotiations. Women who had contact with legal personnel during the investigative phase and established rapport or prepared for and participated in court events were most interested in shaping the outcome of cases.

Most survivors whose cases were tried after victim's rights legislation passed, did receive some official state literature intended for victim-witnesses from police, rape crisis advocates, or victim-witness advocates. However, their use of it was varied, and the literature was vague about the weight of victims' opinions.

Like their coverage of the investigative phase, visual and print media generally neglect crime victims' involvement in the plea process. Thus, survivors did not have a readily available cultural template to guide their self-presentations through the resolution of these cases. Even though some described prior legal experiences with the criminal justice process, they reported little familiarity with this aspect of it.

No women reported anticipating the eventuality of a plea and probing either their legal contacts or prosecutors for information about the way it would unfold or what their possible role might be. When prosecutors contacted survivors by telephone to discuss pleas, the women rarely had their support teams assembled. Prosecutors frequently conducted the conversations about pleas in private witness waiting rooms in courthouses. Supporters not officially recognized as rape crisis or victim-witness advocates were rarely invited into these locations.[7] When prosecutors sought women's immediate responses to terms, they had to rely on the guidance of those who were physically present. Thus, friends and family with legal knowledge and experience, who may have shaped survivors' participation in investigation and their preparation for court, were unlikely to contribute to these interactions.

Notably, victim-witness advocates, who were present when prosecutors initiated discussion of pleas, did not reliably help survivors present their viewpoint to prosecutors. Sara reported her advocate openly siding with the prosecutor, and Carmela said that hers was unhelpful. Advocates who align themselves with prosecutors are not likely to find survivors' desires to pursue a case so that they can confront a defendant or to "take a chance" to be worthy positions to defend.[8] Even independent advocates must maintain good relations with prosecutors to keep avenues of information open, and it is probable that they believe that their support for a woman's contrary views— of either the necessity or substance of the plea—would be interpreted as a violation of work relations.

The absence of emotional support from others in a context in which the prosecutor sought to alter their view no doubt contributed to women's discomfort. When pressure to adopt a perspective that a negotiated resolution was necessary and valuable was coupled with plea terms that significantly undermined their claims of injury, the interaction was fundamentally problematic. It strongly resembled the rape dynamic described by Winkler, wherein the perpetrator imposes his meaning on his victim.[9] Hence, as with their failure to prepare rape survivors for court and as suggested by Madigan and Gamble, well-intentioned prosecutors inadvertently became the means through which the rape survivors experienced re-victimization.[10]

I did not find that rape survivors' social class, as measured by education or employment, was predictive of satisfaction or interest in involvement in pleas. However, I believe prosecutors extended their tendency to exclude minors from discussions to this aspect of the case.

The data are insufficient to assess systematically how rape survivors' conversations with prosecutors shaped the charges and sentences defendants were offered in exchange for pleas of guilt. In a number of cases involving assailants who were past or present intimates, it appears that survivors' stated willingness to testify at preliminary hearings prolonged the time the cases remained in the process. However, I did not find evidence that testifying affected sanctions in any patterned way. Only in Rachel's case were the plea terms achieved after the preliminary hearing less beneficial to the defendant than those presented before it.

When women victimized by men with whom they had been intimate were aggressive about their desire to testify at preliminary hearings, I believe that prosecutors recognized the content of the testimony might give them greater leverage in future negotiations. Prosecutors, who normatively did little to prepare survivor-witnesses for these preliminary hearings, expended little effort for the potential benefit, enabling them to defer negotiations and let the preliminary hearing play out. Rape survivors' offers to testify at trials when they were dissatisfied with plea terms did not offer a comparable gain to prosecutors. Trials presented more work and more uncertainty, while a guilty plea allowed them to dispose of a case and claim a win. It follows logically that survivors who were presented with plea initiatives at or after the preliminary hearings were completely unable to persuade prosecutors to take the cases to trial.

Did participating in the plea process as a result of prosecutorial consultation increase feelings of capability in survivors? For those for whom plea terms were satisfactory and who achieved desired nonlegal outcomes, participation was positive. Those who attempted to reorient prosecutors to their needs but were unable to do so found participation troubling at best and degrading at worst. Those who were the targets of prosecutors' reorientation efforts reported feeling confused, frustrated, angry, depressed, and abused. In short, they felt re-victimized.

After a defendant's guilt is resolved by plea or trial, cases move to sentencing. Probation officers conduct sentencing investigations and issue reports, prosecutors prepare requests, and defendants eventually appear before judges who formalize sentences.

- Once court events in the guilt phase are over and rape survivors' official witness duties are complete, how do they view the rape, the defendant, and themselves?
- Do women whose claims are vindicated through findings or pleas of guilt consider the dispute resolved and their task complete?
- Alternatively, do they have unfulfilled needs and seek further engagement with the criminal justice process?

Most states offer crime victims venues to present their opinions to the court after adjudication is complete. It is possible that involvement at this stage offers rape survivors an opportunity to compensate for the problems they experienced during the process. In the next chapter, I will explore how rape survivors, with the aid of others, evaluate and use the opportunity to be involved in sentencing.

CHAPTER 9

"Having the Last Word": Rape Survivors' Participation in Sentencing

A defendant's guilt may be established through his plea or through a jury's or judge's assessment of evidence. In either case, a judge later conveys the convict's sentence at a formal sentencing hearing. The particulars of sentences have long been guided by state statutes, probation reports, a judge's personal response to crime, and, if relevant, plea agreements. Under relatively recent crime victims' rights (CVR) legislation, rape survivors in many states may also participate in the sentencing process. Most CVR statutes allow them to submit a written statement about the impact of the crime to the sentencing judge, to attend the sentencing hearing, or to make a statement at the sentencing hearing. Survivors in this study described participating in sentencing in a variety of ways and for a variety of reasons.

Gwendolyn, whose assailant pled guilty before the preliminary hearing, wrote a three-page letter to urge the sentencing judge to assign a stiff penalty:

> I didn't want him to get anybody else, and do it to them what he did to me. That was what caused so much rage [in me], not just the injustice that he was still out there, but what he's gonna do to other people.

Francine, whose rapist pled guilty while she waited to testify in the preliminary hearing, returned to speak at his sentencing hearing: "Um, I wanted it [my story] on the record, which I didn't have the opportunity to do."

Arlene wrote the sentencing judge about the emotional impact of the rape after she testified at trial:

> I wrote a very intense letter, I filled it full of as much of my emotional experience as I could possibly dredge up, it was like four pages, typed, it was a very emotional letter ... I was very clear at that point that I would never be the same, and I wanted to be damn sure the judge knew it, and I worked on it really hard, it was an ... another kind of way to purging.

After testifying at trial, Barbara attended the sentencing hearing to speak *to* the stranger who attacked her.

Um, at the time I felt like I wanted to confront him, that I wanted the last word with this guy, and he was sitting in the courtroom, and that's what I wanted, I wanted the chance, even though I was addressing the court, I wanted him to see that um, he couldn't intimidate me. I mean he had intimidated me but that he wasn't getting the last word, I wanted the last word. [...] I knew he was a captive audience, kind of like I had been a captive audience.

As these quotations suggest, participating in sentencing may fulfill needs that participation in the witness role does not or cannot. The opportunity to weigh in without the prospect of being challenged or to confront the defendant directly may offer balance to individuals who have held a responsive, and relatively powerless, legal role. In short, it is possible that participation in sentencing can offset earlier negative experiences. This chapter describes how and when participating in sentencing serves the needs of rape survivors.

Three types of participation are included in this analysis: writing to the court (submitting a completed "victim impact form" or a self-composed letter), speaking in the courtroom (with comments directed to the judge or the defendant), and observing in court. While "observation" has not been examined as a form of participation by other researchers, it must be documented. A rape survivor who goes to a sentencing hearing, even if only to observe, makes an active decision to be a part of the criminal justice process when it is not required. To limit analysis to what we objectively view as having a potential impact on judges' decisions (letters, speaking) prematurely curtails exploration of rape survivors' reality of sentencing.

Motivations to Participate

Influencing the Outcome of Sentencing: Seeking Substantive Justice

Fifty-two percent of the survivors said they intended through their action—speaking or writing the court—to influence the judge to sentence the defendant in a particular way. Women gave three distinct reasons for wanting to influence his sentence. The vast majority sought retribution. They believed their experience of rape was not a trivial matter and wanted to make the rapist pay dearly for injuring them. They asked the judge to impose lengthy periods of incarceration in the most restrictive conditions.

For example, Candace wrote the judge and asked him to "impose the maximum possible sentence" on the stranger who raped her. To support this request, she encouraged him to look at photos of her battered face in the evidence file and emphasized that her attacker would receive a severe sentence in her native country. Barbara, whose assailant negotiated a plea to reduced charges, wanted to make his prison time as uncomfortable as possible and asked the judge to place him in a maximum-security prison.[1]

Eight women were deeply concerned about keeping the man who raped them from raping again. They perceived him to be a general menace and, thus, favored a long period of incarceration to restrict his access to potential victims. In the first opening quotation, Gwendolyn explained that she wrote the court seeking a prison sentence to keep the stranger who raped her from attacking others. Jennifer also took part in sentencing for this reason. She wrote the judge a letter about the impact of the crime and attended sentencing to read it aloud, to achieve her goal:

> I wanted to have the maximum so he couldn't get out and do it to someone else, 'cause he'd already done it. [...] I wanted to let the judge know—he's still the same judge who heard the case—but I wanted to refresh his memory, 'cause it had been months since the trial, and it's not just paperwork anymore, it's actual people.

Mary and Gabriella believed that psychological problems drove the men who attacked them to commit rape and were concerned about their eventual release from prison. To ensure that these men were rehabilitated, they wrote letters and attended the sentencing hearing to ask the sentencing judge to mandate mental health treatment as a condition of incarceration. Mary, emphasized that she did not want to speak publicly in court, but felt that she had to do so to ensure an appropriate sentence. She told the judge, "This man is a sick man and he needs help, therapeutic help, as far as I'm concerned."

In sum, survivors' accounts of their efforts to secure specific sentences reflected philosophies of retribution, deterrence, and rehabilitation found among members of the general population.

Engaging the Criminal Justice Process: Seeking Procedural Justice

The explanations of more than two-thirds of the survivors highlighted their attempts to assert ownership of the injury that criminal justice personnel had appropriated in the name of the state. Eleven of the 17 women in this group (65 percent) explained that, in the absence of a previous opportunity, they wanted to put *their* reality of the rape experience into the official record. Typically, under the controlled circumstances of probable cause hearings and trials, survivors experienced limits on how they discussed their feelings about and experience of the rape. This was due to the question-and-answer framework of direct and cross-examination, the defense attorney's efforts to make answering difficult, and their own efforts to follow prosecutors' directives. The sentencing hearing provided many of them with the chance finally to describe "what happened" in their own way. Other women had no opportunity to publicly testify prior to sentencing, because defendants entered pleas of guilt before evidentiary hearings. This was the situation for Wanda, Marlene, and Francine.

Wanda's desire to tell her story led her back to court after she strongly supported the prosecutor's decision to offer the defendant a 30-year prison term in exchange for a guilty plea:

> The plea-bargain was, on one hand, just an elation, and on the other was a real disappointment. [...] That's why I spoke at sentencing. You know, all through the whole thing I wanted to say my piece. That's why I wanted to go to court.

Francine had suffered a savage beating after the rape, and the plea agreement did not reflect what she felt was a clear attempt to take her life. I provided a brief quotation from her at the opening of this chapter. Below is the longer explanation for her need to return to speak at the sentencing hearing and put her story "on the record."

> When ... when you go through the court system even I think if you get to testify, which I didn't have the opportunity to do, it's under very controlled circumstances and what you say and what you don't say is very closely controlled, and there is objections made if you open your mouth and try to say how you feel. I think it's very important for the victim to have a chance to say, hey, this is how I feel about this, and this is my beliefs about this. [...] Because we're the real people, and what we want is what's important. What affects us, how we feel is what is important, and you have to take that into consideration. [...] In my case, being as I didn't have the opportunity, it was very important to me to have, on some sort of written record, in the court transcripts, what happened that night. I wanted to take everyone in that courtroom to that place, and let them see what happened that night. And get it on the record.

Without consulting Marlene, the prosecutor downgraded charges against her ex-boyfriend to a nonsexual misdemeanor: burglary. She was astonished and dismayed and wrote to the sentencing judge to convey to him that her assailant *had* inflicted a personal injury, which was not captured when his behavior was categorized as a property crime: "I said that he had broken into my apartment. He didn't take any physical thing in my apartment, but he did take part of me, that he raped me."

In spite of prosecutors' imposition of narrow legal categories on the rape event, survivors such as Francine and Marlene had a strong sense of ownership of their own victimization and resisted letting the labels stand unchallenged. They asserted their rights to participate in the sentencing process to remind the judge that "real people" were the impetus for legal cases. While Francine verbalized her belief that the defendant was in fact trying to kill her and Marlene wrote the judge to emphasize her personal injury, not everyone who felt a strong personal stake in the legal case had the fortitude to or was interested in communicating their views to others.

Three women simply attended the sentencing hearing to claim their status as crime victims publicly. Monica's feeling that the state's case truly belonged to her was the sole reason she returned to the court for sentencing. When I asked how she decided to attend she replied: "It wasn't really a decision, I didn't really think anything other than going there, you know, I knew I'd go. Because as I said, I felt it was me against him, not the state."

Survivors' use of the sentencing process to assert a sense of ownership was not tied to a pattern of assertive or confrontational behavior with legal personnel. While Francine actively brought her concerns to the attention of legal personnel during the investigative phase and attended the defendant's arraignment in order to confront him, Monica did not initiate contact during the investigative phase and passively handled disturbing interaction problems with the defense attorney in the preliminary hearing through accommodation.

Five other women who felt a strong sense of ownership attended the sentencing hearing to confirm that their attacker was appropriately processed. They did not feel capable of shaping the outcome or even desirous to do so and talked generally about wanting to see the wheels of justice turn through their final phase, to literally "see justice served." For example, Twyla felt no control over the negotiated resolution of the guilt phase of the case and explained that she went to the sentencing hearing to "make sure that something was being done—that an appropriate sentence was gonna be handed down." In this case, the prosecutor had secured a plea agreement from the stranger who raped her without soliciting Twyla's input, and her assessment of her lack of control over the length of the sentence was accurate.

In sum, more than two-thirds of the survivors had procedural justice concerns. Some were focused on the sentencing event to challenge the responsive role that they held earlier in the process and the resulting lack of attention given to their reality. Others adopted a monitoring role. Although it was passive, it implied the possibility of action, if the survivor perceived that legal procedures were not appropriately followed.

Altering the Balance of Social Power Established through Victimization

Rape is an act of dis-empowerment during which women are at the mercy of their assailant. Whether or not a rapist extends his physical assault beyond sexual violation, sexual assault victims often fear death.[2] When women perceive that criminal justice personnel cater to the rapist's needs by allowing him out of jail on bond, granting him continuances, or meeting his request for a charge or sentence reduction, their feelings of loss of control are intensified.

Twenty-eight percent of survivors explained that they approached the sentencing hearing as an opportunity to eliminate the imbalance of power they felt with the defendant or reduce their fear of him. In the third opening quotation, Barbara, who was raped by a stranger and had difficulty controlling her emotions at trial, explained that part of her motivation to speak at the sentencing hearing was consciously to present an empowered self in his presence.

While Barbara acknowledged that her official audience was technically the judge, she emphasized that her *intended* audience was the defendant. Influencing the length of the defendant's sentence was clearly not her only or even primary goal. She "wanted the last word" and "wanted him to see that um, he couldn't intimidate me."

Mimi gave a deposition but opted not to testify at a preliminary hearing, and she still hesitated to speak in front of the stranger who raped her. However, she attended the sentencing hearing so that she could assert her emergent personal strength relative to him: "I think I got enough courage that I could be in the courtroom with him, but I didn't get up on the stand."

Elisa, who was badly beaten by a home invader and delayed reporting because of fear, was persuaded to attend sentencing by her brother. She had not initiated contact with prosecutors during the investigation and was pleased that they resolved the defendant's guilt without requiring her to testify. While she admitted that her brother's encouragement was her primary impetus to attend, she specifically noted how she wanted the rapist to interpret his presence: "[M]y brother is kind of a big guy, and I thought if he [the defendant] sees that somebody cares ... maybe he won't come back and get me." As she reflected back on her experience after the sentencing hearing, Elisa reiterated her desire to present herself as powerful to her assailant: "Afterwards I was glad I went [...] Like I said, maybe to show him that I'm not as afraid of him as I was. But I was afraid of him, but my being there made me let him think that I wasn't afraid of him."

Two other women who were not comfortable speaking explained that they benefited from seeing their attackers in handcuffs and leg chains. So shackled, the convicts were clearly unable to hurt them further. Trudy, had been involved in apprehending the stranger who raped her and had testified at his preliminary hearing. However, she was fearful that he would retaliate for her part in prosecution. This fear of the consequences of drawing attention to herself kept her from making an oral impact statement—"a ruckus"—at the sentencing hearing; however, she did attend to see her assailant under physical control. She bluntly explained: "I needed to see him [the defendant] hauled off in chains, and um, that's why I went." Natalie likewise emphasized the importance of seeing her assailant in restraints and a convict's clothes, which underscored his fall in social status: "He walked into the courtroom in shackles and a prison uniform and he looked like this is what he deserved [...] because at trial he was in, you know, slacks and a shirt."

A further aspect of women's dis-empowerment through rape is the rapist's denial of their victimization. Rapists often assert during assaults that victims enjoy the forced sexual contact and, then, further deny that their actions were abusive by pleading not guilty to rape charges or admitting guilt only to charges other than rape. For survivors who are not burdened by great fear of their assailant and feel comfortable speaking in public about the specifics of the assault and its effects on them, this denial by the rapist can be a call to action. In the context of the sentencing hearing, which offers no space for a rebuttal by the defendant, the survivor literally has the last word about what transpired between them. For Julianne, the sentencing hearing was a crucial part of the process because she saw it as an opportunity to confront and question the boyfriend who professed his love and then raped her. She felt that he owed her an explanation for his conduct.

> There was NO question I was going to do it [go to sentencing], that I wanted to do it because I felt like I had to see if from point A all the way to point B, and there was no in-between. It was almost my biggest thing. I was going through counseling through all of this, that I had gotten through Victim-Witness [Assistance], which I thank God for. My biggest thing was I needed closure, so there was no question about me going to the sentencing at all. Never in my mind did I question that. [. . .] I said that I wanted to request an opportunity to talk to [the defendant], I felt like I was owed that. I had the right to have him answer a question.

When Julianne spoke at the sentencing hearing, she requested an explanation from the rapist. Surprisingly, he admitted harming her and apologized. Julianne counts this among her successes.

Resolving the Emotional Aspects of Rape

Twenty-four percent of the survivors reported using the sentencing hearing to help them resolve self-doubt, purge their strong emotions, and bring their lengthy emotional ordeal of prosecution to an end. While Francine sought substantive and procedural justice through her oral communication to the judge, another aspect of attending sentencing was putting to rest any doubts she had about the seriousness of the rape and the attention she had devoted to the prosecution.

> Um, I think for a long time right up until the day when I made my statement, I felt that I kept having this irrational feeling that maybe I was blowing it out of proportion. That maybe it wasn't really that serious. Maybe he wouldn't have killed me. Maybe, maybe, maybe, maybe. [. . .] What resolved all that was when I locked eyes on him in there, and saw the absolute rage, that hatred on his face. And it was like; it really was that, wasn't it? I'm not imagining this; I'm not blowing this out of proportion. You really were going to kill me, weren't you?

Arlene testified at the preliminary hearing and actively managed her emotions during cross-examination, then exercised her right to participate in the sentencing process to diminish the intensity of the feelings that remained. She used her written victim impact statement as an opportunity to vent her hurt and anger. Arlene achieved her emotional catharsis by being involved in the sentencing process, but she accomplished this particular goal in part before the sentencing hearing actually took place.

Successive court dates, brought about by unpredictable continuances granted to the defendant, required women to revisit their memories of the assault repeatedly. Thus, it is not surprising that many described their involvement with the criminal justice process as endless and emotionally taxing, and many said that the sentencing hearing was an important symbolic end point. They decided to attend in whole, or in part, because they needed an official way to put their role in the prosecution behind them. This accomplished, they could make their emotional recovery from the assault their primary concern. Jennifer compared being in court for sentencing to "finally closing the door on it [the assault]." Francine likened her participation in the sentencing hearing to reading "the last page of this book" and explained that after speaking to the court she would "close the back cover and put it on the shelf." Julianne's search for emotional closure also comes through strongly in the quotation above.

The Logic of Survivor Involvement in Sentencing

A case-by-case examination of each survivor's involvement in sentencing suggests that the variability in participation is due to the intersection of three factors. First, women perceived their ability to meet their needs through the criminal justice process in different ways. Involvement in particular activities—speaking, writing, or attending—reflected the belief that involvement in sentencing could be *and* was necessary to deliver outcomes they desired. Non-involvement reflected both perceptions that particular goals could not be met through the sentencing process *and* the earlier fulfillment of outcomes they desired. Second, separate from their motivation to use sentencing as an opportunity to heal themselves, survivors differed in their ability to integrate their involvement in the criminal justice process into their emotional healing from the rape. Third, different amounts of external support were available to women who wished to continue to participate in the criminal justice process.[3]

In the remainder of this section, I will show these factors in play using the accounts of 17 women who chose to involve themselves *selectively* in sentencing or *not at all*. Six who knew of their right to participate did not do so at all; 11 others chose to only write letters or to attend sentencing hearings but to avoid speaking.

The Achievability of Desired Legal Outcomes

Some women limited their participation in sentencing because they believed that the time available for oral input—the sentencing hearing—followed critical decisions about charges or the length of the defendant's sentence. These women perceived the personal cost of participation to far outweigh the possibility that they might sway a judge to change his or her mind or to overrule a negotiated settlement.

Anna chose not to attend the hearing or write the judge because these acts would not alter the terms set forth in the plea agreement. In short, her participation in sentencing could not change the substance of the justice process:

> Someone called me. [. . .] She said you have the right to be there, you have the right to say something to the judge, or to write something. And I said, you know, this is my feeling at the time, I may have that right but what good is it going to do? Is he [the judge] going to reverse his [the prosecutor's] decision? Is he [the judge] going to give him [the defendant] some more jail time? Is he [the judge] going to give me back my life? No, no, no, and no. So what good is it going to do? And I said you can tell the judge for me, these were my exact words, I remember this, "it's like he [the prosecutor] just raped me all over again. I just got raped by the system and I got raped by him [the defendant]."

Anna's unwillingness to extend her involvement with the justice system through the sentencing process stands in contrast to the multiple times she took time off from work to appear in court for the rescheduled preliminary hearing.

Other survivors chose to attend sentencing hearings but not to exercise their right to speak there, because their desires were unachievable and expressing them in the courtroom would be pointless. Marlene, who worked hard in the investigative phase to offset blame for the attack, is one such survivor. As discussed above, she wrote a letter to the judge to put the reality of her injury on record. However, she declined to speak at sentencing, because the prosecutor had negotiated a settlement without consulting her and substantially downgraded the sexual assault charges to misdemeanor burglary. Marlene believed that publicly claiming the status of rape victim was risky, because the hearing was not designed to affirm her reality.

> Well, because that's not what this [the sentencing hearing] is for, you know. I mean, I wanna testify to that fact [rape]. I don't wanna testify if it's not gonna be for rape, but [. . .] it's a plea-bargain for burglary and robbery [and] trespassing. What would be the sense of getting up there and humiliating myself about the rape when that really doesn't matter and they probably wouldn't want to hear about it anyway?

Given the specifics of the plea-bargain, the injury that was of personal concern to Marlene was erased; publicly announcing it would only draw attention to the fact that prosecutors did not believe her account of events.

In contrast to Anna and Marlene, four other women elected not to speak at or attend sentencing hearings because the legal outcome they desired had already been achieved. Either an acceptable punishment had been established through a plea-bargain or else an appropriate sentence seemed likely following a guilty jury verdict. In their estimation, their additional oral input was not necessary.

Integrating Participation into Emotional Recovery

A desire to use the criminal justice process as a means to work out feelings of guilt, to purge emotions, and to find closure did not always result in involvement in sentencing. Some who achieved these outcomes early in the process, primarily through testifying in preliminary hearings and trials, lacked the incentive to participate in sentencing. Others found the prospect of participating in sentencing too daunting in spite of its desirability.

Cindy had come to terms with her feelings of anger toward her assailant by confronting him from the witness stand at trial. Given that she had agreed to the plea agreement (achieving substantive justice), she explained that speaking at sentencing would have been "a vengeful kind of thing," which was not necessary for her emotional well-being. Cindy's decision stands in contrast to Francine, whom I quoted earlier. Francine did not have an opportunity to testify and needed a venue to confront the defendant.

Rachel declined to be involved in sentencing because it would undo the emotional closure she had achieved after the preliminary hearing. The betrayal of being assaulted by her "first love" and the father of her children had hurt her deeply. Pursuing prosecution and standing up to him despite a history of manipulation by him was difficult for her. She grappled with self-doubt and was harassed by his family as the case dragged forward and then was harshly cross-examined in the preliminary hearing. When Rachel completed testifying in the preliminary hearing, she declined to testify again, feeling that she had obtained substantive justice through the plea agreement. She explained,

> It was hard for me all the way through, and it was over for me after I finished the preliminary. That was my line. And that was as far as I could go with that. There's only so much a person can handle. [...] It was the hardest thing I'd ever done, and I drew that line, this is ... where it is. This is where I get my life back together, and going to court that day [attending sentencing] would have been bringing it [the rape experience] up for me.

Interestingly, Rachel's fiancé, who had supported her through her involvement in the criminal justice process, did attend the hearing.

Some women find that participating in legal events that constitute the prosecution phase reactivates the trauma of the rape without offering any balancing emotional satisfaction. Therefore, despite their desires for substantive or procedural justice, they view extended involvement in the criminal justice process as an obstacle to their emotional recovery. Twyla and Mimi attended but were unable to speak at sentencing because they remained emotionally vulnerable. While they each *desired* a confrontation that would change the balance of power with their assailant and recognized that the sentencing hearing offered them the opportunity to have one, they were unable to bring themselves to address the court. Pamela, who found that the process of prosecuting her assailant aroused particularly painful memories of being molested as a child, was unable even to mail a letter to the judge (despite composing three) and completely avoided the sentencing hearing, because it might reactivate her pain.

External Support for Survivor Involvement in Sentencing

Survivors' decisions to involve themselves in sentencing were also influenced by others' input. They reported that general encouragement and the suggestion of specific actions by prosecuting attorneys, judges, counselors, and victim-witness advocates led them to write letters and attend sentencing hearings. These legal actors validated their desires to take an active role. Gwendolyn remained too fearful of her assailant to attend the sentencing hearing, but she wrote a three-page letter to the judge at the request of the prosecutor. She described the devastation caused by the rape to the judge and sought substantive justice. The prosecutor invited Gabriella to his office and coached her through preparing a statement to read to the court. She recalled, "He kind of urged me to, kind of maybe focus . . . on the severity of the subject and say exactly what I wanted out of the sentence." Mary spoke at the sentencing hearing because the judge who handled the change of plea hearing had requested that she attend. She recalled that he said, "I'll let you know or we'll let you know when the sentencing is and I want you here." Marlene, who could not see her way to the point of speaking at the sentencing hearing, wrote the sentencing judge because her counselor urged her to do so.

While Jennifer and Gabriella were both motivated to make oral statements in court to achieve substantive justice and received support from prosecutors, media interest in their cases led them to view speaking as an opportunity to reach out to a wider audience. Allowing her statement to be televised, Gabriella explained, enabled her to encourage other women to report their victimization to police.

> I thought that it would be maybe a logical way to get my voice heard, um, about how prominent this problem is and how many women don't, don't speak about it. [. . .] I just felt like it was a way to have my voice heard, to have a voice heard of a woman that'd gone through it, so other women didn't have to. So that was my driving force there.

Not all survivors heard positive messages from prosecutors, however. Several women were dissuaded from maximum participation in sentencing by prosecutors who told them their statements would not change the length of the sentence or questioned their motives. For example, Trudy's inquiries about speaking at sentencing were met with questions, not unqualified support, so she attended the sentencing hearing but did not speak.

> Um well, I asked him if I came to the sentencing, "Could I say something? Could I talk to the judge?" He told me that I was certainly able to talk to the judge, but

he sort of discouraged me a little bit. He asked me, "What good would it do? How would it help you? Would it make you feel better?" What did I hope to do? What did I hope to accomplish by it?

Among women who knew about their participatory rights, positive support for involvement in sentencing from legal personnel or rape counselors and the absence of negative input were associated with *speaking* at sentencing hearings. Of the 15 women who spoke at sentencing, 10 received strong support from others and no negative input. Lack of *any* support for participating in sentencing was associated with the lack of *any* involvement in sentencing. Survivors who attended hearings, but did not speak, or who wrote letters, but did not attend, received mixed levels of support.

Friends and family members were *not* frequently mentioned in the accounts women gave of their motivation to participate in sentencing. Perhaps this is because they granted legal personnel and counselors "expert" status to determine an appropriate course of action with respect to the criminal justice system. However, three survivors explained that family or friends' willingness to *accompany* them to court made their attendance at the sentencing hearing possible. Without moral support, the possible emotional repercussions of appearing in court would have led them to stay home. Other women were accompanied to court by friends or family members, although they did not mention them as an important factor in their deliberations about attending.

Conclusions and Questions for Further Consideration

These women's efforts to achieve procedural and substantive justice are consistent with the three primary reasons for crime-victim participation in sentencing reported by Villmoare and Neto: that is, expressing feelings to a judge, performing one's duty, and achieving a sense of justice.[4] No one has previously reported that crime victims attend sentencing hearings to attempt to rectify a power imbalance with the defendant. However, this motivation is consistent with these survivors' earlier decisions to attend arraignments and assert themselves while testifying.

Through rape, an act of terrorism and anger, perpetrators dominate others. By participating in the process of prosecution, rape survivors make an effort to equalize or reverse that balance of power. When they are not able to achieve a positive emotional state and a feeling of control before being called to testify (through self-preparation, therapy, involvement in the investigation, or attending other court events), they may seek to resolve this issue on the witness stand. However, they have varying degrees of success with this. When cases are pled out before women have the opportunity to testify, the possibility of confrontation and a consequent emotional shift is eliminated. Testifying is also dis-empowering when survivors reexperience the rape and are overwhelmed by emotion in direct examination, feel degraded by the way the defense attorney cross-examines them, or suppress expressions of their anger at the defendant or defense attorney to accommodate requests made by the prosecutor. Rape survivors' failure to shift the balance of power away from the defendant and achieve a positive emotional state through their participation in court events seems to be directly related to their interest in sentencing hearings. In this situation, in which they have more control, rape survivors are able to confront their assailant with their anger as well as their own version of events and counter his domination of them.

Social scientists previously have not reported that crime victims exercise their right to participate in the sentencing phase to deal with the psychological aftermath of victimization. However, this finding about rape survivors is consistent with the assertions of victims' rights advocates that speaking about the physical and psychological impact of the defendant's actions will allow emotional catharsis and promote healing.[5]

Like others studying crime victims, I found that the right to speak at sentencing was used by fewer rape survivors than the opportunity to write the court or simply attend hearings.[6] However, unlike rape survivors studied by Villmoare and Neto, I found women used the full scope of opportunities to participate in sentencing.[7] Villmoare and Neto traced lack of crime victims' participation in sentencing to discouragement by others.[8] My results are in agreement, but I also discovered that positive external support for survivors' participation was predictive of their involvement, especially speaking. Women who made public statements reported being encouraged to do so by prosecutors, judges, and victim-witness personnel. This influence of legal actors on rape survivors' involvement with the criminal justice system is similar to Kerstetter and VanWinkle's finding that police influence rape survivors' decisions to press charges,[9] to Frohmann's finding that prosecutors use the intake interview process to guide survivors to see them as allies,[10] and to results in prior chapters showing that contact between prosecutors and rape survivors increases their initiative in the investigative phase, the amount of their precourt self-preparation, their control over emotions on the stand, and various aspects of their testimony.

Rape survivors' participation in sentencing was also related to their prior involvement in the criminal justice process. Both prior failure to meet specific goals or desires and success in doing so shaped how they directed their behavior. When fulfilling their primary desire seemed unlikely (or it had already occurred), some women focused on fulfilling another goal through sentencing; others curtailed their involvement with the justice system altogether. This finding is generally consistent with previous reports that a crime victim's satisfaction with the outcome or perceived lack of impact on the criminal justice system leads to a lack of participation.[11]

My findings suggest that rape survivors' socioeconomic status and age may be important factors in shaping sentencing behavior. Poor nonwhite survivors did not report that they were discouraged from speaking more than white women did or say that they did not value this aspect of participation, but fewer attended sentencing hearings. All but one speaker was over 28 years of age.

Poor and working-class women may be less able to take time off to attend sentencing hearings or find it difficult to justify the cost of child care or the loss of income to participate in nonessential legal events. For example, Louisa explained that lack of a relative to watch her three children kept her from attending her husband's sentencing, an event she had hoped to use to confront him. Poor and working-class women may be less able to call on similarly situated supporters to attend court with them and, thus, feel less safe about extending themselves at sentencing hearings.

It seems likely the treatment that teenage women received from legal personnel earlier in the process shaped their decisions about participating in sentencing. As discussed previously, prosecutors often cut them out of the communication loop by dealing with their parents. And as a result, some were less likely than older women to initiate contact in the investigative phase or to prepare themselves for upcoming court events. It follows that they would not claim a right to speak publicly without direct support from legal personnel or their parents. Younger women are also more likely to bear the burden of caring for preschool-age children and infants and face the difficulty of finding a sitter during the work day.

I found no direct evidence that rape survivors' involvement in sentencing affected sentences meted out by judges. However, it would be wrong to conclude that letter writing, speaking, and attending to observe the sentencing did not have a substantive effect. I heard the prosecutor tell Candace that her silent presence in court had mattered after the judge handed down the maximum possible aggravated sentence for all counts against her assailant. Several other women reported hearing similar things from prosecutors. Ultimately, it will be necessary to study judges' decision making to understand fully how survivors' participation in the sentencing process impacts sentences.

Almost all the survivors who chose to write letters or speak and attend hearings expressed satisfaction with their participation when their motivation was to secure procedural justice or to resolve emotional issues. No one reported increased fear upon seeing their assailant or a greater sense of loss. All but one who stood up and confronted their assailants silently or verbally reported obtaining a feeling that they had moved beyond the rape event in some emotional way. Those who heard judges call their assailants animals or describe the rape as serious reported feeling vindicated, even when the charges for which their assailant was convicted were not reflective of their experience. Bernice, who was stabbed and raped by a nocturnal intruder in her house explained:

> I remember that the judge called him like an animal, and I remember being really glad that he said that. I was very glad the judge spoke to him and told him what a horrible person he was [...] and condemned him for what he had done and in

particular for the malicious thing [he did and], mentioned at that point the repeated stabbing of me. It was like [...] having someone stand up for me. So that was a real, that was *the* real important thing.

Yet because the court cannot control the defendant's presentation of self, he *can* impact how a rape survivor experiences the sentencing hearing. When an assailant's public performance is inconsistent with what a woman thinks is appropriate for a convicted criminal, she may not successfully resolve the power imbalance established through the rape. For example, Monica noted that, despite being sentenced to nine years, her assailant behaved in a threatening manner:

So any power I may have felt was wiped out by the fact that he still exists. [...] I remember him looking at me and looking at my family and my grandmother came too. He'd turn all the way around in his seat and just stare at me and my family. It just doesn't seem right.

This chapter examines rape survivors' involvement in sentencing, a point at which their participation is clearly optional. In this book, it is the final stage at which I explore rape survivors' agency. But it is important to emphasize that the point at which I end my investigation is not necessarily the point at which survivors resolved the rape experience or ended their pursuit of justice. Some women kept track of their assailant after he was incarcerated. They wrote impact letters when parole hearings were scheduled and actively sought to ensure that he *served* the maximum sentence allowable under law. When Mary's assailant raped again after being released from prison, he was caught and again successfully prosecuted. Prosecutors asked Mary to speak at this second sentencing hearing and she drove more than 800 miles to do so.

Two women pursued civil claims against organizations whose negligence increased strangers' physical access to them and ability to surprise them. Megan pursued justice through her campus judiciary process.

Other survivors became active in the feminist movement to eradicate rape and serve rape victims' needs. These included women whose assailants were found guilty as well as those who were not. One woman became a self-defense instructor. Shortly after I interviewed Sandy, she returned to her volunteer position at the RCC. As noted above, Jennifer and Gabriella spoke to the press about their experiences with the criminal justice process. Others speak publicly at rallies and participate in marches to Take Back the Night.

In the last chapter, I turn to the question of policy—how my findings can improve the way justice is pursued. I take a particular perspective on this question that places rape survivors at the center. Thus, I consider how the criminal justice process can be made to serve the needs of the individuals upon whom its workers rely and our future safety depends: crime victims. My remarks are focused on the specific problems that I have discovered rape survivors encounter in their role as victim-witnesses.

CHAPTER 10

MOVING TOWARD MORE JUSTICE FOR RAPE SURVIVORS IN THE CRIMINAL PROCESS

Somebody needs to teach prosecutors how to look at (and out for) the effects on victims of the state's conduct and attitudes.

—*New York criminal prosecutor Alice Vachss*[1]

Is it acceptable to ask rape survivors to continue to endure the present difficulties and damages associated with fulfilling the victim-witness role? Is it acceptable to leave in place official policies and informal practices that are associated with the historic underreporting of a serious crime, perpetrators' lack of fear of criminal justice sanctions, and broad social tolerance of sexual violence? I believe that, regardless of the outcomes of their particular cases, the women whose experiences are the focus of this book would join me in answering no. We need to move toward a different future.

For decades, feminist scholars and activists have been concerned with improving the prosecution of rape and have sought to bring attention to (1) the significant gap between the estimated rate at which rapes occur and are reported, (2) the attrition rate of rape cases from report to trial, (3) the failure of rape prosecution to result in findings of guilt, (4) the prosecution of a limited range of sexual assaults, and (5) the emotional toll that involvement in rape prosecution has on rape survivors. They have argued that with respect to rape, the criminal justice process fails instrumentally and symbolically. Rapists do not fear swift and severe justice from criminal prosecution and are not deterred from committing further crimes. Community members are not challenged to confront either the full scope of sexual violence in society or to assess their own stereotypical thinking about the crime. Finally, many survivors do not bring their victimization to police attention because they believe there is a greater likelihood that they will be reassaulted in their interactions with defense and prosecuting attorneys than that they will see justice done.

In chapter 1, I provided a legal context for understanding interviewees' experiences; I now will return to the issue of reform.

Proposed Solutions to Continuing Problems

Education

Feminist scholars and activists continue to search for ways to advance societal knowledge about rape and change attitudes that lead to the blaming of women who are victimized. For the most part, this continues to occur via education campaigns directed toward reducing individuals' acceptance of rape myths. However, there have been two important developments in education. The first, occurring on college campuses, is a shift toward engaging men and women in discussions about the need for someone interested in sexual activity to *gain active consent* rather than assume it.[2] This strategy of looking beyond statutes reflects educators' awareness of the ubiquity of rape by known assailants and the social reality that alcohol plays a central role in social life on many campuses. They know that both men and women drink to the point of physically disabling themselves and seek to challenge the assumption that an inebriated individual who does not communicate or physically defend her/himself has de facto given consent to sexual activity. They also endeavor through these discussions to increase bystanders' willingness to challenge the behavior of sexual opportunists who appear intent on committing rape.

RCC activists are the source of the second education development. By focusing on building alliances with police and prosecutorial agencies and on establishing regularized meetings with their representatives, medical providers, and victim-witness assistance agencies, crisis centers have created interlocking groups of people involved in an ongoing process of mutual education and support. RCC representatives engaged in alliance building do not preach a way of doing things, but rather extend themselves to assist other organizations in achieving their missions. However, RCCs maintain a position that the needs of crime victims and prosecution are compatible and hold other organizations accountable for developing processes that are responsive to victims. The result has been recognizable shifts in the stated missions and practices employed by prosecutors and police officers.[3]

Legislation

In most states, a woman's consent to sexual activity is assumed in rape statutes and prosecutors are required to establish that alleged victims communicated their refusal effectively to secure conviction. Given this, removing concern with a woman's resistance continues to be a focus of activism. The most progressive reform efforts mirror the activity on college campuses, passing legislation that specifies rape occurs unless a sexual aggressor obtains active consent: a clear verbal or possibly nonverbal indication of desire for sexual contact.[4]

Some progress has been made on this legislative project. A 2004 *Harvard Law Review* analysis of sexual assault and rape statutes found the following:

(1) 31 states did not mention a rape victim's resistance in statutory language, (2) six states explicitly noted physical resistance was *not* required, and (3) six states and the District of Columbia explicitly separated acquiescence and consent.[5] In 1992, the New Jersey Supreme Court upheld the constitutionality of new statutory language stating, "any act of sexual penetration engaged in by the defendant without the *affirmative and freely given permission* of the victim of the specific act of penetration constitutes the offense of sexual assault."[6] Other progressive definitions of consent passed since then include "cooperation in act or attitude" (Colorado), "positive cooperation" (California), and "word or overt actions by a person who is competent to give informed consent indicating a freely given agreement to have sexual intercourse or sexual contact" (Wisconsin).[7] However, no other states appear poised to pass such legislation.[8]

Conversely, appellate courts have recently made some progressive decisions. Alaska, California, Kansas, Maine, Minnesota, South Dakota, and Connecticut have established that a woman may withdraw consent after penetration. Supreme Courts in California and Indiana have placed restrictions on the "mistake of fact" defense, which allows the defendant to argue he reasonably expected consent.[9]

In the absence of statutory reform, Michelle Anderson[10] proposed shifting the legal meaning of "resistance." She recommended adopting a victim-centered perspective when *examining testimony,* which requires that anything a woman says or does must be interpreted as communication of her will. Through this lens, resistance of *any* type must be interpreted as indicating a woman's lack of desire and, thus, her lack of consent to sexual activity. Following this logic, submitting *any* evidence of physical or verbal resistance occurring before sexual activity would demonstrate that a defendant overcame a woman's will and accomplished it by some force or coercion.

Legal scholar and former prosecutor Andrew Taslitz's focus is on altering problematic features of the rape trial that contribute to the rape survivor's experience of a second assault or jurors' failures to convict.[11] He proposes that victim-witness participation in trials must be *meaningful.* Their testimony must have the capacity to influence jurors, and they must experience the activity of testifying as communicating *their* perspective. He argues that under current trial procedures, rape survivors' participation is not meaningful in either way. Jurors lack accurate background knowledge to adequately interpret and fairly evaluate rape survivors' narratives. Defense attorneys also disrupt rape survivors' acts of telling by halting direct examination through objections and tactically cutting off rape survivors' answers during cross-examination. Defense attorneys break rape survivors' narratives into bits that are incomprehensible to jurors and greatly fluster rape survivors, making it difficult for them to form statements they feel are intelligible to others.

Taslitz has proposed making three changes in trial procedures to protect rape survivors' ability to convey their reality to jurors and to limit their experience of being under attack by defense attorneys. He has suggested that rape survivors be allowed to describe the rape event without interruption in direct examination. Second, he has recommended that an intermediary be introduced into cross-examination to lessen defense attorneys' ability to dominate rape survivors through the way in which they ask questions. This individual with social service training would "translate defense counsel's questions into less abusive forms."[12] To avoid a perception of procedural bias and unfairness, the intermediary would, however, also be used in direct examinations. Third, Taslitz has urged the passage of legislation to enable the use of a new type of expert in rape trials to counter the negative impact of pervasive cultural stereotypes.[13] Prosecutors would introduce the experts to provide jurors with information about the social context of rape, women's indirect communication styles, and how human reasoning processes—such as those upon which jurors rely—tend to block the development of empathy for victims.[14]

Taslitz grounds his proposals in the "external costs" that are currently associated with rape trials.[15] He argues that the language practices currently in use in these trials "constitute the practice of subordination itself"[16] and induce "linguistic trauma,"[17] which reduces the reliability of a rape survivor's testimony. Less-reliable testimony in conjunction with jurors' typical reliance on stereotypes results in a failure to convict when other evidence strongly supports conviction. This deprives the state of security. Furthermore, when a rape victim's broken testimony does not effectively convey her experience of violation, jurors leave courtrooms as misinformed about the realities of rape as when they entered them. The impact of linguist trauma does not end there, though. The failure of prosecution to convict in individual cases sends messages to *all* women about the narrow scope of behavior that is acceptable for them. These messages place limits on women's liberty, especially on their full participation in the public sphere. When women do not fully participate in the public sphere, the impact they can have on public deliberation is reduced and the full airing of their concerns about any subject is unlikely. This limits the development of a society in which women are fully equal. In short, Taslitz's premise is that altering trial procedures in rape cases serves the ultimate end of greater gender equality.

Patricia Martin is interested in providing rape survivors with meaningful participation opportunities.[18] She shares Taslitz's concern with creating a *courtroom* situation that would allow rape survivors to convey their reality with a minimum of disruption, and thus not damage them, but she is also interested in increasing their access to procedural justice. Martin recommends that rape survivors be provided with an opportunity to shape the outcome of the process, not just to increase the capacity of their testimony to influence others who make decisions. In short, Martin seeks for rape survivors a role that extends beyond what is traditionally recognized as the "witness's place" in prosecution.

The proposal in Martin's book, *Rape Work*, which is directed toward the end of procedural justice, is to expand the availability of restorative justice programs (RJPs) that parallel the criminal justice process.[19] These programs are typically run through community organizations and are focused on reintegrating offenders into society. They are also focused on giving crime survivors a chance to speak directly to their victimizer about their experiences and injuries as well as a direct role in negotiating their victimizer's consequence. Most RJPs in operation are experimental and funded through grants rather than state budget lines. Programs directed to rape and sexual assault survivors are not available to all rape survivors. They are limited to first-time offenders, who know their victims, used low levels of force to compel sexual activity, and are willing to admit their guilt.[20]

Evaluating the Current Policy Agenda

Education

We must continue to have a robust public education campaign that pertains to rape and sexual assault. This should include expanding the reach of existing programs to dispel myths that limit what is recognized as criminal behavior and who is seen as a legitimate victim. It should also involve incorporating discussions of consent and resistance now central to education on campuses and feminist legal writing.

This individual education serves several purposes. First, it may reduce the actual incidence of rape, by making sexual opportunists aware they are violating women and the law and by making bystanders more willing to intervene. Second, it may increase the efficacy of the criminal justice process. Making more potential jurors aware of the empirical realities of rape has the potential to increase conviction rates in the minority of trials they adjudicate. Perhaps even more important, legal personnel gauge their discretionary decisions on their perceptions of jurors' views. Changing social attitudes toward rape should make prosecutors more secure about changing the way in which they *charge* and *plead* cases, affecting the *majority* of claims that enter the process.

While "rape experts" are now a recognized resource to rape survivors in many communities, the public is the source of "others" on whom rape survivors most frequently rely to make decisions about reporting, for decisions about taking a role in investigation, and for support in preparing for court and testifying. Recognizing this, we should expand efforts to educate the public about what completing a forensic rape exam entails, stages of the criminal justice process, and the rights of victims as well as defendants within that process.

Our efforts can build on existing rape-awareness campaigns to reach individuals who are adults, but we would achieve a great deal more by targeting high school government and civics curricula for expansion. We need 18-year-olds, who fall within the highest risk groups of both rape victimization and perpetration, to understand more than the legislative process. They should grasp the basic steps of criminal justice prosecution and the mechanisms that are in place to protect the rights of both defendants and victims. Given the variation in criminal law and procedure among states, this will require the production of materials to augment mass-marketed textbooks and thus a commitment of financial resources from state or national governments.

In the absence of a historic program to educate the public about the criminal justice process, mass media is the primary source of public knowledge and attitudes about it. People draw their views from factual programming and from entertainment programming that provides a plethora of police, lawyer, and criminal investigation shows. Much entertainment, including "reality" programming, inaccurately portrays the criminal justice process and the crime victim's place in it. Thus, in tandem with expanding the content of public education, we need to work to clarify the line between legal reality and fantasy. This requires identifying and actively countering misinformation about legal procedures that appears on television and in movies, particularly as it relates to sexual assault and rape.

Colleges and universities may be in a unique position to contribute to this effort. Faculty in journalism, sociology, political science, communications, legal studies, criminal justice, and education can engage students in conducting scientifically valid studies of legally oriented television programs to identify areas of inaccuracy. The results of systematic reviews conducted by students can then be shared with the public through local news outlets.[21] College students may personally benefit from conducting this kind of research, because they fall within the age sector in which sexual assaults are most frequent.[22]

The formation of organizational networks through which mutual education occurs among rape processors must continue to be part of the education agenda. These alliances are a critical component of rethinking the way in which justice is done on a *daily* basis. They are our best hope for developing mechanisms to engage rape survivors fully in investigations and plea-bargaining and to ensure that their right to participate in sentencing exists in practice, not just in theory. State and federal funds should be made available to support such networking efforts.

But RCCs may not be the only organizations that are capable of developing and sustaining such alliances. Women's Centers at colleges and universities should engage in such a project, as should the campus staff who currently advocate internally on behalf of rape victims. Likewise, campus health units and campus health education units are another valuable resource for these alliances, because their staff are knowledgeable about the habits of students and barriers to their reporting.[23] In addition, health staff can combat stereotypes of wayward "co-eds," which are a barrier to successful prosecution and seem to be a particular problem when more liberal campuses are situated in generally conservative rural areas.[24]

No doubt, there will be institutional resistance to university staff sharing information that can unsettle public perceptions of a safe campus. However, the reporting requirements of the Clery Act have already done that to some extent, undermining this objection.[25] In addition, colleges and universities have a vested interest in seeing such ties develop, because the costs of litigation associated with their failed efforts to use campus judiciary processes to manage rapes will only increase.[26] Finally, many colleges and universities have difficult relations with the governments and populations of the larger communities in which they are located. Leadership in building alliances that support women's access to justice in the broader community could help ease these tensions.

Statutory Revision of Crime Definitions

Altering rape statutes to require affirmative consent probably would increase the likelihood that jurors will find guilt in cases involving known assailants. New statutes could also affect the way in which legal personnel approach charging and pleading. However, the full implementation of most new statutes is hampered by constitutional challenges, so a time lag must be expected before legal personnel alter their practices. In addition, new laws of evidence would not alter *how* defense attorneys question rape survivors and could increase their reliance on tactics of intimidation.

Altering the Criminal Justice Procedure

I have no doubt that Martin's proposal to expand RJP could offer rape survivors who are primarily interested in resolving the power imbalance with the rapist, resolving the emotional impact of the rape, or seeking to make an official record of their experience an opportunity to achieve this.[27] The parallel process would also save some women from domination by defense attorneys in adversarial court interactions or by prosecutors in plea-bargains. However, I object to compensating for shortcomings of the criminal justice process by creating an alternative process for handling sexual assault and rape. I have three specific concerns.

David Rauma found that a diversion program for batterers created to *expand* the formal handling of victims' reports did not have this effect. Michigan prosecutors used it to shift prosecutable but "lesser cases" out of the criminal justice process. Rauma described this phenomenon as "going for the gold" and suggested it was due to limited resources.[28] I am concerned that legal personnel will similarly view RJPs for rape and sexual assault as a resource to reduce their workload—as a tool to limit the passage of difficult cases into the criminal justice process—or to build up their win-loss record.

Could RJP be insulated from selective pressures if *rape survivors*, not prosecutors, make the choice? Unfortunately, I believe not. My research and other studies show that legal personnel actively try to influence rape survivors to withdraw from the criminal justice process before significant resources are expended on investigation and arrests are made, and actively seek to alter their perspectives on plea terms that are under discussion.[29] Thus, it seems likely that some legal personnel will work to guide, if not pressure, rape survivors who fit the participatory criteria for RJP to make early decisions to commit to the alternative process. Furthermore, I expect that stereotypical beliefs about the needs of particular groups of rape survivors will be used to justify guiding individuals into RJP, and that usage patterns for RJP will soon show demographic biases.[30] In particular, I expect young women (the most likely targets of juveniles) and women raped by current and former intimates will be directed out of the criminal justice process. Cases involving both types of victims are seen as difficult to prosecute under existing law and procedures.

Second, for many years, and perhaps indefinitely, many raped women will have only the option to pursue justice through the criminal justice process because a state-funded RJP has not yet been created in their jurisdiction, the offense committed against them does not fit the criteria for participation, or the defendant does not wish to participate. Some rape survivors may also place a high priority on the state's capacity to incarcerate or to bestow an official criminal label on their assailant and the crime and be unwilling to forgo these options to achieve other goals. If the effort to develop parallel restorative processes takes pressure to meet the needs of all victims off criminal justice personnel and legislators, rape survivors will continue to suffer in their victim-witness roles.

Third, replicating the restorative justice model described and recommended by Martin (RESTORE) may prove to be quite difficult. Despite the commitment of academics and mental health and criminal justice professionals in Tucson, Arizona, it took years of collaboration to implement the program. Establishing processes to move rape survivors smoothly out of the criminal justice process may be difficult in jurisdictions where there is no history of cross-agency collaboration. Some features of the model may not correspond well to certain sectors of the survivor-defendant population. Specifically, the RESTORE model works when the family and community are geographically close to support both defendant and survivor.[31] This is usually the case for juveniles who live with or near their guardians, but it is less likely for young adults who travel to find work opportunities or pursue their education. Although communities can certainly be created in such settings, they may not include the significant others who are central to survivors' and defendants' conceptions of self. The RESTORE program commitments not to create documents that can be used in legal proceedings and to expunge records, when a defendant has completed the program, are inconsistent with my findings that some rape survivors seek to create a public record of the crime. Despite their interest in confronting the defendant, they may opt out on this basis. Secrecy about the details of penalties also does not work to increase community awareness of sexual assault and rape and its consequences.

Taslitz's recommendation that rape survivors be given the opportunity to testify in an uninterrupted fashion would enhance the likelihood that they perceive their testifying to be meaningful. Likewise, introducing expert witnesses as a general practice to provide a context for making sense of rape survivors' testimony should enhance a juror's ability to reach a conclusion of guilt. However, if these procedural changes are only applied in trials, the larger number of rape survivors who testify only at preliminary hearings will be left unprotected. Furthermore, defensive behaviors they adopt to protect themselves at trial, as a result of their preliminary examination experiences, can have external costs for prosecution.

Introducing intermediaries in direct and cross-examination at trial may also produce some unintended negative consequences. Given my findings that rape survivors currently manage multiple layers of interaction in courtrooms, adding an additional party with whom they must interact is troubling. The intermediary would certainly be a buffer between a rape survivor and her historic adversary, the defense attorney, but the intermediary would also be a buffer between her and her potential ally, the prosecutor. Specifically, imposing a third party between prosecutor and rape survivor would limit prosecutors' ability to assist rape survivors' emotion management. Prosecutors could not engage in the largely nonverbal interaction that they currently use to assist rape survivors with crafting a narrative that reduces the likelihood of recall and becoming emotionally overwhelmed. In addition, an absent prosecutor certainly could not physically impose him- or herself between the defendant and rape survivor to ease the intimidation factor. In sum, adding an intermediary to the courtroom, whom the survivor does not know and with whom she has no rapport, may result in her greater emotional isolation as well as increased difficulty in fulfilling her testifying obligations.

Furthermore, I have discovered that rape survivors monitor prosecutors' nonverbal responses to their testimony, and this affects how they construct subsequent answers in both direct and cross-examination. Because rape survivors recognize that they are witnesses for the state and often seek to strengthen the state's case, their desire to do this will not diminish. Removing the prosecutor from the courtroom removes a source of feedback for rape survivors that may lead them to rely further on observing supporters in the courtroom or even to try to "read" the intermediary.

Finally, if the process is altered to incorporate intermediaries without the physical removal of any other actors—the defendant, prosecutor, and defense attorney—then rape survivors will have another interaction to manage. Some will be involved in simultaneously carrying on four or five interactions, further complicating their work as witnesses.

The theory that the survivors' problems in court result from the defense attorney's behavior during cross-examination justifies employing intermediaries in the courtroom. The result of this study shows, in contrast, that the difficulties many rape survivors have in court, and their feelings of oppression and, consequently, dissatisfaction, emanate from the nature of the interactions they have (or fail to have) with prosecutors. In short, intermediaries will not improve their testifying experiences because they do not have an impact on the source of their problems. In fact, the vast majority of rape survivors, whose cases are resolved short of trial by prosecutors, will not be affected at all by this procedural shift.

Implementing RJPs on a large scale will require the collaborative work of many rape-processing agencies. Altering courtroom procedures will require legislative action, and thus, at best, are years away.

My focus in the rest of this discussion is on the kinds of changes in organizational practice that could immediately improve rape survivors' experiences in the criminal justice process or have an immediate positive impact on the success of prosecution. They are the kind of changes that could be the aim of organizational alliances focused on responsive processing. I present my suggestions in this book, which is intended for a general audience, because it is my hope that (1) legal personnel will see their value and seek latitude to change their practices within their organizations, and (2) rape survivors and their professional and lay supporters will demand changes and hold legal personnel accountable for developing a more humane justice process.

How to Move Toward a Better Criminal Justice Process

How do we move toward a better process? I next turn to the conceptual project and then discuss some concrete alterations in the doing of justice that could ameliorate some of the difficulties experienced by rape survivors and make the witness role more meaningful, in both Martin's and Taslitz's senses of the word.

Identifying the Parameters of Good Organizational Practices

In 1993, sociologists Patricia Martin and Marleen Powell argued that all people involved in processing rape "victims" must be reflective about the impact of their actions and institute "practices that prioritize rape victims' well-being in legal (and allied) organizations."[32] My academic publications built on and extended their agenda.[33] In *Rape Work*, Martin expands her analysis of the organizations that process rape, and puts forward an agenda presented by Koss and colleagues, to create "a more victim-centered justice response to sexual assault."[34] Such a response would involve the development of processes that

> (1) establish victims' safety; (2) offer options for cases where there is evidence supporting probable cause that a sexual assault occurred, which under the *status quo* would be rejected for charging; (3) respond to victims' concerns about having choice, being treated as autonomous individuals, having face-to-face contact, and voicing the impact of their experience; (4) [shorten] the time between crime and consequence, to reduce victim stress; (5) [give] victims input into the consequences faced by the offender; and (6) [. . .] help them [victims] obtain reparations and gain a feeling of *moral satisfaction*.[35]

Having now analyzed how rape survivors move all the way through the process—from reporting to sentencing—and are involved in investigations and pleas as well as negotiating the dynamics of courtroom interaction, I find this comprehensive agenda a good point of departure. However, I would modify number six, given the concerns I have described above, and add three items:

- Victim centering requires development of practices that prioritize rape survivors' well-being throughout the criminal justice process and facilitate their use of existing confrontation opportunities to achieve social reintegration and obtain moral satisfaction.
- Victim centering requires the provision of information and support that maximizes rape survivors' ability to meaningfully fulfill their testifying obligations.
- With respect to the need for the criminal justice process to serve the broader cause of legitimacy, processes need to be developed that consciously minimize the impact of social inequalities on rape survivors' ability to engage with the criminal justice process fully. Such inequalities include class, race/ethnicity, and age.

Developing the capacity of the criminal justice process to serve rape survivors' needs requires rethinking victimization and victims outside the confines of cultural stereotypes and legal constructions. I agree with Martin's argument that organizational frames of reference that treat rape survivors as liars or as unpredictable, in particular, need to be replaced.[36] There is no reason to assume that the experience of sexual violation inevitably produces these traits, and there is no reason to assume that rapists restrict their selection of victims to women who have these traits. Imposing these assumptions on rape survivors creates rather than alleviates problems.[37] Change will happen much more quickly if alternative ways to coherently conceptualize rape survivors are presented to supplant views that exist.

To this end, Martin has emphasized the importance of organizations adopting interpretive frames that are responsive to rape survivors. Such frames necessarily acknowledge that the rape survivor is an injured person when she makes a report and implicitly acknowledge that she remains so despite the legal transfer of her injury to the state. Such frames also acknowledge that the rape survivor's recovery from her injury is as important as the prosecutorial agenda.[38] State practices, therefore, must not contribute further harm or unnecessarily prolong the rape survivor's recovery period. Andrew Taslitz has also urged prosecutors to change their domineering approaches and "treat rape victims as equals."[39] At a minimum, an orientation toward equality requires acknowledging that, although constructed as passive, rape survivors are not indifferent to the trial process. They have interest in the prosecution of their injury and have the intellectual and emotional capacity to be involved. Although Taslitz makes his recommendation in a discussion about preparing rape survivors for trial, I see no reason not to extend it to the entire scope of interactions prosecutors have with rape survivors. More completely, however, treating rape survivors as equals requires that state practices be developed with an understanding of their *full humanity.* This would involve recognizing that rape survivors engage the criminal justice process like any other human activity, despite the oppressive circumstances that lead to the need for it.

The Result of the Legal Erasure of Rape Survivor Injury and Interests

An uncritical acceptance of the legal transfer of the injury of rape from individual to state has shielded prosecutors from scrutiny, limited acknowledgment of rape survivors' full involvement in and contributions to the criminal justice process, and consequently limited the scope of problems activists have recognized and sought to address.

When raped women report the injury of their body and self to authorities, they legally lose "ownership" of their victimization to prosecutors who take up action on behalf of the state. Prosecutors *legally* appropriate the rape survivor's grievance against her attacker—his violation of her body—and determine what crime to adjudicate and the extent of resources to invest in pursuit of substantive justice. Their adversary in the criminal justice process is the attorney who represents the defendant. I submit that if we think of ownership of crime in this way—as something only one party can have at a time, it restricts how we think about "injuries" as well as how we treat the people from which ownership has been transferred—the "victims."

In relation to legal personnel, witnesses exist primarily as objects; their capacity to narrate what they have observed or experienced is their value, and prosecutors apply it to achieve the ends they desire. When ownership of a crime transfers to the state, the crime survivor's "victim" status is symbolically encapsulated *in* the victimizing event. The crime victim is thought of as someone whose body *was* injured, not someone whose body *is* injured, and she is relevant to the prosecution as a *witness to her past.* The role that accompanies the *legal* status of "witness" is thus, passive.

Sole state ownership of crime is a *legal fiction,* a socially constructed, not subjective, reality for crime victims. Nevertheless, it operates to preserve the scope of unfettered discretion that legal personnel can exercise. The crime victim has no legal standing from which to challenge a prosecutor's decisions about charging and prosecuting, including setting terms for a plea. The social construction of the witness role as passive also discourages legal personnel from recognizing behaviors that demonstrate rape survivors' initiative and current investment in their dispute with the defendant *for what they are.* This ignorance of rape survivors' expression of their interests reinforces the belief that they do not have an independent agenda—that they are passive. When legal personnel perceive the typical rape survivor to be passively oriented toward prosecution, they can pursue their own agendas while holding the belief that the actions they take are in "rape survivors' best interests."

If we feel empowered to act for another human's best interest, it is unlikely that we will scrutinize our own behavior as a cause of damage to the other for whom we act. Rather, we will view our adversaries as theirs as well. Following this logic, if prosecutors conceive of themselves as acting *for* rape survivors, it is unlikely they will consider their own actions as a cause of rape survivors' dissatisfaction. Rather, they will probably explain the negative experiences that rape survivors report with the criminal justice process as arising from their interactions with defense attorneys (prosecutors' formal adversaries).

But the legal fiction that denies crime victims' subjectivity and a legal basis on which to engage the defendant directly hides another reality when the crime victim is a *rape survivor*. American culture, from which jurors are drawn, frames rape as an ongoing trauma, and the rape survivor must appear as a subject with an emotional investment in her dispute with the defendant or be viewed as failing in her performance as a witness. Thus, prosecutors seek contemporary performances of victimization from rape survivors in the courtroom, and directly and indirectly guide rape survivors to achieve them. Because they see themselves as acting on behalf of witnesses, prosecutors are not inclined to consider whether their efforts to get rape survivors to perform victimization in the courtroom might be experienced negatively. So prosecutors tend to expect rape survivors to *perform as victims* for public consumption, while they refuse to recognize them as *being or existing as victims* who are still fundamentally connected to the defendant through their injury. Rape survivors experience this as a contradiction, and many view it as an inherently hypocritical aspect of the criminal justice policy.

If we seek to make the criminal justice process more victim-centered, we must not accept constructed legal fictions about crime victims *as* their subjective reality, and we must investigate and come to understand the varied ways in which prosecutors are deeply implicated in rape survivors' negative experiences. In addition, we must explore whether treating crime victims solely as prosecution resources maximizes their capacity to fulfill their witness roles and maximizes the state's position in criminal prosecution.

Rethinking Rape Victims: Acknowledging Humanity

Below, I propose a sociological model for thinking about rape survivors outside the mold of legal or cultural stereotypes.[40] It is a model against which organizational practices may be evaluated; through which individual legal personnel may gauge their behavior toward rape survivors; and that friends and family can use to think through their efforts to assist rape survivors. It is also a model that rape survivors can use to understand their actions as rational and reasonable, to press for their right to participate in the process, and to reject treatment they experience as victimizing.[41]

Humans are interpretive actors. We develop lines of action as we define situations and focus on and respond to the behavior of other people. We attribute
meanings and motives to others' behavior—whether it is intentional communication directed at us or not—with reference to roles they occupy in the situation and our understanding of social expectations. Our world views and
preexisting knowledge of specific types of situations and roles guide, but do
not determine, the actions we take.

If we apply this approach to rape survivors, we see that while reporting
decisions will be guided by preexisting perceptions about the legal process
and about rape, rape survivors' future lines of conduct are constructed with
reference to meanings, motives, and capacities they attribute to legal personnel. Because motivation can be imputed to inaction as well as action, what
legal personnel say *and* don't say will have an impact both on how rape survivors perceive themselves to be viewed and on what they do. Legal personnel
who recognize the interpretive nature of rape survivors' behavior are in a
much better position to decrease their perception of being judged and foster
rather than hinder their commitment to the state's agenda.

Humans generally find entering situations in which they are unfamiliar
with the social roles available to participants and the rules of interaction to be
embarrassing and emotionally taxing. Few of us are capable of complete role
immersion in these situations, because we spend a great deal of effort monitoring the fit between what we are doing and what we think is going on. We
press on in these situations, however, because we assume that others will help
us maintain our self-presentations.

The dynamics of the courtroom are foreign to most rape survivors upon
entry into the victim-witness role. If rape survivors are not educated about
the roles actors take on in the courtrooms and the rules of interaction that
pertain to them, they are not positioned to interact with ease. Awareness of
the lack of preparation results in anxiety about participation. When defense
attorneys do not support rape survivors' efforts to stay within their roles, and
in fact work to derail them, it makes the project of constructing testimony
extremely daunting and frustrating. However, if prosecutors comprehensively
socialize rape survivors into the courtroom setting and their witness roles,
they can reduce survivors' precourt anxiety and facilitate their ability to convey their meaning in direct and cross-examination.

Most important, humans are not isolated individuals. We are socially situated, connected to others through our familial and public social roles. We seek
to act responsibly in relation to these preexisting relations, in particular, protecting those who depend on us. Our orientations toward these relationships
tend to persist as long as we maintain our definitions of them.

The immediate social relations rape survivors have with others that predate
the sexual attack—mother, daughter, wife, lover, friend, employee, neighbor,
and so forth—have bearing on every aspect of their involvement with the
criminal justice process. Their reporting decisions and desires to be involved

(or not) with later stages of prosecution are shaped by their obligations to protect others, including their children and spouses (including the assailant) and to protect their public image. Social relationships influence who rape survivors seek out for assistance preparing for court and for support in court. And, the desire to protect relationships and specific others affects rape survivors' testimony—both their ability to maintain emotional control and the content of their speech. Rape survivors' preexisting social relations also influence who feels empowered to act for them and in what ways. Legal personnel who build rapport with rape survivors and seek to understand them as socially situated individuals are much more likely to be able to convey the rationality of their behavior to juries. Likewise, they are able to anticipate ways in which survivors' court performances may be shifted away from the state agenda, before they occur.

Broader social networks and economic resources have bearing on humans' ability to draw on others for social support and information, and rape survivors are no exception. Both influence whether rape survivors have access to specialized information, can engage in discretionary court events, and are able to engage in the process through its entire length. Legal personnel who recognize the impact of economic marginality can facilitate the participation of survivors by providing alternatives to traditional social supports.

The human self is an identity and a process—always becoming—and is *also* an emblem of one's social roles and social status. An injury to the self also exists in these forms. It alters an individual's sense of "who I am," evolving as the individual finds ways to reconfigure a sense of wholeness, and it affects the way in which others respond to the individual. The self is not something one person can transfer to another, nor is an injury to the self. Rape causes serious damage to an individual's personal and social identity and the legal transfer of the "injury of rape" from a victimized individual to the state is fundamentally at odds with how humans socially experience such damage.

The injury of rape—sexual domination—involves the rape survivor's core sense of being. Resolution of the injury requires the rape survivor to regain a sense of positive social value and a place in the social fabric from which she was torn. Central to this resolution is receiving social recognition of the reality and seriousness of the injury. Participating in group counseling is one way to achieve social recognition of one's victimization, and it can help some survivors move through and beyond the experience of domination inherent in the assault event. However, taking on the victim-witness role currently provides rape survivors with the only means to secure a *criminal* label for the assault event and offers them the only opportunity to shift the balance of power *directly away* from their dominator. In the absence of formal alternatives, the criminal justice process will be a medium for many to resolve their injury. Legal personnel who recognize that their agenda overlaps with, but is distinct from, rape survivors' need to resolve the rape experience are much less likely to reproduce the dynamics of domination in interactions with them.

Furthermore, they are much more likely to be able to help rape survivors direct their energy toward the state agenda.

Achieving a More Humane Criminal Justice Experience

The Case for Early Contact with Rape Survivors

After reporting there is often a comparatively long period before rape survivors are called to fulfill their testifying responsibilities. The investigation continues, arrests are made, charges are filed, and early plea discussions take place. Regular contact between rape survivors and legal personnel is the exception during this period. It is more typical that police detectives or prosecutors initiate contact sporadically or not at all, depending on whether they need something from the rape survivor. Rape survivors' efforts to establish contact to gain information or contribute information meet with mixed success.

On the basis of contacts and their absence, rape survivors form an evaluation of state investment in the case during the investigative period. Unless positive contact with legal personnel takes place, women who draw negative conclusions about legal personnel are unlikely to shift their views before initial court events. As a result, they are likely to form a defensive orientation toward their testifying responsibilities.

Although little is needed from rape survivors during the investigation and the period before probable cause is established—their resource value is low—much can be gained from legal personnel prioritizing early contact with rape survivors, ensuring that their initiatives receive a response and they have means to track case developments. Through these efforts, prosecutors will communicate competence, commitment, and caring and engage survivors in the stated mission of prosecution.

First, legal personnel who make early contact can build the rapport that is necessary for trust. Trusting survivors are more likely to be open about their anxieties and more likely to see themselves as members of a team and share their plans with legal personnel before implementing them. Second, prosecutors who make early contact gain an opportunity to correct inaccurate information before it becomes the basis of rape survivors' lines of action, such as when the national or local media outlets extensively cover a sexual assault or rape prosecution that is procedurally atypical. Third, prosecutors who explain the nature and scope of their legal obligation to share information with the defense encourage survivors to openly communicate concerns that could be an impetus to control information.

My interviews underscore that prosecutors should assume that women will seek to fill in perceived gaps in their legal knowledge and do what they believe is necessary to win the case. They will carry out appearance work, rehearse their testimony, manage their emotions, build courtroom teams, research their roles, and procure evidence, all to enhance the strength of the case and their ability to perform their witness roles. Much of the time, survivors' efforts will be consistent with the goals of prosecution. However, when guided by an understanding of the issues involved in the case that is different than that held by prosecutors, their efforts can work at cross-purposes with prosecutors' plans. Legal personnel who educate survivors about the prosecution process are more likely to become aware of their initiatives and be able to guide their activity so that it reinforces rather than undermines the prosecutorial agenda. Those who learn of rape survivors' initiatives are positioned to gain additional but unanticipated relevant evidence.

A critical aspect of improving rape survivors' experiences of pleas is ensuring that they are never caught unawares by this development. They and other crime victims need to be told early on about the proportion of cases of all kinds that are resolved through pleas. Crime victims need to learn about their structural position in pleas before they are confronted by the reality. Under current law, a right to be consulted does not imply an individual right to demand a specific outcome. The state's legal ownership of the case allows the prosecutor to dispose of the case before trial if she or he determines that resolution serves state needs.

Survivors who participate in the RESTORE program are prepared before they encounter their assailants. The mediator informs them about the scope of possible penalties and the reparation options that are available through the program, so they do not enter into interaction with unrealistic expectations. It is logical to incorporate such a discussion about the sanctions actually imposed in a given jurisdiction into the early discussions all investigators and prosecutors have with rape survivors.[42]

Contact that makes legal personnel aware of rape survivors' precourt initiative also enables them to reevaluate initial impressions they have formed of rape survivors and to reduce systemic bias that tends to follow from the application of organizational stereotypes. Studies of real and hypothetical rape reporting have found that women who are raped by men they know, without weapons, and experience few injuries in addition to the rape are less likely to report their violation to police.[43] A common extrapolation made from this information is that late reporters will be less-willing witnesses and less committed to the prosecution process. I found, however, that women whose experiences were least consistent with stereotypes and hesitated the longest in making reports to police were among the *most* active in working toward prosecution. This counterintuitive finding is important. It suggests that the documented practices of not bringing charges against suspects or plea-bargaining when rape survivors delay in making police reports, or when they experienced something other than a stereotypical rape, excludes women from the prosecution process who otherwise would be committed to it. Specifically, it excludes women willing to devote time, energy, and personal funds to have the opportunity to see their assailant held accountable for his actions. With evidence that reluctant reporters do "come around" to be committed witnesses, prosecutors should be more willing to prosecute cases that they currently perceive to be hard won.

Rape survivors' involvement in early court events—bail hearings, arraignments, and motions of various kinds—can be facilitated by legal personnel who establish and maintain contact with them. While the rape survivor is *not necessary* for prosecution purposes, these court events offer venues for them to confront their assailants as crime victims and begin to overcome feelings of domination. Rape survivors' progress in reconstituting their selves before probable cause hearings and trials has the potential to reduce anxiety about testifying and to reduce the impact of the defendant in the courtroom, thereby increasing their ability to manage emotions, interaction, and information as needed. Opportunities to confront defendants in early court events might also lessen feelings of personal loss, which are associated with plea negotiations that take place before rape survivors have an opportunity to testify at probable cause hearings or trials. Participating in early court events allows rape survivors to see the "doing of justice" and thus may contribute to their positive assessment of procedural justice.

The Case for Detail in Precourt Preparation of Rape Survivors

Sometimes prosecutors prepare rape survivors well ahead of court events, but many times, as discussed in chapter 4, this information is not provided until court events are in process, if at all. In addition, information about influencing the judge or jury is often given at the expense of information about the survivor's place in the interaction and her ability to shape its development. The typical "witness" that is constructed before the majority of probable cause hearings and a large minority of trials is, thus, anxious and unprepared to perform her role gracefully. Her lack of general and case-specific information sets her up to be re-victimized. She is not knowledgeable about the situation into which she will enter or about her ability to control the question-answer interaction and, as such, is open to attack by the defense attorney. Additionally, lack of discussion about how to manage the discomforting aspects of testifying leaves the rape survivor exposed.[44] In short, when prosecutors do not thoroughly inform rape survivors, they contribute to the survivors' dis-ease and anger as well as frustrate their efforts to regain a superior position relative to the defendant and defense attorney. From the standpoint of securing convictions, this is counterproductive.

Lack of accurate information leads rape survivors to be anxious and to act on the basis of their fears. Before court events, prosecutors should fully inform them about the witness role, the roles of others with whom they will interact, and the formal and informal rules of interaction. Providing rape survivors with detailed information about defense attorneys' questioning practices and the possible ways they make constructing answers difficult acknowledges fear of a second assault. Disabusing women of any expectation that cross-examination will have the "normal" ritual qualities of conversation, or that they will be extended sympathy by the defense attorney, should assist them in avoiding or at least anticipating feelings of shame, embarrassment, and hurt. Discussing problems openly also sets the stage for prosecutors to explain how they will participate in cross-examination *with* the rape survivor. Survivors should be told what objections are intended to achieve and how and when the prosecutor is likely to use them. Even in cases of stranger rape, women should be told what protection they can reasonably expect under the state's rape shield, so they can think through management of their social identities. These discussions must be tailored to the known specifics of cases, as rape survivors' relationships with defendants will expose them to various questions.

Prosecutors will benefit from matter-of-factly discussing the ways in which rape survivors might independently respond to interaction problems or threats to their presentations of self during cross-examination. Once they address the full scope of resistance strategies—accommodating defense attorneys' behavior, manipulating and halting interaction—and their potential pitfalls, prosecutors are positioned to introduce preferred ways to handle problems. Prosecutors can identify nonverbal ways for survivors to communicate "help me, I am being shut down," so they can ask for assistance in protecting their speaking turns.

The defendant and the defense attorney are sources of intense feeling that compete for a rape survivor's attention whether or not they are in conversation with her. Prosecutors can (1) ensure that the survivor has someone who will provide friendly eye contact by assisting supporters in finding seats that are out of the line of sight of the defendant and (2) introduce an alternative audience toward whom the rape survivor can direct her responses (such as an advocate) if she wishes to turn away from the defendant or defense attorney. In the event that a survivor does not have a support network, it is in the prosecutor's best interest to assist her in securing an advocate through local agencies. If prosecutors are aware that rape survivors are in counseling, they can encourage them to work on mentally erasing or diminishing the defendant.

Discussion of formal rules and established practices must be accompanied by a matter-of-fact conversation about the potential conflict a rape survivor will find between the obligations of the witness role and her social identities. Prosecutors or advocates should solicit a rape survivor's concerns about social exposure, and they should discuss any strategy they have for managing specific information about her. Should she indicate any serious conflict with her self-image, the prosecutor should address this. One approach is to facilitate the rape survivor's access to alternative courtroom supports (such as victim-witness assistance) during the periods when testimony is perceived to be troubling. Another is to seek a middle ground in terms of informational openness with the survivor, and to craft a set of questions collaboratively to lead her through the minefield.

In sum, it is urgent that prosecutors rethink their relationship to rape survivors with respect to interaction management and information management. If women do not see *prosecutors as resources*, with concrete capabilities to protect them from what they fear during court events, they will manage problems that occur in court by themselves. When they manage alone, their strategies may or may not be aligned with the state's case. In particular, if trial is a possibility, prosecutors must consider the potential negative ramifications of letting unprepared witnesses endure preliminary hearings so they can assess their fortitude and the strength of the evidence. This is a recipe for heightened self-protective behavior in all of its manifestations, and the rape survivor who has the tenacity to continue with prosecution is likely to interpret the prosecutor's failure to act as lack of capability or interest. Unless she is very knowledgeable and confident, neither of these assessments will encourage *her* to initiate communication should the case go to trial. Once a survivor has a negative view of a prosecutor, it is an uphill battle to build rapport and gain trust, both of which are necessary to produce a single collaborative strategy at trial.

The Case for Collaboration and Facilitating Rape Survivor Control

Prosecutors should never assume that rape survivors abdicate their ownership of the rape and the responsibility that implies when serving as a witness. Prosecutors must expect that rape survivors can and will act to protect their ability to provide answers and to control how they are represented throughout court events.

Within the context of the courtroom, my interviews suggest that prosecutors are primarily concerned with surface expressions of emotion—such as tears, tones of voice, and facial expressions—that are available to the judge and jury and give the appearance of feelings of pain, terror, and anger. Likewise, they appear to be interested in controlled emotional displays: tears without convulsive weeping and tears that can be brought to a halt through the application of tissues, water, and short breaks from testifying. A desire for surface level expression of emotion is inconsistent with the emotional intensity of many survivors' testifying experiences. The pain, anger, and terror associated with seeing one's assailant, reliving the assault, seeing one's parents' pain, and so forth, are intensely felt and survivors expend a great deal of energy to manage these feelings in order to carry out the responsibilities of their witness role. They are not dispassionate, but achieve an apparent "rationality" and calm demeanor to protect their selves. In some cases, their successful cultivation of anger, which is inappropriate from a feeling rule standpoint, may be what stands between their coherent testimony and incoherent sobbing. Thus, prosecutors must accept the fact that, while they can inform rape survivors of the emotional displays that are most likely to sway a jury, they cannot dictate rape survivors' emotions. They will, out of necessity, work to protect their selves.[45]

Prosecutors can avoid contributing to sudden rushes of emotion by showing rape survivors photographs and other physical evidence before they introduce them into the courtroom. Moreover, prosecutors may increase their key witnesses' confidence by giving them a nonverbal cue to use when they are in trouble, are close to losing emotional control, and desperately need a break. It is very doubtful that these two mitigation tactics will eliminate the surface expression of emotions from the courtroom; however, they should make the management of interaction somewhat less difficult for rape survivors and make it easier for them to align with prosecutorial concerns about emotional expression.

During court events, prosecutors must carry through any agreed-on information management strategies and respond to any nonverbal calls for support or intervention.

The Case for Transparency, Procedural and Substantive Justice, and Formal Opposition in Plea-Bargaining

Plea-bargaining is critically important because it affects the majority of rape survivors whose cases are prosecuted after they make reports to police. Yet there is not a robust discussion about it within the scholarly and activist community concerned with rape prosecution. Prosecutors maintain their discretion in pleas by standing behind the legal construction of state ownership of crime. The conflation of rape survivors' interests with state interests has also been used to justify the value of any plea of guilt that is obtained. However, a criminal justice process that is responsive to rape survivors' needs cannot be achieved while setting aside the plea component. Drawing on my findings, this section suggests some important features of a process that will achieve greater substantive and procedural justice for rape survivors.

Prosecutors must not reduce the charges in rape cases substantially more than they do in cases of comparable nonsexual assaults and robbery. Prosecutors must not extend defendants in sexual assault or rape cases a greater plea benefit in terms of official label, type of sentence, or sentence length, because of their selection of victim or their mode of attack. While the need to offer pleas may reside with cultural stereotypes, the logic of pleas that are offered does not need to be based on extralegal features of cases. However, historic patterns of bias in rape prosecution and the limited comparative research conducted on pleas in an adversarial system like our own strongly suggest that a persistent pattern of bias should be *assumed* in most jurisdictions.[46] Until such time as research establishes otherwise, prosecutorial organizations should seek to moderate the plea benefit made available to defendants in sexual assault and rape cases.

Eliminating the practice of doubly rewarding defendants for guilty pleas is a place to begin. Reduction in the severity of sexual assault and rape charges should not consistently be accompanied by sentence reductions. When it is organizational practice for prosecutors to file complaints with the maximum possible complement of charges that can be derived from the rape survivor's report to police, charge reductions achieved through negotiations are quite obvious, and this practice would be fairly straightforward to implement and monitor. However, it will not work in jurisdictions such as Urban County, where felony complaints are filed with minimal charges—in order to secure early pleas—unless prosecutors acknowledge their starting points as reductions. When pleas are negotiated before probable cause is established through a grand jury or preliminary hearing, this may not be possible. However, if a rape survivor provides sworn testimony in a preliminary hearing in Urban County, giving evidence of a more serious crime, her reality should be acknowledged as the starting point.

Second, following Taslitz's line of argument about the broad impact of silencing women in trials, we need to recognize that negating the meaning of their testimony at any stage in the process subverts the cause of justice for *all* women. When the version of victimization that state representatives formally enter into law is substantially different from the experience a rape survivor has formally conveyed, the plea process functions to silence all women. Formal practices should be created to hold prosecutors accountable when they negotiate a plea that results in the elimination of the sexual component of the crime. Minimally, they should provide written justification of the action. However, I favor implementing a mandatory review before the prosecutor can formalize the plea agreement. This review, conducted by a superior, would require that the rape survivor be given an opportunity, accompanied by an advocate of her choosing, to convey her concerns about the plea terms.

While I encourage setting some limits on prosecutors' discretion in negotiating rape and sexual assault cases, we must recognize that they need to maintain latitude in deciding when to commit to trial. Given this, there needs to be formal recognition of the potential divergence of rape survivors' and the state's interest in pleas. Prosecutors must consult with rape survivors before agreements are finalized: inform them in a timely way that plea discussions have been opened, tell them what terms are being offered and how they differ from initial charges, and allow them an opportunity to ask questions and to offer support or opposition. Prosecutors should not be required or expected to achieve the rape survivor's agreement to plea terms, however, because the structural lack of authority rape survivors have makes this a recipe for these interactions to become dominating and assault-like. Rape survivors who object to plea agreements should be *invited* to state their opposition to renaming or devaluing their injury publicly in court, as well as in writing, before a judge officially accepts the plea and validates the prosecutor's discretionary decision. Encouraging rape survivors to publicly express their opposition to legal reconstruction of their experience initiates public discussion of the reality of rape that is suppressed when they do not have an opportunity to testify. It also challenges state mechanisms that deny to the public the women's reality, which Taslitz builds as a strong case is in violation of women's collective 14th and 1st Amendment rights.[47] Furthermore, presenting public opposition in the context of a judicial hearing reasserts the responsibility that the judiciary has to secure a just process. If bias is persistent in plea agreements it occurs because judges condone it. Rape survivors' public expressions of opposition to pleas are one small step toward holding the judiciary accountable.

To acknowledge rape survivors' experiences of victimization fully, it is logical for prosecutors to present disputed plea agreements to the court in ways that recognize the differences in the state's and the rape survivor's interests. Prosecutors should not claim that they pursued a plea to meet a particular victim's need for a speedy case resolution or to allow her to avoid testifying unless the rape survivor truly made that request. Instead they should acknowledge that their decision to negotiate reflects organizational needs, including an interest in avoiding the costs and time associated with trial. They should also be free to state that the decision to negotiate does not reflect their own personal beliefs about the rape survivor's credibility.

The Case for Facilitating Rape Survivor Involvement in Sentencing

As many of the quotations in this book demonstrate, survivors of rape are unhappy with their exclusion from a series of decisions and events that matter a great deal to them.[48] When given the opportunity to assert their ownership of the rape publicly and exercise their right to speak and write to the court or simply to attend hearings, many take advantage of it.

Some critics have focused on the possibility that victims' exercise of their rights to participate will hurt defendants—by capriciously lengthening sentences. Yet empirical research has not shown this to be a consistent outcome of sentencing reform.[49] Other critics have pointed to failure of the reforms to change sentencing practices substantially as a weakness. A. Walsh, for example, argues against extending the right to participate in sentencing to crime victims on the grounds that it does not equate to shifts in substantive outcomes, producing consistently longer sentences.[50] He implies that there may be a cathartic result for individuals, but he dismisses that as a secondary outcome, calling it a "placebo."

While Walsh places a priority on substantive justice, many of the rape survivors who participated in this study did not give more weight to obtaining substantive justice than resolving the emotional impact of the rape event. In fact, some women who sought to equalize the imbalance of power with the defendant and sought emotional closure did not express any interest in obtaining substantive justice through their participation in sentencing. Furthermore, if substantive justice seemed unlikely, even if desirable, women participated in sentencing to achieve other ends. In sum, survivors did not give more weight to affecting systemic outcomes than to preserving themselves. To characterize their behavior as succumbing to a placebo is to ignore their lived experiences and their agency.

To the extent that rape survivors come to feel a new balance of interpersonal power between themselves and the defendant, they have achieved a more equitable relationship.[51] This is a clear benefit to them that does not increase harm to others. Orth and Maercker's findings that crime victims' feelings of "moral satisfaction" are significantly associated with fewer posttraumatic symptoms years later are consistent with these results.[52] Rape survivors' efforts to use the sentencing process to achieve substantive and procedural justice, to reduce the imbalance of power with the defendant, and to overcome the emotional impact of the rape should thus be encouraged.

Facilitating survivors' participation in sentencing has several components. One goal should be to provide every woman with a venue to achieve her goals.[53] Toward this end, legislative activism should focus on broadening crime victims' rights to encompass speaking and writing the court in all jurisdictions. A second goal should be to ensure that all rape survivors are enabled to use all legal means to participate in the process. All women must be informed of their legal rights to participate, and we must work to address any social conditions that work against the participation of particular groups of women. Instead of relying on prosecutors to pass on information to rape survivors, RCCs and victims-witness advocates should become part of the information chain. But the education effort should not stop with institutions identified with servicing victims, as many women do not avail themselves of these services. Churches and pastors and other women's social organizations may be the primary resources and supports for some women.

Victims' rights must not remain privileges extended by a small portion of legal personnel. Thus, a third goal should be to engage prosecutors in actively supporting rape survivors' participation, which is logically coupled with improving their reliability as information sources. Following court events that are resolved through pleas or findings of guilt, prosecutors can reinforce rape survivors' claims of ownership of the rape, by encouraging them to put *their* stories on record, if they have a desire to do so.

The Case for Vertical Prosecution

Early contact, detailed preparation, development of a courtroom strategy, and honest and complete consultation about pleas are not possible when prosecutors are not able to develop rapport with rape survivors. Our best hope for achieving this comes from so-called vertical prosecution, in which one prosecutor sees a case through from filing the complaint to resolution. He or she has an opportunity to see a rape survivor develop a sense of her victim-witness role and understand her motivations to participate. The rape survivor also has an opportunity to see the prosecutor demonstrate competence, caring, and commitment. Yet vertical prosecution in the context of scarce resources can lead prosecutors to concentrate their energy on cases that are further along in the process, consequently negating its potential as an avenue to rapport. Thus, adequate state funds are crucial to the improvement of rape survivors' experiences, a more just process, and collaborative arrangement between prosecutors and their key witnesses.

The Case for the Involvement of Rape "Experts"

Many survivors and the others who helped them reach reporting decisions believed the content of education campaigns conducted by RCCs and the opinions of rape crisis advocates to be authoritative. Conversations with rape crisis advocates led women who experienced sexual assaults that differed from cultural stereotypes of rape to define them as serious, criminal, and worth bringing to police attention. These conversations and recollected education also led women to attempt to preserve evidence on their bodies, resisting any inclination they had to remove vestiges of their assailant's physical domination and rejecting sincere gestures of support that come in the form of offers of drinks of water and coffee. In two instances, advocates alerted survivors that medical personnel had failed to act expeditiously to collect evidence, and the women made a second effort to provide a forensic basis for prosecution.

This apparent social recognition of rape expertise residing outside the criminal justice process supports Martin's argument that working relationships should be established and interdepartmental training should be conducted between rape crisis, law enforcement, prosecution, victim-witness, and medical organizations.[54] In particular, it would be advantageous for rape crisis advocates as well as victim-witness advocates to receive detailed training about the basics of plea-bargaining, courtroom roles and rules of interaction, and methods of responding to domineering questioning strategies, because survivors incorporate them into their courtroom teams.

Victim-witness and rape crisis advocates present a solution to the conflicts posed by many rape survivors' would-be team members. They are concerned, but *not* personally invested, supporters. Furthermore, agency advocates can make a commitment of sustained involvement to survivors throughout the lengthy process of a criminal case, whereas friends or family members may not be able to make such a commitment because of work or other activities. Working-class and poor women, whose family members and friends are more likely to be engaged in hourly wage work, might benefit substantially from this aspect of formal support programs. Given the important contributions advocates make to survivors' comfort in the courtroom and ability to carry out their victim-witness roles, it would be wise to continue state funding of these programs. It is necessary to extend them as well so that advocates are available should rape survivors desire support discussing a plea or attending arraignments, changes of plea, and sentencing hearings.

Increasing rape survivors' involvement with advocates could also relieve prosecutors from "social work" tasks, as advocates address fears and instill a "positive attitude toward the criminal justice system" in witnesses.[55] However, *turning over* preparation of rape survivors to victim-witness advocates is unlikely to meet rape survivors' needs fully for two reasons. First, advocates who do not work closely with prosecutors, who are housed in other parts of the criminal justice process like sheriffs' departments, or who work for an independent agency like that in Urban County are rarely privy to case specifics and cannot give rape survivors much information relevant to crafting their stories, managing known defense stories, or identifying qualities of the defense attorney. Second, in jurisdictions like Rural County, where advocates are intimately tied in with prosecution, they may be reluctant to reveal information to rape survivors that might "jeopardize" the prosecution effort, thus replicating the problem of lack of relevant information. Worse yet, their alignment with prosecution may exacerbate rape survivors' feelings of being dominated and coerced. Another consideration about relying on victim-witness advocates to ensure adequate preparation is the lack of availability of advocates in all jurisdictions at this time.

The Case for Written Material

Accomplishing the goal of educating rape survivors requires not just a commitment on the part of prosecutors to view them as collaborators or access to advocates, but also relevant written materials to guide these discussions that rape survivors can retain and review at their leisure. Developing such materials will require a fiscal commitment by law enforcement and prosecutorial organizations. However, this effort is already in process, as social scientists concerned about rape survivors' experiences in court and the success of prosecution have produced some publications that are suitable for adaptation. Amanda Parriag, Edward Renner, and Christine Alksnis have written an analysis of the false logic at the base of defense questioning strategies and compiled a useful table that systematically summarizes their discussion.[56] In another publication specifically for witnesses, Renner and Parriag explain how rape survivors can respond to particular types of questions that are intended to challenge their credibility as victims.[57]

It is possible within the parameters of the U.S. criminal justice process to achieve more humane treatment for individual rape survivors and achieve the broader societal goal of gender equity. Recognizing the behavior of rape survivors as willful and understanding that responding to their needs can support the state's mission of prosecution are key to this effort. Progress will be facilitated through collaboration among processing agencies, through expansion of education, and through the individual activism of rape survivors and their supporters.

NOTES

Chapter 1

1. Miller, Cohen, and Wiersema (1996) estimate that the fiscal cost of rape to adult victims (out-of-pocket expenses) is close to $127 billion annually.

2. In 2002, the Federal Bureau of Investigation (FBI) announced that someone had raped or attempted to rape 64.8 of every 100,000 women and girls in the United States. However, the Bureau of Justice Statistics' National Crime Victimization Survey (NCVS), conducted to determine the nature and extent of *unreported* crime, produced a substantially higher figure in the same time period: 103 attempted or forcible rapes per 100,000 women and girls.

3. See Kilpatrick and Ruggiero (2004) for a discussion of the strengths and weaknesses of various ways rape has been measured.

4. See Holmstrom and Burgess (1983).

5. See Konradi (1994) for the interview schedule.

6. My goal was to develop an analysis with maximum fit among all the interviews, following the logic of analytic induction. See Katz (1983). See Konradi (1994) for more detailed discussion of methodology.

7. I employed the perspective of symbolic interaction that arose from the pragmatic philosophy of Mead (1964) and that was systematized by Blumer (1969). I also drew on the interactionism of Goffman (1959, 1961, 1967) and others who emphasized that human collectivities maintain stability because members share certain rules about *how* to interact.

8. States formed from regions once controlled by the Spanish and French reflect the legal systems of their forebears as well.

9. Bienen (1980: 47) reports that in New Jersey the rape law in effect in 1976 was "essentially the same as the one enacted in 1796, which in turn was derived from an Elizabethan statute first enacted in 1576."

10. Proof of penetration shifted as new techniques for examining the body emerged. The ability to detect semen by looking through a microscope replaced visual inspection that was adequate to establish the hymen was torn. DNA tests are the most recent development in establishing the source of sperm.

11. See *Yale Law Journal* (1972).

12. See Brownmiller (1975); Estrich (1986); LeGrand (1973); Robin (1977); Schwartz and Clear (1980); Schwendinger and Schwendinger (1974); and Williams (1984).

13. See Caringella-MacDonald (1984).

14. See LeGrand (1973: 935); emphasis mine.

15. See Bohmer (1974); Loh (1981); and Polk (1985).

16. See LeGrand (1973).

17. See Bevacqua (2000); Matthews (1994); and Schwartz and Clear (1980).

18. See Bienen (1977); Estrich (1986); Loh (1981); and Rose (1977).

19. See Berger (1977); Bienen (1976, 1977, 1980); and LeGrand (1973).

20. The *Harvard Law Review* (2004) reported that, in 2004, 31 states and the District of Columbia did not mention resistance in statutory language, while six states explicitly noted that resistance was not required for rape to occur. Lyon (2004) notes that currently one state retains the old common law requirement of utmost resistance.

21. Lyon (2004) reports that removal of the marital exemption was mostly accomplished in the 1980s, when the number of states that dropped them increased from 9 to 42. Currently, 2 states maintain a broad immunity, while 24 states and the District of Columbia have abolished it completely. However, the *Harvard Law Review* (2004) reports that 13 states require separation or divorce, unless the rape is accomplished by force.

22. Kessler (1992: 82) described rape shields as follows: "All rape shield laws limit the admissibility of evidence concerning a rape complainant's prior sexual history to some extent. Some statutes categorically exclude evidence involving the prior sexual history of the victim with third parties. However, other statutes provide that evidence may be admitted for certain narrowly prescribed purposes, for example, to dispute a material fact like the origin of pregnancy or venereal disease or to raise a motive for the complainant to have fabricated the accusation. Still others direct trial court judges to weigh the probative value of proffered evidence against its likely prejudicial effects." Most states now have a rape shield, but many include exceptions for patterns of conduct or a prior relationship. See Gruber (1997) for a discussion of variation in statutes. See Berry (2002) for an evaluation of current statutes.

23. See Boeschen, Sales, and Koss (1998) for a discussion of the scientific legitimacy of using expert testimony about rape trauma syndrome in the courts and Hoeffle (2001) for a discussion of its current legal status.

24. The Massachusetts District Attorney's Association (www.mass.gov/mdaa/courts/king.html) reported in September 2005 that the Massachusetts Supreme Court ruled, in *Commonwealth v. King*, that the first person a rape survivor speaks to can provide evidence of that fact and give details about the victim's mental and physical condition. This opinion is notable for its direct rejection of rape myths.

25. See Frazier and Haney (1996); Martin (2005); Martin, DiNitto, Byington, and Maxwell (1992); and Rose (1977).

26. This medical exam also allowed survivors to get immediate medical care. This included the opportunity to obtain hormone pills to prohibit pregnancy and antibiotics to ward off venereal disease.

27. Martin (2005) has argued that Rape Crisis Centers (RCCs) are now more common than ever, but they are concentrated in urban centers, leaving women living in rural areas without support.

28. See Ledray (1999).

29. See Bevacqua (2000); Berger, Searles, and Neuman (1987); Campbell, Self, Barnes, Aherns, Wasco and Zaragosa-Diesfeld (1999); Caringella-MacDonald (1984, 1988);

Estrich (1987); Frazier and Haney (1996); LeBeau (1988); Loh (1981); Martin (2005); and Spohn and Horney (1992).

30. See Frohman (1991); and Stanko (1981). LaFree (1980); Rose and Randall (1982); and Kerstetter (1990) report that rape survivors' races and other personal attributes factor into police officers' decisions to do the investigative work necessary to bring cases to the attention of prosecutors. Chandler and Torney (1981); Frohmann (1991); LaFree (1981, 1989); and Stanko (1981) report they also factor into prosecutors' decisions to file felony charges and pursue them through to trial. Schafran (1993) explains how judges' sentencing decisions continued to demonstrate a concern with nonlegal factors of cases, such as a rape survivor's relationship to her assailant, her marital status, her race, and her class.

31. Kessler (1992) shows some judges defined a single case of contact as patterned behavior. Recent appellate rulings go both ways on this issue. Toutant (2004) reports that the Supreme Court of New Jersey ruled a defendant could introduce information about previous nonsexual interactions he had with the victim several years before the rape. However, in February 2004, the Pennsylvania Supreme Court ruled in *Commonwealth v. Watkins* No. 2997–01 that a defendant could not introduce testimony about sexual interactions the victim had with the defendant's brother. See the *Pennsylvania Discovery and Evidence Reporter* (2004).

32. See Matoesian (1993, 1995); and Taslitz (1999). Ehrlich (2001) draws similar conclusions about the prosecution of rape in Canada.

33. The majority of cases were prosecuted in California, four each came from Arizona and Louisiana, and the rest were spread among Virginia, Illinois, Iowa, Montana, New Jersey, Kansas, and Washington. Sixty-two percent of the women were involved in prosecuting cases in California; 59 percent of those took place in the Urban County.

34. I have used 1987 for comparison because Searles and Berger (1987) published a comprehensive state-by-state analysis of rape laws in that year. When I began this research four years later, no one had updated it.

35. Maria and Louisa.

36. See Larcombe (2002); Matoesian (1993); and Sanday (1996).

37. Feminists typically refer to rape "myths" to underscore the lack of factual support for rape stereotypes. To readers interested in the complicated political and historic genesis of rape myths in the United States, I recommend *A Woman Scorned: Acquaintance Rape on Trial*, an anthropological analysis written by Sanday (1996). For a discussion of the infiltration of social myths about rape into the law in the United Kingdom see Stevenson (2000). The deeply racist nature of rape myths is discussed by Schwendinger and Schwendinger (1974) and Davis (1981). Matoesian (1993) provides a short but systematic comparison of the facts of rape to the psychopathological model of rape—implicit in prevailing stereotypes—and to an alternate structural alternative put forward by feminists in "The Social Facticity of Rape" a chapter of *Reproducing Rape*. Those who are interested in the degree to which the general population believes rape myths can find an extensive body of psychological literature on the subject. Typing "rape myths" or "rape stereotypes" into any general Internet search engine will produce a plethora of lists, many on university and college Web sites. Vachss (2003), a New York criminal prosecutor, discusses the way in which myths shaped public discussion of Kobe Bryant and his victim (originally published in the *Washington Post*).

38. For example, forced oral intercourse may be prosecuted as rape, sexual assault, sodomy, or involuntary deviant sexual intercourse, depending on the state.

39. See Martin (2005) for a cogent argument in favor of using the term "victim" when discussing the behavior of organizations that process rape. See Young and Maguire (2003) for a thorough review of social science literature pertaining to the naming debate.

40. One need only review the press coverage of the victims involved in prosecuting Kobe Bryant, Mike Tyson, and William Kennedy Smith to grasp this concept.

Chapter 2

1. Survivors include Wanda, Isabel, Bernice, Janice, Crystal, Susan, Mimi, Nan, Mary, Marlene, Francine, Lauren, Natalie, Candace, Trudy, Emily, Gwendolyn, Cindy, Connie, and Sara.

2. Survivors include Mimi, Susan, Natalie, Wanda, Lauren, Isabel, and Francine.

3. Strangers raped three of these women, an acquaintance raped one, and three were raped by their spouse/partners. Men who attacked Barbara, Rosanne, and Nellie brandished weapons, and Jennifer's assailant implied he had a gun. Louisa and Katherine were battered shortly before being assaulted; Maria was battered during the assault. Louisa, Katherine, and Maria each perceived the violence in her relationship with the assailant to be escalating. All the assailants threatened further violence to the survivors or their families if reports were made to police.

4. The rapist did not indicate that he knew Rosanne reported. He did not attack her daughter.

5. The detective who took Katherine's statement renamed "forced sex" as "rape." With the new name for her experience, she suddenly understood why the police were so intent on apprehending her assailant.

6. Survivors include Julianne, Carmela, and Rachel.

7. See Brison (2002); Cahill (2001); and Winkler (2002).

8. See Burgess and Holmstrom (1976, 1979).

9. Survivors include Arlene, Monica, Gabriella, Frida, Elisa, Sandra, Anna, and Leslie.

10. Survivors include Barbara, Francine, Lauren, Trudy, Connie, Emily, Gwendolyn, Cindy, and Candace.

11. Pierce-Baker, an African American rape survivor, shows in *Surviving the Silence* (1998) that race is certainly salient in some reporting decisions.

12. Hollander (2001) makes the important point that others contribute to victims' perceptions of vulnerability and dangerousness on a daily basis. Prior conversations likely contributed to some women taking their assailants' threats more seriously than others did.

13. See Dukes and Mattley (1977).

14. See Martin (2005).

15. Candace's efforts to look at her assailant resulted in him pummeling her about the face. This increased the violence of the assault and appears to have contributed to the prosecutor's view of the rape as an aggravated assault.

16. I believe that the failure of a jury to convict Rosanne's assailant was tied to their inability to understand that a rape victim was capable of strategic thought and behavior. How could a raped woman invite her assailant to return (even if she planned to set him up for arrest)?

17. See Dukes and Mattley (1977); Greenberg and Ruback (1985); Rennison (2002); and Rennison and Rand (2003).

Chapter 3

1. Like many defendants, this individual was released from custody on bond.

2. I use the term prosecutor to indicate a *function* within the criminal justice process. In vertical prosecution, a single prosecuting attorney handles the case from start to finish. In a horizontal process, a supervisor or a small team makes filing decisions, after which cases are passed on to deputies who pursue establishing probable cause. The case may again be transferred to another attorney for trial or sentencing.

3. Investigation may continue between the probable cause hearing and trial.

4. The average number of kinds of requests made of women attacked by strangers was 2.5, compared with the 1.1 requests made of women who knew their assailants.

5. Spohn, Beichner, and Davis-Frenzel (2001) report that inability to locate victims was the second most common reason prosecutors in their study dropped cases. See also Stanko (1982).

6. This message resulted in the apprehension of the suspect.

7. Most survivors expressed no desire to see the defendant before hearings for probable cause.

8. Survivors' relationships to rapists, other assault attributes (such as use of a weapon or injury), the speed with which they made reports, and their capability to decide and act alone were not indicative of their efforts to initiate interaction with the investigation.

9. I believe that Marlene's report of rape would have been quickly unfounded and her assailant gone uncharged without her persistence in the investigative phase.

10. See Kerstetter (1990).

11. See Frohmann (1998); Kerstetter (1990); and Spohn, Beichner, and Davis-Frenzel (2001).

12. See Conley and O'Barr (1990).

13. Spohn, Beichner, and Davis-Frenzel (2001) recognize that rape survivors likely pursue their own agendas and may opt out of prosecution when they feel they have achieved their goals.

Chapter 4

1. Some of the modes of preparation can have an impact beyond the category to which I have assigned them. However, thinking in terms of these categories helps us understand the impact of certain patterns of preparation on rape survivors. For example, a woman who is only prepared to attend to the credibility of her self-presentation may well have difficulty testifying if she is not well informed about the scope of her witness role.

2. Survivors received *court process information* before 70 percent of probable cause hearings and before 50 percent of trials.

3. Seventy percent of survivors received this preparation before preliminary hearings and 64 percent of survivors received this before trials.

4. This information was not conveyed to them before court events, possibly because the prosecutors believed that they would make trouble.

5. Hochschild (1979, 1983) describes how the production or suppression of specific emotions for display to others, in order to conform to feeling rules, is a form of psychological labor called emotion work.

6. Prosecutors were interested in appearances and were not concerned whether women actually felt the emotions they exhibited.

7. One woman noted the only information she received came from the detective assigned to the case, because the prosecutor could not or would not make any time for her.

8. Barbara was told probable direct questions, that she would be excluded when others testified, and briefly how she might manage emotionally difficult aspects of the courtroom.

9. See Holmstrom and Burgess (1983).

10. This is an important issue because defense attorneys may be more abusive in preliminary hearings than trials with a jury audience. See Matoesian (1993).

11. See Frohmann (1991).

12. See Davis (1981); and Sanday (1996).

Chapter 5

1. Some of the survivors who did not request this kind of support did not know it was available or did not want it.

2. Survivors called both victim-witness advocates and crisis workers to get answers to questions that attorneys ignored. When crisis workers could not provide answers to survivors' questions, they were sometimes able to pressure prosecutors to get the information that survivors needed. It is probable that advocates were cautious about saying things that could undermine the prosecutor, because victim-witness programs are often associated with the district attorney's office in some way.

3. Many survivors also read books about coping with the trauma of rape that included chapters on criminal prosecution, which suggests a possible continuum of "research" activity.

4. The defense attorney asked Julianne about previous occasions during which she had initially resisted sexual intercourse and then acquiesced, and he introduced some Polaroid photographs that depicted her bound in provocative poses. The judge called the preliminary hearing to a halt and recommended an immediate resolution. A plea agreement to significantly lesser charges was quickly arranged.

5. See Greenberg and Ruback (1992).

6. See Conley and O'Barr (1990).

Chapter 6

1. These women experienced their lack of power in the courtroom as the defendant's continued violation of them through institutional means.

2. It is possible that "they" in this quotation refers to the defendant as well as the defense attorney. That is, the defense attorney traps and continues to torment the rape survivor for the defendant. This would be consistent with survivors' experience of paralysis when seeing the defendant, described earlier.

3. They engaged in deep acting as described by Hochschild (1979, 1983).

4. Survivors made the greatest number of unsolicited references to the role of judges in the legal proceedings in connection to their efforts to help when the women were in distress.

5. See Bohmer and Blumberg (1975); Holmstrom and Burgess (1983); Lurigio and Resick (1990); and Madigan and Gambel (1989).

6. See Mills and Kleinman (1988).

7. See Shott (1979).

8. See Clark (1987, 1990); and Goffman (1959, 1967).

9. See Hochschild (1979, 1983).

10. See Holstein and Miller (1990); Konradi (1996a); and McCaffrey (1998).

11. This finding supports Bennett and Feldman's (1981) and Matoesian's (1993) contentions that the prosecutor is a participant in the production of direct and cross-examination testimony.

Chapter 7

1. Atkinson and Drew (1979: 113) argue that silence is so dangerous in a courtroom that even accused defendants, who have a right to remain silent, really cannot.

2. Survivors reported the following cross-examination problems (number of court events/percent of court events): defense attorney's demeanor (17/43 percent), repetitious questions (17/43 percent), blaming questions (13/33 percent), personal and graphic questions (12/30 percent), overly detailed questions (10/25 percent), illogical questions (10/25 percent), negative declarative statements (9/23 percent), and needling (3/8 percent).

3. Before the trial, the prosecutor prepared Janice in more detail. This preparation combined with her prior hearing experience made her feel much more knowledgeable, and she handled cross-examination alone.

4. The "two or three shots of southern comfort" she reported having during the lunch break, just before she confronted the defense attorney, may have contributed to her daring to do so.

5. Bennett and Feldman (1981: 121) report that lawyers in direct examination phrase their questions to give witnesses "cues about how broadly to answer a question, what to volunteer, and what to anticipate in the next question." Sanford (1987) and Kebbell, Deprez, and Wagstaff (2003) also found that prosecuting attorneys, like their defense counterparts, used question constructions that directed rape survivors' answers, including restrictive questions to narrow the rape survivors' direct testimony.

6. Both cases resulted in guilty verdicts.

7. The emphasis in this quotation is mine.

8. The emphasis in this quotation is mine.

9. Natalie later said that she held nothing back when she testified.

10. Unfortunately, as discussed in chapter 5, the defense did bring the photographs in as evidence to challenge her denials of equivocating about sexual activity.

11. This case was tried before DNA typing was used. Thus, the source of semen was not an issue.

12. See Rice (2003); and Valdez (1986).

13. See Danet, Hoffman, Kermish, Rafn, and Stayman (1980). Rice (2004) also found strategic introduction of information in the transcripts of preliminary hearings of rape cases she analyzed.

14. Atkinson and Drew (1979: 181) discovered that witnesses gave replies "designed to address (and even directly answer) *future* questions in projected sequences" ensuring them "opportunities to give replies to questions whose (future) production they [could not] guarantee."

15. See Matoesian (1993).

16. See Rice (2003).

17. In U.S. culture, demands to share what one knows generally are interpreted in the present context. From this perspective Arlene's answer was untrue, because she believed at the time of the trial that she had seen the defendant several days before he attacked her.

Chapter 8

1. See Kerstetter (1990); and Mack and Anleu (2000).

2. Respectively, this was 58 percent and 59 percent of the subsamples.

3. See Holmstrom and Burgess (1983); and Renner and Parriag (2002).

4. This "means to an end" way of conceptualizing charging is similar to the way in which prosecutors typically describe charges.

5. Parole practices also would alter these benchmarks; however, few survivors were attentive to this issue.

6. Both Frohmann (1998) and Kerstetter (1990) reported that during these face-to-face interactions prosecutors sought to reorient the perceptions of rape survivors with whom they did not agree. Specifically, they worked to convince some women who were interested in seeing charges filed that they would be better off if their injury was not prosecuted.

7. Julianne's account of working out the plea terms with the prosecutor *and* her father is anomalous.

8. Davis, Kunreuther, and Connick (1984) discovered that victim-witness advocates housed in prosecutors' offices had to carry out their responsibilities under restrictions placed on them by prosecutors and were often likely to identify with the prosecutor's interests.

9. See Winkler (2002).

10. See Madigan and Gambel (1989).

Chapter 9

1. The women were unaware that corrections officials generally determine where convicts serve their time.

2. See Holmstrom and Burgess (1983); and Shapland, Willmore, and Duff (1985: 107).

3. Women engaged in all forms of participation—speaking, writing, and attending—regardless of their relationship with the defendant, whether or not they sustained injuries, and their socioeconomic status and education. Survivors' relationships with defendants also did not differentiate their motivations to participate in sentencing.

4. See Villmoare and Neto (1987).

5. See Erez (1990); Kilpatrick and Otto (1987); and McLeod (1986).

6. See Erez and Guhlke (1988); Erez and Tontodonato (1990); McLeod (1987); and Villmoare and Neto (1987).

7. See Villmoare and Neto (1987).

8. See Villmoare and Neto (1987).

9. See Kerstetter and VanWinkle (1990).

10. See Frohmann (1991, 1998).

11. See Erez and Guhlke (1988); and Villmoare and Neto (1987).

Chapter 10

1. See Vachss (1993: 46).

2. In 1993, Antioch College introduced an affirmative consent requirement in its code of conduct. In 1994, the fourth Annual International Conference on Sexual Assault and Harassment on Campus held its first workshop titled "Sex without Consent." See Sanday (1996) for further discussion.

3. See Martin (2005) for a full discussion of the development, maintenance, and potential of these alliances. See also Martin and Powell (1994); and Schmitt and Martin (1999).

4. See Sanday (1996) for a review of this development and Pineau (1989) for an early statement.

5. The *Harvard Law Review* (2004: 2351–2352).

6. See Sanday (1996: 281); the emphasis is mine.

7. Similar statutes have passed in Illinois, Minnesota, Washington, and the District of Columbia. See *Harvard Law Review* (2004: 2350–2351).

8. See Lyon (2004).

9. In 1992 the California Supreme Court ruled in *People v. Williams* that the relevant issue is consent to intercourse, not consent to "spend time" with the defendant. In 1993 the Indiana Court of Appeals specified "an honest and reasonable belief that a member of the opposite sex will consent to sexual contact in the future is not a defense of rape." See *Harvard Law Review* (2004: 2352).

10. See Anderson (1998).

11. See Taslitz (1999).

12. See Taslitz (1999: 115).

13. See Taslitz (1999).

14. In some, but not all states, appellate courts established that prosecutors may introduce experts to testify about rape trauma syndrome to provide grounds for understanding a rape survivor's nonstereotypical behavior. See Boeschen, Sales, and Koss (1998) and Hoeffle (2001) for further discussion.

15. Taslitz (1999) maintains that the 1st and the 14th Amendments of the Constitution support the logic of his proposals. He considers the general emotional toll associated with confronting defendants and testifying about intimate assault to be an internal cost.

16. See Taslitz (1999: 112).

17. See Taslitz (1999:125).

18. See Martin (2005).

19. Martin (2005) describes research conducted by Koss, Bachar, Hopkins, and Carlson (2004). See Strang and Braithwaite (2002); Weitekamp and Kerner (2003); and Zehr (1990) for information about the restorative justice movement and practices in the United States and abroad.

20. Many existing restorative justice programs are limited to juveniles.

21. The print media and visual media should then be pressured to present the results on these studies to the public as a public service.

22. The American Bar Foundation is a source of funds for small-scale research projects focused on legal education.

23. See Konradi (2003) and Konradi and DeBruin (2003) for discussion about the possible logic of students' resistance to reporting and accessing SANE.

24. See Konradi and DeBruin (2003).

25. Public and private colleges and universities in the United States are required to publish incidents of crime that occur on and near their campuses as a result of the Jeanne Clery Disclosure of Campus Security Policy and Campus Crime Statistics Act. The law is enforced by the U.S. Department of Education.

26. Security on Campus (www.securityoncampus.org) focuses on the handling of rapes on college and university campuses.

27. See Martin (2005).

28. See Rauma (1984).

29. See Frohmann (1998); Kerstetter (1990); Spohn, Beichner, and Davis-Frenzel (2001); and Martin (2005).

30. See Frohmann (1991, 1998). Koss, Bachar, Hopkins, and Carlson (2004) report they are currently following usage patterns in their demonstration program, which should address these latter concerns

31. See Koss, Bachar, Hopkins, and Carlson (2004).

32. Martin and Powell (1994: 862); internal quotations omitted.

33. See Konradi (1996a, 1996b, 1997, 1999); and Konradi and Burger (2000).

34. See Martin (2005: 215–216); and Koss, Bachar, Hopkins, and Carlson (2004: 1442).

35. See Martin (2005). See Koss, Bachar, Hopkins, and Carlson (2004: 1442); my edits are in brackets.

36. See Martin (2005: 2230).

37. See Martin (2005: 2230).

38. See chapters 3–5 in Martin (2005) for discussion of frames that are imposed and chapter 6 for a discussion of discursive politics.

39. See Taslitz (1999: 116).

40. This model is based on symbolic interactionist and dramaturgical understandings of human behavior.

41. In *One Night*, Winkler (2002) explains how women can move to "victim as survivor-activist" (VISA) status by critically analyzing the institutional treatment they experience as painful and degrading. I believe having a framework for understanding their behaviors as ordinarily human can facilitate this process.

42. See Koss, Bachar, Hopkins, and Carlson (2004: 1451).

43. See Greenberg and Ruback (1992).

44. This is an important issue because defense attorneys may be more abusive in preliminary hearings than trials with a jury audience. See Matoesian (1993).

45. As Thoits (1996: 98) points out, "research has long shown that uncontrolled venting of emotion is not beneficial to individuals."

46. See Mack and Anleu (2000).

47. See Taslitz (1999).

48. This is consistent with what others have found: Hernon and Forst (1984); Kelly (1984); Konradi (1997); and Shapland, Willmore, and Duff (1985).

49. See Erez and Roeger (1995). Kelly and Erez (1997) review the known impact of victim participation on the administration of justice and sentences.

50. See Walsh (1986).

51. Several studies suggest that equity theory, as it is applied to crime victims should be elaborated in light of the sociology of emotions: Erez and Bienkowska (1993); Kilpatrick and Otto (1987); and Tontodonato and Erez (1994).

52. See Orth and Maercker (2004: 223).
53. See Joutsen (1987).
54. See Martin (2005).
55. See Finn and Lee (1985: 27).
56. See Parriag, Renner, and Alksnis (1998).
57. See Renner and Parriag (2002).

BIBLIOGRAPHY

Anderson, Michelle J. 1998. Reviving resistance in rape law. *University of Illinois Law Review* 1998 (4): 953–1001.

Atkinson, John, and Drew, Paul. 1979. *Order in Court: The Organization of Verbal Behavior in Judicial Settings.* London: Macmillan.

Bennett, W., and Feldman, M. 1981. *Reconstructing Reality in the Courtroom.* New Brunswick, NJ: Rutgers University Press.

Berger, Ronald, Searles, Patricia, and Neuman, W. Lawrence. 1987. The dimensions of rape reform legislation. *Law & Society Review* 22: 329–357.

Berger, Vivian. 1977. Men's trial, women's tribulation. *Columbia Law Review* January: 1–103.

Berry, Tracey A. 2002. Comment: Prior untruthful allegations under Wisconsin's rape shield law: Will those words come back to haunt you? *Wisconsin Law Review* 1237: 1243–1244.

Bevacqua, Maria. 2000. *Rape on the Public Agenda: Feminism and the Politics of Sexual Assault.* Boston: Northeastern University Press.

Bienen, Leigh. 1976. Rape I. *Women's Rights Law Reporter* Winter: 45–57.

———. 1977. Rape II. *Women's Rights Law Reporter* Spring: 90–137.

———. 1980. Rape III. *Women's Rights Law Reporter* Spring: 170–225.

Blumer, Herbert. 1969. *Symbolic Interactionism: Perspective and Method.* Berkeley: University of California Press.

Boeschen, Laura E., Sales, Bruce D., and Koss, Mary P. 1998. Rape trauma experts in the courtroom. *Psychology and Public Policy* 4 (1/2): 414–432.

Bohmer, Carol. 1974. Judicial attitudes toward rape victims. *Judicature* 57: 303–307.

Bohmer, Carol, and Blumberg, Ann. 1975. Twice traumatized: The rape victim and the court. *Judicature* 58: 391–399.

Brison, Susan J. 2002. *Aftermath: Violence and the Remaking of a Self.* Princeton, NJ: Princeton University Press.

Brownmiller, Susan. 1975. *Against Our Will: Men, Women, and Rape.* New York: Simon and Schuster.

Burgess, Ann W., and Holmstrom, Lynda L. 1976. Coping behavior of the rape victim; Rape trauma syndrome. *American Journal of Psychiatry* 133 (4): 413–418.

———. 1979. *Rape Crisis and Recovery.* Bowie, MD: Robert J. Brady.

Cahill, Anna J. 2001. *Rethinking Rape.* Ithaca, NY: Cornell University Press.

Campbell, Rebecca, Self, Tracy, Barnes, Holly E., Aherns, Courtney A., Wasco, Sharon
    M., and Zaragosa-Diesfeld, Yolanda. 1999. Community services for rape survivors:
    Enhancing psychological well being or increasing trauma? *Journal of Consulting
    and Clinical Psychology* 67 (6): 847–858.
Caringella-MacDonald, Susan. 1984. Sexual assault prosecution: An examination of
    model rape legislation in Michigan. *Women in Politics* 4 (3): 65–83.
———. 1988. Marxist and feminist interpretations of the aftermath of rape reforms.
    Contemporary Crises 12: 125–144.
Chandler, Susan M., and Torney, Martha. 1981. The decisions and the processing of
    rape victims through the criminal justice system. *California Sociologist* 4: 155–169.
Clark, Candace. 1987. Sympathy, biography, and sympathy margin. *American Journal of
    Sociology* 93: 290–321.
———. 1990. Emotions and micropolitics in everyday life: Some patterns and para-
    doxes of place. In *Research Agendas in the Sociology of Emotions*, edited by Theodore
    Kemper, 305–333. Buffalo: State University of New York Press.
Conley, J., and O'Barr, W. 1990. *Rules versus Relationships: The Ethnography of Legal Dis-
    course*. Chicago: University of Chicago Press.
Danet, B., Hoffman, K., Kermish, N., Rafn, H., and Stayman, D. 1980. An ethnography
    of questioning. In *Language and the Uses of Language*, edited by R. Shuy and A.
    Shnukal, 222–234. Washington, DC: Georgetown University Press.
Davis, Angela. 1981. *Women, Race, and Class*. New York: Vintage.
Davis, R. C., Kunreuther, F., and Connick, E. 1984. Expanding the victim's role in the
    criminal court dispositional process: The results of an experiment. *Journal of
    Criminal Law and Criminology* 75: 491–505.
Dukes, R., and Mattley, C. 1977. Predicting rape victim reportage. *Sociology and Social
    Research* 62 (1): 63–84.
———. 2003. *State Court Sentencing of Convicted Felons, 2000, Statistical Tables*. Bureau of
    Justice Statistics (NCJ 198822). http://www.ojp.usdoj.gov/bjs/abstract/scsc00st.htm.
Erez, E., and Bienkowska, E. 1993. Victim participation in proceedings and satisfaction
    with justice in the Continental systems: The case of Poland. *Journal of Criminal
    Justice* 21: 47–60.
Erez, E., and Guhlke, V. 1988. Victims in the court. Paper presented at the World Soci-
    ety of Victimology 6th International Symposium, Jerusalem, Israel.
Erez, E., and Roeger, L. 1995. The effect of victim impact statements on sentencing
    patterns and outcomes: The Australian experience. *Journal of Criminal Justice* 23:
    363–375.
Erez, E., and Tontodonato, P. 1990. The effect of victim participation in sentencing on
    sentence outcome. *Criminology* 28: 451–474.
Erez, Edna. 1990. Victim participation in sentencing: Rhetoric and reality. *Journal of
    Criminal Justice* 18: 19–31.
Estrich, Susan. 1986. Rape. *Yale Law Journal* 95 (6): 1087–1184.
———. 1987. *Real Rape*. Boston: Harvard University Press.
Finn, P., and Lee, B. 1985. Collaboration with victim-witness assistance programs: Pay-
    offs and concerns for prosecutors. *The Prosecutor* 18 (4): 27–36.
Frazier, Patricia A., and Haney, Beth. 1996. Sexual assault cases in the legal system:
    Police prosecutor and victim perspectives. *Law and Human Behavior* 20 (6): 607–628.
Frohmann, Lisa. 1991. Discrediting victims' allegations of sexual assault: Prosecutorial
    accounts of case rejections. *Social Problems* 38: 213–226.

———. 1998. Constituting power in sexual assault cases: Prosecutorial strategies for victim management. *Social Problems* 45: 393–407.

Goffman, Erving. 1959. *The Presentation of Self in Everyday Life.* Garden City, NJ: Doubleday.

———. 1961. *Encounters.* Indianapolis: Bobbs-Merrill.

———. 1967. *Interaction Ritual: Essays on Face-to-Face Behavior.* New York: Pantheon Books.

Greenberg, Martin S., and Ruback, R. Barry. 1985. A model of crime victim decision making. *Victimology* 10: 600–616.

———. 1992. *After the Crime: Victim Decision Making.* New York: Plenum Press.

Gruber, Aya. 1997. Pink elephants in the rape trial: The problem of tort-type defenses in the criminal law of rape. *William & Mary Law Review* 4: 203–225.

Harvard Law Review 2004. Acquaintance rape and degrees of consent: "No" means "no," but what does "yes" mean? *Harvard Law Review* 117 (7): 2341–2364.

Hernon, J., and Forst, B. 1984. *The Criminal Justice Response to Victim Harm.* Washington, DC: National Institute of Justice.

Hochschild, Arlie. 1979. Emotion work, feeling rules, and social structure. *American Journal of Sociology* 85 (3): 551–575.

———. 1983. *The Managed Heart: Commercialization of Human Feeling.* Berkeley: University of California Press.

Hoeffle, Janet C. 2001. The gender gap: Revealing gender inequalities in admission of social science evidence in criminal cases. *University of Arkansas at Little Rock Law Review* 24: 41–79.

Hollander, Jocelyn A. 2001. Vulnerability and dangerousness: The construction of gender through conversation about violence. *Gender & Society* 15 (1): 83–109.

Holmstrom, Lynda, and Burgess, Ann. 1983. *The Victim of Rape: Institutional Reactions.* New Brunswick, NJ: Transaction.

Holstein, James, and Miller, Gale. 1990. Rethinking victimization: An interactional approach to victimology. *Symbolic Interaction* 13: 103–122.

Joutsen, M. 1987. Listening to the victim: The victim's role in European criminal justice systems. *Wayne Law Review* 34: 95–124.

Katz, Jack. 1983. A theory of qualitative methodology: The social system of analytic fieldwork. In *Contemporary Field Research*, edited by Robert Emerson, 127–148. Boston: Little Brown.

Kebbell, M., Deprez, R., and Wagstaff, S. 2003. The direct and cross-examination of complainants and defendants in rape trials: A quantitative analysis of question type. *Psychology Crime and Law* 9 (1): 49–59.

Kelly, D. P. 1984. Victims' perceptions of criminal justice. *Pepperdine Law Review* 11: 15–22.

Kelly, D. P., and Erez, E. 1997. Victim participation in the criminal justice system. In *Victims of Crime*, 2nd ed., edited by R. C. Davis, A. Lurigio, and W. G. Skogan, 231–244. Thousand Oaks, CA: Sage.

Kerstetter, Wayne A. 1990. Gateway to justice: Police and prosecutorial response to sexual assault against women. *Journal of Criminal Law and Criminology* 81: 267–313.

Kerstetter, Wayne A., and VanWinkle, B. 1990. Who decides? A study of the complainant's decision to prosecute in rape cases. *Criminal Justice and Behavior* 13: 268–283.

Kessler, Elizabeth. 1992. Pattern of sexual conduct evidence and present consent: Limiting the admissibility of sexual history evidence in rape prosecutions. *Women's Rights Law Reporter* 14 (1): 79–96.

Kilpatrick, D. G., and Otto, R. K. 1987. Constitutionally guaranteed participation in criminal proceedings for victims: Potential effects on psychological functioning. *Wayne Law Review* 34: 7–28.

Kilpatrick, Dean G., and Ruggiero, Kenneth J. 2004. *Making Sense of Rape in America: Where Do the Numbers Come From and What Do They Mean?* Violence Against Women NET. www.VAWnet.org.

Konradi, Amanda. 1994. *Taking the Stand: Rape Survivors' Agency Reporting, Preparing, and Testifying in the Criminal Justice Process*. Ph.D. Thesis, Board of Studies in Sociology, University of California, Santa Cruz.

———. 1996a. Preparing to testify: Rape survivors negotiating the criminal justice process. *Gender & Society* 10: 404–432.

———. 1996b. Understanding rape survivors' preparations for court: Accounting for the influence of legal knowledge, cultural stereotypes, and prosecutor contact. *Violence Against Women* 2 (1): 25–62.

———. 1997. Too little, too late: Prosecutors' pre-court preparation of rape survivors. *Law & Social Inquiry* 22: 1101–1154.

———. 1999. "I don't have to be afraid of you": Rape survivors' emotion management in court *Symbolic Interaction* 22: 45–77.

———. 2003. A strategy for increasing post rape medical care and forensic examination. *Violence Against Women* 9 (8): 955–988.

Konradi, Amanda, and Burger, Tina. 2000. Having the last word: An examination of rape survivors' participation in sentencing. *Violence Against Women* 6 (4): 351–395.

Konradi, Amanda, and DeBruin, Patricia L. 2003. Using a social marketing approach to advertising sexual assault nurse examination (SANE) services to college students. *Journal of American College Health* 52 (1): 33–39.

Koss, Mary, Bachar, Karen, Hopkins, C. Quince, and Carlson, Carolyn. 2004. Expanding a community's justice response to sex crimes through advocacy, prosecutorial, and public health collaboration: Introducing the RESTORE program. *Journal of Interpersonal Violence* 19 (12): 1435–1463.

LaFree, Gary D. 1980. The effect of sexual stratification by race on official reactions to rape. *American Sociological Review* 45: 842–854.

———. 1981. Official reactions to social problems: Police decisions in sexual assault cases. *Social Problems* 28: 582–594.

———. 1989. *Rape and Criminal Justice: The Social Construction of Sexual Assault*. Belmont, CA: Wadsworth.

Larcombe, Wendy. 2002. The "ideal" victim v. successful rape complainants: Not what you might expect. *Feminist Legal Studies* 10: 131–148.

LeBeau, James L. 1988. Statute revision and the reporting of rape. *Sociology and Social Research* 72: 201–207.

Ledray, Linda. 1999. *Sexual Assault Nurse Examiner, SANE: Development and Operation Guide*. Washington, DC: U.S. Department of Justice, Office of Justice Programs, Office for Victims of Crime.

LeGrand, Camilla E. 1973. Rape and rape laws: Sexism in society and law. *California Law Review* 61: 919–1041.

Loh, Wallace. 1981. Q: What has reform of rape legislation wrought? A: Truth in criminal labeling. *Journal of Social Issues* 37 (4): 28–52.

Lurigio, A., and Resick, P. 1990. Healing the psychological wounds of criminal victimization: Predicting postcrime distress and recovery. In *Victims of Crime: Problems, Policies, and Programs*, edited by A. Lurigio, W. Skogan, and R. Davis, 50–68. Newbury Park, CA: Sage.

Lyon, Matthew R. 2004. No Means no? Withdrawal of consent during intercourse and the continuing evolution of the definition of rape. *Journal of Criminal Law and Criminology* 20 (1): 45–52.

Mack, Kathy, and Anleu, Sharyn Roach. 2000. Resolution without trial, evidence law and the construction of the sexual assault victim. In *Feminist Perspectives on Evidence*, edited by Mary Childds and Louise Ellison, 127–148. London: Cavendish Publishing.

Madigan, Lee, and Gamble, Nancy. 1989. *The Second Rape: Society's Continued Betrayal of the Victim*. New York: Lexington Books.

Martin, Patricia Yancey. 2005. *Rape Work: Victims, Gender, and Emotions in Organizational and Community Context*. New York: Routledge.

Martin, Patricia Yancey, DiNitto, Diana, Byington, Diane, and Maxwell, M. Sharon. 1992. Organizational and community transformation: A case study of a rape crisis center. *Administration in Social Work* 16: 123–145.

Martin, Patricia Yancey, and Powell, Marlene. 1994. Accounting for the "second assault": Legal organizations' framing of rape victims, *Law & Social Inquiry* 19 (4): 853–888.

Massachusetts District Attorneys Association. 2005. From the courts/recent court decisions: *Commonwealth v. King*, Supreme Judicial Court, September 29. www.mass.gov/mdaa/courts/king.html.

Matoesian, Gregory. 1993. *Reproducing Rape: Domination through Talk in the Courtroom*. Chicago: University of Chicago Press.

———. 1995. Language, law, and society: Policy implications of the Kennedy Smith rape trial. *Law & Society Review* 29: 669–702.

Matthews, Nancy. 1994. *Confronting Rape: The Feminist Anti-rape Movement and the State*. London: Routledge.

McCaffrey, Dawn. 1998. Victim feminism/victim activism. *Sociological Spectrum* 18: 263–284.

McLeod, M. 1986. Victim participation at sentencing. *Criminal Law Bulletin* 22: 501–517.

———. 1987. An examination of the victim's role at sentencing: Results of a survey of probation administrators. *Judicature* 71: 162–168.

Mead, George Herbert. 1964. *On Social Psychology: Selected Papers*. Chicago: University of Chicago Press.

Miller, Ted, Cohen, Mark, and Wiersema, Brad. 1996. *Victim Cost and Consequences: A New Look*. Washington, DC: U.S. Department of Justice. www.ncjrs.org/txtfils/victcost/pdf.

Mills, Trudy, and Kleinman, Sherryl. 1988. Emotions, reflexivity, and action: An interactionist analysis. *Social Forces* 66: 1009–1027.

Orth, Ulrich, and Maercker, Andraes. 2004. Do trials of perpetrators re-traumatize crime victims? *Journal of Interpersonal Violence* 19 (2): 212–227.

Parriag, Amanda, Renner, K. Edward, and Alksnis, Christine. 1998. Is logic optional in the courtroom? An examination of adult sexual assault trials. www.carelton.ca/erenner/nsap.html.

Pierce-Baker, Charlotte. 1998. *Surviving the Silence: Black Women's Stories of Rape.* New York: W. W. Norton and Co.

Pineau, Lois. 1989. Date rape: A feminist analysis. *Law and Philosophy* 8 (2): 217–243.

Polk, Kenneth. 1985. Rape reform and criminal justice processing. *Crime and Delinquency* 31 (2): 191–205.

Rauma, David. 1984. Going for the gold: Prosecutorial decision-making in cases of wife assault. *Social Science Research* 13: 321–351.

Renner, K. Edward, and Parriag, Amanda. 2002. Supporting adult witnesses: How you can present yourself effectively. www.napasa.org.

Rennison, Callie M. 2002. *Rape and Sexual Assault: Reporting to Police and Medical Attention, 1992–2000.* Washington, DC: U.S. Department of Justice, Office of Justice Programs, Bureau of Justice Statistics, August (NCJ 194530).

Rennison, Callie M., and Rand, Michael. 2003. *Criminal Victimization.* Washington, DC: U.S. Department of Justice, Office of Justice Programs, Bureau of Justice Statistics, August (NCJ 199994).

Rice, Liane Tai. 2003. *Powerful Sentences: Domination through Courtroom Discourse in Rape Hearings.* Unpublished BA Thesis. Department of Psychology, Swarthmore College, Swarthmore, PA.

———. 2004. Powerful sentences: Domination through courtroom discourse in rape hearings. Association of Women Psychologists, February 28, Philadelphia, PA.

Robin, Gerald. 1977. Forcible rape: Institutionalized sexism in the criminal justice system. *Crime and Delinquency* 23 (2): 136–153.

Rose, Vicki McNickle. 1977. Rape as a social problem: A byproduct of the feminist movement. *Social Problems* 25: 75–89.

Rose, Vicki McNickle, and Randall, Susan Carol. 1982. The impact of investigator perceptions of victim legitimacy on the processing of rape/sexual assault cases. *Symbolic Interaction* 5 (1): 23–36.

Sanday, Peggy Reeves. 1996. *A Woman Scorned: Acquaintance Rape on Trial.* New York: Doubleday.

Sanford, Stephanie. 1987. *The Nature of Discourse in the Courtroom: The Complete Rape Trial.* Unpublished Ph.D. Dissertation. Department of Sociology, Indiana University, Bloomington.

Schafran, Lynn Hecht. 1993. Maiming the soul: Judges, sentencing and the myth of the nonviolent rapist. *Fordham Urban Law Journal* 20: 439–453.

Schmitt, Frederika E., and Martin, Patricia Y. 1999. Unobtrusive mobilization by an Institutionalized Rape Crisis Center: "All we do comes from victims." *Gender & Society* 13 (3): 364–384.

Schwartz, Martin D., and Clear, Todd R. 1980. Toward a new law on rape. *Crime and Delinquency* 26 (2): 129–151.

Schwendinger, Julia R., and Schwendinger, Herman. 1974. Rape myths: In theoretical and everyday practice. *Crime and Social Justice* 1: 18–26.

Searles, Patricia, and Berger, Ronald. 1987. The current status of rape reform legislation: An examination of state statutes. *Women's Rights Law Reporter* 10 (1): 25–43.

Shapland, J., Willmore, J., and Duff, P. 1985. *Victims in the Criminal Justice System.* Aldershot, United Kingdom: Gower.

Shott, Susan. 1979. Emotion and social life: A symbolic interactionist analysis. *American Journal of Sociology* 84: 1317–1334.

Spohn, Cassia, Beichner, Dawn, and Davis-Frenzel, Erika. 2001. Prosecutorial justifications for sexual assault case rejection: Guarding the "gateway to justice." *Social Problems* 48 (2): 206–235.

Spohn, Cassia, and Horney, Julie. 1992. *Rape Law Reform: A Grassroots Revolution and Its Impact.* New York: Plenum Press.

Stanko, Elizabeth. 1981. The impact of victim assessment on prosecutors' screening decisions: The case of the New York county district attorney's office. *Law & Society Review* 16: 225–239.

———. 1982. Would you believe this woman? Prosecutorial screening for "credible" witnesses and a problem of justice. In *Judge, Lawyer, Victim, Thief,* edited by Nicole Rafter and Elizabeth Stanko, 63–82. Boston: Northeastern University Press.

Stevenson, Kim. 2000. Unequivocal victims: The historical roots of the mystification of the female complainant in rape cases. *Feminist Legal Studies* 8: 343–366.

Strang, H., and Braithwaite, J. 2002. *Restorative Justice and Family Violence.* Melbourne: Cambridge University Press.

Taslitz, Andrew. 1999. *Rape and the Culture of the Courtroom.* New York: New York University Press.

Thoits, Peggy. 1996. Managing the emotions of others. *Symbolic Interaction* 19: 85–109.

Tontodonato, P., and Erez, E. 1994. Crime punishment and victim distress. *International Review of Victimology* 3: 33–55.

Toutant, Charles. 2004. High court takes pass on reviewing exceptions to N.J. rape shield law. *New Jersey Law Journal* February 2. www.law.com/jsp/nj/index.jsp.

Vachss, Alice. 1993. *Sex Crimes: Ten Years in the Front Lines Prosecuting Rapists and Confronting Their Collaborators.* New York: Random House.

———. 2003. The charge of rape, the force of myth. *Washington Post,* November 2.

Valdez, G. 1986. Analyzing the demands that courtroom interaction makes upon speakers of ordinary English: Toward the development of a coherent descriptive framework. *Discourse Processes* 9: 269–303.

Villmoare, E., and Neto, V. V. 1987. *Victim Appearances at Sentencing Under California's Victims' Bill of Rights.* Washington, DC: National Institute of Justice.

Walsh, A. 1986. Placebo justice: Victim recommendations and offender sentences in sexual assault cases. *Journal of Criminal Law and Criminology* 77: 1126–1141.

Weitekamp, E., and Kerner, H. J. 2003. *Restorative Justice in Context: International Practice and Directions.* Devon, United Kingdom: Willan.

Williams, Linda. 1984. The classic rape: When do victims report? *Social Problems* 31 (4): 459–467.

Winkler, Cathy. 2002. *One Night: Realities of Rape.* New York: Alta Mira Press.

Yale Law Journal. 1972. The rape corroboration requirement: Repeal not reform. *Yale Law Journal* 81 (7): 1365–1391.

Young, Stacy L., and Maguire, Katheryn C. 2003. Talking about sexual violence. *Women and Language* 26 (2): 40–51.

Zehr, H. 1990. *Changing Lenses: A New Focus for Crime and Justice.* Scottsdale, AZ: Herald Press.

INDEX

About the Author

AMANDA KONRADI is currently a visiting associate professor at Loyola College of Maryland. She has served on the editorial boards of *Gender & Society* and *Teaching Sociology* and reviews proposals for the Woodrow Wilson Foundation Women's Studies Dissertation Fellowship program. She has published three editions of *Reading Between the Lines* and professional articles in *Gender & Society, Violence Against Women, Law & Social Inquiry*, and *American Journal of College Health.* She has received awards for her teaching at the University of California–Santa Cruz and Ohio University.